William Henry Whitmore

A bibliographical Sketch of the Laws of the Massachusetts Colony

From 1630 to 1686 In Which are Included the Body of Liberties of 1641

William Henry Whitmore

A bibliographical Sketch of the Laws of the Massachusetts Colony
From 1630 to 1686 In Which are Included the Body of Liberties of 1641

ISBN/EAN: 9783337251314

Printed in Europe, USA, Canada, Australia, Japan

Cover: Foto ©Suzi / pixelio.de

More available books at www.hansebooks.com

A BIBLIOGRAPHICAL SKETCH

OF THE

LAWS OF THE MASSACHUSETTS COLONY

From 1630 to 1686.

IN WHICH ARE INCLUDED

THE BODY OF LIBERTIES OF 1641,

AND THE

RECORDS OF THE COURT OF ASSISTANTS, 1641-1644.

ARRANGED TO ACCOMPANY THE REPRINTS OF THE
LAWS OF 1660 AND OF 1672.

BY WILLIAM H. WHITMORE, RECORD COMMISSIONER.

Published by Order of the City Council of Boston.

BOSTON:
ROCKWELL AND CHURCHILL, CITY PRINTERS.
1890.

TABLE OF CONTENTS.

	PAGES
PREFACE	V–XVII
CORRECTIONS OF MASSACHUSETTS RECORDS, VOLS. I. AND II.	XIX–XXIV
RECORDS OF COURT OF ASSISTANTS, 1641–1644	XXV–XLIII
BIBLIOGRAPHICAL INTRODUCTION	1–138
(CONTAINING ALSO, THE BODY OF LIBERTIES OF 1641)	29–68
INDEX	139–150

PREFACE.

The City of Boston has caused to be issued *fac-simile* reprints of the Colonial Laws of Massachusetts, of the two editions of 1660 and 1672. The reproduction of the edition of 1672 was first made in 1887, and contained no bibliographical preface; the reprint of the Laws of 1660, made in 1889, contained an introduction of 117 pages. As these two books are printed from electrotype plates, and may not improbably be re-issued from time to time, it has seemed best to recast the Introduction and make it applicable to either volume.

Although the State has published the Records of the Massachusetts Colony from 1629 to 1686, these do not supply the necessary information in regard to the laws. The entire code known as the Body of Liberties was enacted in 1641, but not entered on the Records. Again, in each Revision changes were made in codifying and condensing, and of course such revision superseded the older forms of the separate acts. Hence it is most desirable to have easy access to copies of the Laws of 1660, because from that date onward they embodied all the active general legislation. It must be conceded that any law of a general nature which was not included by Secretary Rawson and the committee in such codification, must be considered as repealed and null after that date.

Owing to the scarcity of copies of the Laws of the Colony and Province, the Legislature, in 1812, appointed Nathan Dane, William Prescott, and Joseph Story a committee "at the expense of the Commonwealth to collect the Charters and the public and general Laws of the late Colony and Province of Massachusetts Bay; and . . . . to add in an appendix any other documents or laws which they may deem proper to explain the jurisprudence of this Commonwealth." One thousand copies were issued at the public expense, and this is the volume so often quoted in decisions as "Ancient Charters and General Laws."

Useful as this compilation has proved, it will be of necessity entirely superseded by recent publications. The State has commenced and nearly concluded the publication of all the General Laws of the Province from 1692 to the Revolution, a work which is enriched with every kind of illustrative notes gathered by the industry of the indefatigable editor, A. C. Goodell. It has also published all of the Records of the Great and General Court and the Assistants, prior to 1686, carefully reproduced under the care of the late Dr. N. B. Shurtleff. Now the City of Boston has supplemented these by these two volumes of Laws, viz., the Liberties of 1641 and Revision of 1660, and the Revision of 1672 and Supplements.

The student will therefore have, in print, everything which the Commissioners of 1812 had to use mainly in manuscript. One suggestion indeed is made with the utmost diffidence by the present editor. In the Preface to Ancient Charters the editors say: "A number of colony acts of importance, especially in a historical view of our laws, have been found in the original records, not included in the edition of 1672; these have been selected and printed in this volume wherever found to have remained a material part of the colonial system."

In other words, the committee of 1812 did not reprint either the edition of Laws of 1660 or of 1672 complete, but they made a new compilation with a new arrangement of chapters, and inserted such general laws, evidently, as they considered "to have remained a material part of the colonial system."

With the utmost deference to the honored memory of Dane, Prescott, and Story, it is certain that we now know much more of the history of Massachusetts as a colony than was known in 1812. Such antiquaries as Farmer, Savage, Winthrop, Palfrey, Trumbull, Dexter, and Ellis, with the innumerable lesser historians, have added immensely to the true knowledge of the events of that period. Hence it may not be presumptuous to suggest that the selections made in 1812, even by such eminent lawyers, were not always wise, and by no means complete.[1]

---

[1] One instance may be cited. The present editor, after the Laws of 1672 was issued, received an inquiry from a prominent lawyer, asking for the reason for the omission of Section 19 of Chapter XVIII., of Ancient Charters. It will be found therein on p. 61, and refers to the punishment for Blasphemy. Now, it will be found that in 1641, Liberty No. 94, § 3, gave the first simple act punishing blasphemy. In 1646 (Records, II., 176-177), this Section 19 was passed as printed. But in 1660 (and presumably in 1649), the Revised Statutes cut down the act to the form printed as Section 3 of this very chapter in Anc. Char., p. 58. The editors in 1812 reprinted the first Act of 1646 as well as the revised form, but surely thereby they darkened counsel instead of aiding the student, who would suppose this §19 to be a different and continuing statute. — W. H. W.

Preface. VII

During the past year the City of Boston has obtained for its Public Library the famous manuscript duplicate of the records of the Massachusetts General Court, formerly owned by Gov. Hutchinson, later by Col. Thomas Aspinwall, and last by Hon. Samuel L. M. Barlow of New York city. This acquisition has revived an interest in the question of the method in which our early official records of the legislature were kept, and especially in the matter of the literary importance of this manuscript.

This copy is a manuscript of 313 pages, beautifully written, the first 224 pages being in the well-known hand-writing of Thomas Lechford. As he left Boston August 3, 1641, the date of this portion is settled approximately. The manuscript begins thus: "A true copie of the Court booke of the Governor and Society of the Massachusetts Bay in New England." It is therefore avowedly a copy, not a duplicate original, and its great value lies in the fact that it is a wonderfully exact copy, so that it can be safely taken as an authority for all such passages as are missing or illegible in the original record now at the State House.

The Records preserved in the State House, and printed by Dr. Shurtleff, are contained in five volumes, but it should be noted that the third volume, as numbered and printed, is not part of the series. The periods covered by each, are:

Vol. I. March, 1628-9 to Dec. 10, 1641.
  II. May 18, 1642 to Oct. 17, 1649.
{   IV. pt. 1, May 22, 1650 to Dec. 19, 1660.
  IV. pt. 2, May 22, 1661 to March 11, 1673-4.
  V. May 27, 1674 to May 20, 1686.

These volumes contain the record of the Company of the Massachusetts Bay previous to the removal to New England, beginning in February, 1628-9. The entries continue along to a meeting at Southampton, Eng., March 18, 1629-30, then a Court of Assistants aboard the Arbella, March 23, 1629-30, and next "the first Court of Assistants, held at Charlton [*i.e.* Charlestown], August 23, 1630." From that date the record was presumably complete. Volume 1 contains records of the General Court and also of the Court of Assistants, but none of the later volumes record the proceedings of the Assistants.

There is no reason to doubt that these volumes were kept officially by the Secretaries, with some clerical aid duly noted by Dr. Shurtleff, and especially by Increase Nowell as to volumes 1 and 2, and by Edward Rawson as to volumes 4 and 5. We have a very clear statement as to the shape of our records in the letter of Joseph Hills, dated in 1682, hereinafter printed, (Introduction, p. 127). He says that in preparing for the printed Code of 1649 he consulted, "the two old books of records, the book of liberties, and the great book then and since in the hands of Mr. Rawson." This seems to be an exact description, leaving out the lost manuscript Book of Liberties, of the existing records, vols. I. and II., pp. 312 and 217, respectively, and the great volume IV., of 736 pages.

So again in 1652 it appears that there were "two old books of records belonging to the General Court" as the following order testifies : * —

"Forasmuch as their are two old bookes of Records belonging to the Generall court wherin are many Things involved which are of great concernment as well as in Rights and bounds of Lands as other material things ; which bookes are decaid and very Imethodicall, as Well in finding out any Record, as allso in Severall circumstantiall errors in entreing Some of the orders ; for Regulating whereof,

This Court orders that a committe be appointed in the vacancy of the court to overlooke those two books of Records afforsaid, and to correct all such circumstantiall errors in words in them contained, but not to alter anything for substance and matter ; and after the said books be vieued and Corrected as before, then the Secretary is to take care that the said bookes bee truly transcribed into new books of Good paper, well bound, and covered with velume or parchment, and marginall abreviats of each order colected, an alphebeticall table affixed for finding out of all orders therein, and all due chardge for transcription of the said bookes be duly paid unto the Secretary by the country.

The Magistrates have past this with reference to the consent of our brethren, the Deputies.

JO. ENDECOTT, Govr."

"The Deputies thinke meete a Comittee shall examine all the records that are not extracted, abbreviated, or composed into the bookes of the printed lawes, and shall make amendment of all circumstantial errors without altering the substance, and present the same to the next sessions of court which may take care of the transcribing them ; and Mr. Hill, Capt. Johnson and the Secretary are desired to Joyne with some of the magistrates as a comittee for that end.

WM. TORREY, Cleric."

"The Magistrates have voted Mr. Bellingham and Mr. Glover to Joyne with the Comitee of the brethren the Deputies to serve in the courte of election.

EDWARD RAWSON, Secret."

"Consented to by the Deputyes,

WM. TORREY, Cleric."

---

* I am greatly indebted to my friend, Mr. A. C. Goodell, jr., who kindly called my attention to the above important order which is preserved in Mass. Archives, Vol. 88, page 386.

As to the occasion for which Lechford's copy was made, nothing certain is known. We may say however that it would be strange if no duplicate had been made, especially when there was in Boston such an admirable scrivener, already employed in similar work, and starving for lack of it. I agree with those who think that the following entry in Lechford's Note Book (printed p. 256) refers to this copy. It seems to bear date in June, 1640.

"The Court booke at 16 d a sheete, 102 sheetes for Mr Endecott, cometh to £6, 16s." Following this is an entry in short-hand, which as read by Mr. Upham, is as follows: "Money received upon my book as appeareth 38£, 8s, 5d, or thereabouts, beside the debts owing were 8£, 18s 10d. Cast 2, (5). 1640."

It is simply incredible that Lechford should have made a second copy of this large manuscript without an order, or that he should have omitted to record it in his Note-Book. Circumstantial evidence is also very strong to prove the identity of the Endecott copy with this Barlow one. The 102 "sheets" doubtless mean leaves, or 204 pages. In the Barlow copy page 204, the upper half, ends with the record of a Quarter Court, 2d day, 4th mo., 1640. This is the month when Lechford enters his charge against Endecott. Then there is a break in the transcribing for several months, as will be shown. Lechford resumes his work with a new ink, finishes the last three lines of that Quarter Court record, and adds the Assistants' Court of 31st, 5th mo. 1640, on p. 204. Then, pp. 205–214 are covered by him, the last entry being the Court of 28th, 11th mo. 1640, or February, 1641, modern style. He adds pp. 215–221, with miscellaneous papers.

Mr. Upham points out that not only was the ink changed, but a noticeable change in penmanship occurs, on p. 204. Up to that point Lechford made his letters "f" and long "s" with a straight line to the bottom. He uses the same forms in his Note-Book; but in this latter book between the 12th and 14th March, 1640-41,

---

Although it has all the marks of an order duly passed by both branches of the Legislature, it will not be found in the printed journals.

The date must be 1652, since that is the only year giving us the necessary coincidence of Bellingham and Glover as magistrates. Glover served only in 1652 and 1653, but in the latter year Bellingham was deputy-Governor, and ever afterwards till 1664, except in 1654 when he was governor. I feel sure that with the care taken in bestowing honorary titles at that date, Bellingham would not have been termed simply a magistrate when he was deputy-governor.

This order probably was acted upon, and the report, as amended by the Deputies, was, I presume, presented to the Court in 1653, which "took care of the transcribing" by passing the order of Sept. 10, 1653, printed by me, *post*, p. 116.

The phrase which occurs in this order of 1652, " records that are not extracted, abbreviated or composed *into the books of the printed laws*," may perhaps be cited as an additional proof that at that date there were *two* printed books of the laws. viz. the Code of 1649 and the supplement of 1650, as discussed by me. *post*, p. 80. — W. H. W.

he adopted the style of a round looped bottom to these two letters, and so continues to the end. Hence the last ten pages written by Lechford were written between March and August, 1641, and presumably very soon after the date of the session of the last Court (Feb., 1641), entered by him. This would entirely agree with the theory that this copy is Endicott's, completed first to June, 1640, and then added to in March or April, 1641, prior to Lechford's departure.

After Lechford had finished, the work was continued by two or three other writers. It is useless to go into the details here, but the copy of the official record is made with similar accuracy through p. 313, being the Court of Elections, 14th, 3d mo., 1643. This copy also contains the records of the Court of Assistants from Oct. 28th, 1641 to March 5, 1643–4, *which are wanting in the official journals* preserved at the State House and printed by Shurtleff.

Little is known as to the subsequent ownership of this manuscript after Gov. Endicott received it. The following memorandum was written by Gov. Thomas Hutchinson on a fly-leaf of the book: —

"This book belonged to Edward Hutchinson of Boston who being employed by the Government to enter upon a Treaty with a Tribe of Indians in 1675 was treacherously waylaid and mortally wounded by them and died and lies buried in the town of Marlborough, the first English settlement to which he could be carried. In the year 1769 an old man of the name of Rice died in *Marlborough* (Worcester), who was present and perfectly remembered having seen Mr. Hutchinson brought into Marlboro'. Rice died at the age of 102. Edward Hutchinson received the freedom of the Colony in 1634, Sept 3^d (see p. 81), and Mr William Hutchinson, his father, received his the 4th of March following. p. 82."

We know of nothing to explain the ownership by Capt. Edward Hutchinson, whose only civil office was that of representative in 1658, from Boston, and who was not connected with Endicott by blood or marriage. We do know that Edward's son, Elisha Hutchinson, was greatly interested in the records, and in 1680 was on the committee for reprinting the laws. His priceless collation of the Code of 1672, with its Supplements, and his manuscript copy of the Body of Liberties, are now in the Boston Athenaeum.

There is a remarkable coincidence between the time covered by the Barlow manuscript and the third volume of Records printed by Shurtleff. That volume, as already stated, contains only the proceedings of the Deputies, from 14th, 3d mo. 1645 through May 6, 1657. It seems to stand alone, without a predecessor or successor, for though Shurtleff writes (preface, p. vi) "it is evident that the popular branch of the Colonial Legislature continued a record of its proceedings until the time the Colony Charter was vacated." (*i. e.* 1686), he adds "no copy of these valuable volumes can be found in the archives of the Commonwealth extending beyond the period embraced in these pages, nor are any positively known to exist any where else." I am unaware of the grounds of Shurtleff's belief that other volumes once existed, but Mr. Goodell is confident that he has met with references thereto. The accounts of the fire at the State House, in 1747, declare that many unspecified records were then destroyed.

I am unable thus far to find any order for the preparation of this third volume. In March, 1643-4, the famous vote was passed by which the separate sessions of the two branches was ordered; but this volume does not begin at that date.

The regular pagination of this Volume III. begins with the session of May 14, 1645. On p. 21 (Records, iii. p. 28), it is entered under date of June 18, 1645, that "Edward Rawson is chosen and appointed clerk to the House of Deputies for one whole year, to enter all votes passed in both houses, and those also passed only by them, into their book of records." Again, November 4, 1646 (Records, iii. p. 83), " it is ordered that Edward Rawson shall have twenty marks allowed him for his pains, out of the next levy, as Secretary to the House of Deputies for two years past." This last entry is probably intended to go back only to May, 1645, because the earlier manuscript, for part of 1644, is not in Rawson's writing but in that of Capt. Robert Bridges of Lynn, one of the deputies. In fact, November 7, 1646 (Records, iii. 78), at the beginning, it is stated that Capt. Robert Keayne was chosen " Speaker for the first day of sitting, and Capt. Robert Bridges was chosen secretary for the first day of sitting "; and then Bridges was chosen Speaker for the whole session.

A careful examination of the volume shows that it was bound in June, 1781, according to a memorandum at the end; that Rawson's part begins with the Court of May, 1645; and that the few pages dated in 1644, written by Bridges, were no part of the original record. Of course the record of the first year may have been lost, since it is most reasonable to presume that a deliberative body would keep an exact journal from its organization.

If however the Deputies had acquired the Endicott manuscript, they would have had in the custody of their Clerk, a transcript of all the records as complete as that in charge of the Secretary for the Magistrates.

That there was at first some lack of formality in keeping the House Journals, may be inferred from the order of October 18, 1648 (*post*, p. 78), which provides that "as there is a Secretary amongst the Magistrates" . . . ." so there shall be a Clerk amongst the Deputies to be chosen by them from time to time." The duties of the Clerk were very fully set forth in the act, and it must be presumed that Rawson attended to the chief part of his duties, namely the special record of the proceedings of the Deputies, although he was evidently remiss in the preparation of the "Deputies' book of copies of record."

Shurtleff notes (Rec. iii. 105) that William Torrey, who was a Deputy in 1648 and 1649, wrote pp. 107-110, of the proceedings of 26 May, 1647, and that up to p. 253, when Torrey was chosen Clerk (May 22, 1650), he supplied many pages of the record which Rawson was presumed to prepare as Clerk. Very probably as Rawson was at this latter date promoted to the office of Secretary in place of Increase Nowell, the pressure of his new duties will account for the irregularities in the Deputies' books and papers. It is worth noticing that William Torrey was Clerk to the last; and in 1650 (Records, iv. part 1, p. 33), Oct. 13, 1650, Torrey was granted State Island "in consideration of his entering the orders of Court for two or three Courts, not yet entered in the Deputies book, so as he do it in one year next coming, and perfect the book as far as he can." But Nov. 12, 1659 (Records, iv. part 1, p. 407), the island was confirmed to him on the conditions of the old grant, "he having now perfected the Deputies book of copies of records."

The reader can draw his own inferences from the following vote of May 15, 1672 (Records, iv. part 2, p. 509) : —

"This Court doth order, that all records of this Court and of the Council, from the first beginning thereof, be fairly transcribed in a legible hand, so as there may be a fair copy thereof besides the original, that in case of fire or other accident the country may not suffer so great a damage as the loss of their records would be; and the Treasurer [Russell] and Secretary [Rawson] are ordered to procure the same to be done timely and on as reasonable terms as they can; and the comparers (who shall be appointed by this Court) shall, upon their oaths, declare the copy transcribed to be a true copy."

Gov. Hutchinson claims that the Barlow manuscript belonged to his great-grandfather Edward Hutchinson who was killed in

1675. If so, it probably descended to Elisha Hutchinson and thence to his grandson, Thomas. It is supposed that Col. Aspinwall bought this manuscript in England.

This priceless manuscript has been carefully examined by William P. Upham, Esq., who reports that in many places it completes the deficiencies of the printed text, and that a critical collation of the two is very desirable. It supplies also ten pages to Vol. I. and two pages to Vol. II., as Shurtleff notes *in his second edition*. (See *post*, p. XIV.) It also adds the records of the Court of Assistants for some three years, new and valuable information nowhere else extant.*

In the reprint of the Laws of 1660, I reproduced the pages from Shurtleff's second edition which showed the additions from the Barlow manuscript to p. 346 of Volume I., and pp. xiv, xv and xvi, of Volume II.; the earlier part covering ten pages relating to proceedings in England did not seem of sufficient importance to be reprinted herein. See *post*, pp. XIX–XXIV. I now add to this edition the pages which contain the records of the Court of Assistants, so fortunately recovered, *post*, pp. XXV–XLIII.

For a full understanding of the subject, I also reproduce a portion of my former Preface, explaining the state of the printed editions issued by the Commonwealth under Dr. Shurtleff's supervision.

In 1853 (Resolves, chap. 63) the Governor was directed to have printed one hundred copies of the first two volumes of the General Court's Records. By chap. 5 of Resolves of 1854, eleven hundred more copies were ordered, and twelve hundred copies of Volumes III., IV., and V. The work was done under the supervision of the late Dr. N. B. Shurtleff, the first two volumes bearing the imprint 1853, and the others that of 1854.

In 1855 (Resolves, chap. 19) the Governor was directed to have printed five hundred additional copies of the first volumes of said Records.

In 1856 (Resolves, chap. 9) the Secretary was empowered to allow the State printer to publish an edition for public sale, as a private enterprise, the permission being for three years from June 4th. (Resolves, chap. 87, 1856.)

---

* The careful Catalogue of the Records of the Supreme Court, prepared by the Clerk and issued in August, 1890, shows that he has the custody of the "Second Book of Records of the Court of Assistants, begun March 3, 1673," continued through April, 1686, suspended till Dec. 24, 1689, and then continued into 1692. The first book seems to be utterly lost. — W. H. W.

In the "Boston Daily Advertiser" for March 6, 1865, Dr. Shurtleff published a letter in regard to certain changes made by him in the stereotype plates after the first edition was issued. The following extracts cover the main point: —

"Soon after the issue of the edition ordered by the Legislature in 1853, my excellent friend, Col. Thomas Aspinwall, came back to his American home, bringing, with his historical treasures collected during a long residence in London, a manuscript copy of the first volume of the old records, and of a portion of the second volume, extending, I think, to the year 1646. This manuscript contained a large portion of the lost records, namely, a portion of the proceedings of the 23d of March, 1628–9, the proceedings of the 30th March, 2d, 6th, 8th, 13th, 16th, 27th, and 30th of April, 1629, and also portions of the proceedings of the 10th of December, 1641 (being part of Volume I.), and the commencement of the record of the General Court of Elections, commencing on the 13th of May, 1642, being the beginning of Volume II."

"Fortunately the succeeding Legislature passed an order for the issue of another edition of Volumes I. and II.; and, consequently, an opportunity was afforded for completing the printed volumes of records from the material furnished so opportunely by Colonel Aspinwall's copy. *The stereotype plates were revised, and the lost parts of the original records were artistically supplied,* so that the second impression from the stereotype plates contains all that exists of the old colonial records of Massachusetts."

It appears that the changes made in the stereotype plates after the first edition was printed were as follows: In Volume I. ten pages were inserted, marked 37 *a* to 37 *j*, inclusive, and on p. 346 enough was added to complete that page. In Volume II. (which begins, in the first edition, with p. 3), two whole pages were inserted, numbered 1 and 2, and the first half of page 3. The former page 3 was cancelled, the two bottom lines (concerning one Gregory Taylor) being carried over to page 4, and the spaces on page 4 being readjusted, so that page 4 ends alike in both editions.

I believe that I am correct in saying that no change was made in the title-pages to this second edition of Volumes I. and II., that no notice was given of the corrections and additions (except a short note on p. 344 of Volume I.), and that no alterations were made in the Index of either volume.

As to the additions made in the first volume, their value is merely antiquarian. But the pages added in the second volume contain the organization of the government for 1642, an order about votes in the General Court, and a law respecting constables, (which is in the Code of 1660, the first clause of section 2, and not cited in the margin as passed in 1642, the whole section being referred to Anno 1646). There are also two laws, one relating to the pay of the Elders when employed by the General Court, and the other empowering any Court having two magistrates to admit church members to be freemen: both laws copied into the Code of 1660.

For these two laws I spent many hours in fruitless search, till I learned the fact of there being two editions. In the lack of any definite information of the number of copies printed by the State printer under his license, I conclude that fully two-thirds of the copies of the first two volumes of the Records now in circulation and use are defective. The stereotype plates of these books were destroyed in the great fire in Boston in 1872, and I have therefore reproduced the four pages, one (p. 346) of Volume I., and three pages of Volume II., in order that any one who wishes to verify my citations, and who is unfortunately the owner of the first edition only, may have the full copy before him.

It is useless to criticise Dr. Shurtleff's peculiar method of altering the plates of such an important book. Any one taking up a copy of State Records issued by authority of the Legislature naturally relies upon its entire accuracy. I am sorry to say that this reliance is misplaced in many small matters of textual correctness, as I have discovered; but the fact that three or four pages of proceedings are to be found in one edition, and not in another, is one which calls for the greatest publicity. I fear that many of the highly valued copies of the first edition were placed in public libraries, and are the only ones accessible to many students.

The legislation of the Andros or Inter-Charter period remains still in manuscript, and deserves to be printed as the only missing link in the chain of entire continuity from A.D. 1629 to the present time.

As this Preface and Introduction is intended to serve hereafter for any reprint of either the edition of 1660 or that of 1672, I would note that the bibliographical information in regard to the edition of 1672 is contained in the special Introduction to that volume. The reprint of the edition of 1660 consists of two impressions, each of some 400 copies. The copy used for the text was that preserved in the State Library, and the supplements were copied from the beautiful volume formerly owned by Secretary Edward Rawson, now in the library of the American Antiquarian

Society at Worcester. Later on, my attention was called to a copy formerly owned by Judge Story, now in the Law Library of Harvard University. Although it lacked some of the Supplements, it contained those for 1668 and 1669 complete. I was thus enabled in the second impression to add nine pages, besides perfecting two others, and it is hoped that the Supplements are now complete. Extra copies of these added pages were furnished to those having the first impression only.

I have devoted much time to the Body of Liberties, as it has hitherto not received the recognition to which its importance entitles it. This Code was first rediscovered by the late Francis Calley Gray, and printed by him in 1843. But being published only in a volume of the Collections of the Massachusetts Historical Society, a knowledge of it has been confined to very few persons. I have merely followed out Mr. Gray's line of unanswerable arguments proving the certainty of the identification of his copy of this Code, but I have added a Table of Contents, Index, and Notes, which may assist the student in using it.

The reprints have been made by the Photo-electrotype process, which has proved to be peculiarly adapted to such work. The Indexes to both volumes were prepared by Frederick E. Goodrich, Esq.

It is reasonable to think that the ground covered by these two volumes is now completely covered, even should some fortunate chance restore to us a copy of the edition of 1649. But there is room, and almost a necessity, for some qualified person to work up this material into a concise and well-digested history of the jurisprudence of Massachusetts. A thorough consideration of the Body of Liberties will prove that our ancestors were far more enlightened than their English contemporaries, and that the influence which they sent forth has continued to affect most powerfully our laws, customs, and thoughts to the present time.

Especially to be forever remembered, for their pious care and intuitive perception of the value of these records, are Edward Rawson, Elisha Hutchinson, and Francis Calley Gray.

The Introduction is a recasting and amplification of that prefixed to the reprint of the Laws of 1660. Considerable new and important matter has been incorporated therein, and I trust that the whole is now placed in a more symmetrical and convincing form. The first edition of any essay upon a new topic must be imperfect, and publicity must tend to correction and improvement. I venture to hope that the public interest in these matters created by the publication of these two reprints, bore fruit in the munificent appropriation by which the Trustees of our Public Library were enabled to purchase the Barlow manuscript together with so many other literary treasures.

WILLIAM H. WHITMORE.

CITY HALL, BOSTON, Sept. 26th, 1890.

ADDITIONS MADE IN THE SECOND PRINTED EDITION OF THE RECORDS OF MASSACHUSETTS,

AND NOT TO BE FOUND IN THE FIRST EDITIONS.

[P. XXI. IS P. 346 OF VOLUME I.]

[PP. XXII.–XXIV. ARE THE BEGINNING OF VOLUME II.]

THE RECORDS OF THE COLONY.

M{rs} Marg{t} Winthrope hath her 3000 acres of land formerly granted her, to bee assigned about the lower end of Concord Ryver, near Merrimack, to bee layde out by M{r} Flint & Leift Willard, w{th} M{r} Oliver, or some other skilfull in measuring, so as it may not hinder a plantation; & any p̄t thereof they may purchase of any Indians that have right to it./

1641.
10 December.
M{rs} Winthrops 3000 ac{rs}.

Upon the petition of M{r} Willi: Tynge, it was ordered, that M{r} Bartholomew, George Giddings, & John Whipple should set a dewe valuation upon the house & ground w{ch} Willi: Whitred did effeofe to M{r} Tyng aforenamed./

It was ordered, that Sara, the late wife of James Hubberd, should have fourty pound of the estate of her said late husband, & the use of the childrens stock till they come to the ages mentioned in the will, & then the eldest sonne./

At this Court, the bodye of laues formerly
    sent forth amonge the ffreemen, &c.,
    was voted to stand in force, &c./

[The last paragraph is in the handwriting of Governor Winthrop. The following is restored from an early copy of the records in the possession of Thomas Aspinwall, Esq.]

M{r} Atherton Hoffe is graunted foure hundred acres of land in regard of fiftie pounds disburssed in the ioint stocke.

M{r} HoTes 400 acres.

M{r} Davies was denied libertie to sell drinke, or ale, or to keepe a cookes shopp, because there are others sufficient in the towne of Boston, and his carriage hath bin formerlie offensiue.

W{m} Davies.

M{rs} Dunster is graunted hir farme with the bondaries from Sudburic bounds, a straite line running south easterlie and north westerlie to the great ponnd over against that place, where the river issueth outt of itt on the other side, the line cutting y{e} said pond over unto the said issue, then following the streames vnto the place where Sudburic cutteth againe the river, & soe along by the river within Sudburie line, as itt is agreed betweene the towne of Sudburie and hir: the line lying in forme is described in the plott subscribed by M{r} Thom̄ Flintt & Thom̄ Mayhewe.

M{rs} Dunster farme.

M{r} Samuell Mavericke is remitted 40{li} of his fine of 100{li}, formerlie sett vpon him, if hee pay y{e} remaining 60{li} in due valuation.

M{r} Sam: Mavericke fine remitt.

M{r} Mayhewe his accounts were referred to the Treasuro{r} & M{r} Duncum; & for the bridge by the mill over the Charles River, the Co{rt} doth conceiue itt to belong to the towne or townes in w{ch} itt lyeth.

Thomas Bartlett is appointed leivetenant & Hugh Mason ensigne to Captaine Jeanison, Waterton.

Military officers.

MASSACHUSETTS RECORDS.

THE RECORDS OF THE COLONY OF THE MASSACHUSETTS BAY IN NEW ENGLAND.

[The manuscript of the second volume of the Massachusetts Colony Records commences on the third page, at the place indicated by an asterisk. The first portion of the volume is lost, and the first eighteen pages of what remains are in a very decayed condition. By the aid of ancient transcripts of the volume, made apparently very early, and by a duplicate leaf in the handwriting of the Secretary who wrote the volume, the decayed portions have been restored. The volume is mainly in the chirography of Secretary Nowell, although occasionally passages, and sometimes pages, are in that of Mr. Edward Rawson, who succeeded Mr. Nowell as Secretary in 1650.]

1642. [*The Generall Court of Elections, the 18th Day of y̓e 8d Month, 1642.*

18 May.   PRESENT, The Governoʳ,   Mʳ Bradstreet,
                    The Depᵗⁱᵉ Governoʳ,   Mʳ Staughton,
                    Mʳ Dudley,   Mʳ Flintt,
                    Mʳ Bellingham,   Mʳ Increase Nowell.
                    Mʳ Saltonstall,

Deputies p̃sent:

Wᵐ Hilton,	Robert Bridges,	Elea: Lusher,
Wᵐ Walderne,	Mʳ Wᵐ Ting,	Wᵐ Heath,
Wᵐ Hayward,	Capt Edw: Gibbons,	Wᵐ Parkes,
John Saunders,	Ralph Sprague,	Mʳ John Glover,
Edward Rawson,	Thomas Line,	Mʳ Nat: Duncum,
Matthew Boyse,	Capt Geo: Cooke,	Alex: Winchester,
Maximi: Jewett,	Mʳ Nat: Sparhawke,	Wᵐ Cheesborough,
Mʳ Sam: Simonds,	Capt Wᵐ Jeanison,	James Parker,
John Whipple,	Mʳ Simon Eyres,	Edw: Bates,
Mʳ Ema: Downing,	Symon Willard,	Jos: Pecke,
Edm: Batter,	Peter Noyse,	Edm: Hubberd.
Edw: Hollioke,	Edw: Allen,	

Govern͛   JOHN WINTHROPP, Esqʳ, was chosen Governoʳ for this yeare and till new bee chosen, and tooke his oath.

Dep. G.   John Endicott, Esq , was chosen Depᵗⁱᵉ Governoʳ, & tooke his oath.

Assistants.   Thom: Dudley, Esqʳ, was chosen an Assistant, & tooke his oathe.
            Rich: Bellingham, Esqʳ, was chosen an Assistant, & tooke his oath.

VOL. II.   1   (1)

Preface.

THE RECORDS OF THE COLONY OF

Rich: Saltonstall, Esqr, was chosen an Assistant, & tooke his oath.
Mr Symon Bradstreet was chosen an Assistant, & tooke his oath.
Mr Increase Nowell was chosen an Assistant, & tooke his oath.
Mr Israell Staughton was chosen an Assistant, & tooke his oath.
Mr John Winthrop was chosen an Assistant.
Mr Wm Pinchen was chosen an Assistant, and tooke his oath.
Mr Thomas Flintt was chosen an Assistant, and tooke his oath.
Mr Tyng was chosen Treasurer.

It was ordered that a warrant should bee sentt to Salem for a new election of a new deputie to be ioined with Mr Downing, because the Court is doubtfull of ye choyse, & Mr Edmund Batter was sent.

Mr Staughton & Mr Ting, Treasuro^r, were appointed a comittee to advise Goodman Johnson aboutt ye amunition.

An order was made for the pssing 4 horses, to goe wth Mr Collecott and his companie (if they cannot hire wthout pssing) to helpe them to carrie necessaries to run the south line.

Cape Anne is to bee called Gloscester; John Sadler is chosen constable thereof, and tooke his oath.

John Sadler had comission to traine the men att Gloscester.

Obadiah Brewen is appointed Surveyer of ye Armes att Gloscester.

George Norten is appointed to keepe an ordinarie att Gloscester.

Richard Gibson was comitted to the marshall for his seditious practises, & vpon his submission & acknowlegement of his fault vnder his hand hee was dismissed with an admonition.

Watertowne delivering in a transcript of thier lands, nott being perfect was lent them backe againe.

Leivetenant Symon Willard & Edward Converse are appointed to view Shawshins, & to certifie whether the land that is free bee fitt for a village or nott.

Goodman John Johnson had order to lend six carabines to Mr Collecott & his companie wch are to run the south line.

Itt was ordered, that the Treasuro^r should defray the charges of the elders, when they are imployed vpon anie speciall order from the General Co^rt.

The lawes were read over the 20th of the 3^d month.

John Pemberton was bound in 20^{li} to appeare att the nextt Court att Ipswich.

The order for hempe & flax seed to passe att twelve shillings the bushell is repealed.

The orders for restraint of wheat are repealed.

There is power given to everie Co^rt wthin o^r jurisdiction y^t hath two

XXIII

1642.
18 May.

Treasurer.
Deputye.

Pressinge of horses.

Gloster.

Gibson.

Waterton.

Shawsin.

South line.

487—
Charges.

20 May.
Lawes.
Pembleton.

488—
Flaxseed,
12^s bush.
Repeale.

489—
Freemen,
admission.

THE MASSACHUSETTS BAY IN NEW ENGLAND.

1642.
20 May.

magistrates to admitt anie church members that are fitt to bee free, & to give them the freemens oath, & to certifie thier names to the Secretarie att the next Generall Courtt.

490-
Votes in Courts. Repeale.

The order formerlie made for writing things before they bee voted, is declared nott to concerne matter of forme, butt to bee meant of things that are to bee matters of record.

White.

Phillip White, for drunkenesse, was fined 10ˢ, & for misdeamenoʳ, wᶜʰ 10ˢ Richard Wayte vndertooke for White.

Posture of Warre.

The Deputy Governoʳ, Mʳ Staughton, Capṫ Gibbons, Captaine Jeanison, Capṫ Cooke, Mʳ Rawson, Leivetenᵗ Willard, & Mʳ Parker, these or the greater number of them, are appointed to putt the countrey in a posture of warre.

491-
Officers duly to receiue forraine prisoners.

Itt is ordered, yᵗ when anie person shall bee tendred to anie officer of this jurisdiccon by anie constable or other officer belonging to anie forreigne jurisdiction in this countrey, or by warrant from anie such authoritie, hee or shee shall bee presentlie receiued and conveyed forthwith from constable to constable till the partie bee brought to the place to which hee or shee is sentt,

Hue & cry.

or before some magistrate of this jurisdiction, who shall soe dispose of the partie as occasion & the justice of the cause shall require, & thatt all hew and cryes shall bee dilligentlie receuived & pursued to full effect.]

[*1.]
492-
Ordʳ about hue encryˢ

Whereas the country is put to great charge by the Courts attendance vpon suites coffenced or renewed by either appeales, petition, &ᶜ, it is ordered, that in all such cases, if it shall appeare to the Coʳᵗ that the plainṫ in any such action of appeale, petition, &ᶜ, in any Coʳᵗ, hath no iust cause of any such proceeding, they shall take order that the said plaintiff shall beare all the charges of the Coʳᵗ wᶜʰ they shall iudge to have beein expended by his occasion, & may further impose a fine vpon him if the merrit of the cause shall so require ; & if they shall finde the defendant in fault, they shall impose the charges vpon such defendant./

William Aspinwall, upon his petition & cirtificat of his good carriage, is restored againe to his former liberty & freedome./

The Court left it to the liberty of the townes to send but a deputy a peece, if they please, to the next session of this Court./

The marshall hath leave to go to Coñecticut, leauing a deputy./

The beaver tradʳˢ are appointed to bring in what is due to the countrey at the next session./

Edward Bendall hath liberty to make vse of any of the cables, & other things belonging to the worke, as he needeth, alowing for the hurt of them./

Gregory Tayloʳ, being chosen constable of Water Towne, tooke his oath to discharge that place./

RECORDS

OF THE

COURT OF ASSISTANTS

OF THE

COLONY OF THE MASSACHUSETTS BAY

IN

NEW ENGLAND.

From October 28, 1641, through March 5, 1643-4.

NOW FIRST PUBLISHED FROM A CONTEMPORANEOUS COPY RECENTLY OWNED BY SAMUEL L. M. BARLOW, ESQ., AND NOW IN THE POSSESSION OF THE BOSTON PUBLIC LIBRARY.

RECORDS OF THE COURT OF ASSISTANTS

FROM OCTOBER, 1641, TO MARCH 5, 1643-4.

NOW FIRST PUBLISHED FROM THE MANUSCRIPT COPY, RECENTLY OWNED BY S. L. M. BARLOW, ESQ., AND NOW PRESERVED IN THE BOSTON PUBLIC LIBRARY.

[NOTE. — It is well-known that the first volume of the Massachusetts Colony Records contains not only the proceedings of the General Courts, but also those of the Magistrates or Assistants sitting in special courts. These records are recorded in regular order as they were held, the Quarter Court of September 7, 1641, being on pp. 334-336, and the General Court of October 7, 1641, covering pp. 336-343, and (as continued December 10, 1641), pp. 343-346. In the second and subsequent volumes, only the proceedings of the General Courts are recorded. As already noted, the Clerk of the Supreme Court finds his earliest volume is marked "Court of Assistants, second booke of Records, beganne the 3rd of March, 1673." This *hiatus*, from 1641 to 1673, has long been deplored; and it is with great pleasure that I am now enabled, by the kindness of the Trustees of the Boston Public Library, to supply a part of the missing records. In the so-called Barlow copy of the early part of our Colonial records, at the latter part of the volume, a contemporary copy was made of the proceedings of the Assistants, from October 28th, 1641, through March 5th, 1643-4.

The portion here printed begins on p. 277, 15th line.

The last preceding order "The comission above, wth the alterations was confirmed the 5th m^{o}, 1645" etc., is numbered in margin 2839. (See Records of Mass., Vol. II., p. 65.) This copy was made by William P. Upham, Esq.

W. H. W.]

[277] At a Co^{rt} the 28th 8th Moth 1641.
Present The Governo^{r} Mr Winthrop.
Mr Dudley. Increase Nowell.

2840. James Luxford was Ordered to bee delivered to his three Credito^{rs}. Luxford.
2841. Mr Symon Voysey for striking Mr Constable was comitted, & fined Voysey fined. to give Mr Constable, 10^{lb}
2842. Mr Henry Waltham, & James Brittaine, were bound for Gawen Waltham. Brittaine bound for Wilson his appearance at ye next Co^{rt}. Wilson.
2843. John Knight is comitted vntill hee find sureties. Knight comitted.

At a Quarter Co^{rt} at Boston the 7th of the 10th Mth 1641.
2844. Jacob Eliot deposed to the will, & Inventory of John Tee. Eliot. Tee.
2845. John Smith is graunted five shillings against William Prichard. Smith. Prichard.
2846. John Richardson appearing & testimony given of his good car- Richardson riage, hee, & his sureties were discharged. discharged.

Wilson, & sureties discharged.	Gawen Wilson appearing, hee, & his sureties were discharged.	2847.
Vocar fined or whipt.	John Vocar was censured to pay ten shillings, or bee whipped, the 1st Mo^{th}.	2848.
Capt. Williams, Richardson.	Capt. Williams was p'ssed, & promised to endeavo', & doe what in him lay to bring backe John Richardson.	2849.
Richards fined.	Walthian Richards was vpon his p'sentment fined 5^{lb}, & enjoyned to pay the witnesses, which were Edward Bennet, & his wife; Richard Silvester, & his wife; Arthur Warren, Thomas Rawlings, Thomas Penny, Mr Waltham, & Mary Smith, after 2^s p day, & to make a Publique.	2850.
Finch his wife ill.	Samuel Finch his wife was certified to bee ill.	2851.
Braintree.	The Inhabitants of Braintree, for the bridge over Minotocot River are respited till the Generall Court.	2852.
Hingham.	Hingham hath time till the first of the 3^d Mo^{th} to finish the bridge over Layford's-liking, which they are to doe by that time vpon paine of 5^{lb}.	2853.
Barnes.	Thomas Barnes about lace, was admonished, & discharged.	2854.
Jobson.	John Jobson for vnadvised exp'ssions, was admonished, & discharged.	2855.
Hands discharged.	Marke Hands for want of proofe was discharged.	2856.
Dorchester fined.	Dorchester for defective wayes was fined 5^s, & had [time] [*interlined*] till the 2^d Mo^{th}.	2857.
Marklin recompence Pen.	It was referred to indifferent men to judge, what recompence Marklin Knight should returne to James Pen.	2858.
Davies fined, bound.	William Davies for keeping an house of disorder, by giveing enterteinement against Order, was fined 20^s, & bound in 10^{lb} not to sell ale, strong beare, wine, or strong-water.	2859.
Chidley.	Mr Chidley was gone out of the Countrey before Co't.	2860.
Hawkins fined.	Thomas Hawkins for makeing bread to light was fined 5^s and enjoyned to give one witnesse, Edward Bates, 2^s 6^d.	2861.
Boston fined.	Boston for defective *was* towards Roxbury is fined 10^s, & enjoyned to mend them, by the 24th of the 2^d Mo^{th}, vpon paine of five pounds.	2861.
Cambridge fined.	Cambridge for a defective way to Charlestowne is fined 5^s.	2862.
Fuller.	Fuller was respitted till the next Quarter Co't.	2863.
Knight. Carters wife.	John Knights Cause to be tryed by Action. Carters wife was admonished, & discharged.	2864.

[278] At a Co't at Boston the 27th 11th Mo^{th} 1641.
Present The Governo^r Mr Winthrop.
Mr Dudley. Increase Nowell.

Knowers estate.	The administration of the estate of Thomas Knower is grannted to James Browne & William Stitson Gosse, & his wife, to bee brought to the next Co't, to answer things objected against them.	2866.
Wilsmore.	Elizabeth Wilsmore had warrant to the Constable of Watertowne, to provide hir a place in service, or otherwise.	2867.
Williams. Reed.	David W^{ms} hath put himselfe to John Read for 4 yeares, from the 12th of this p'sent Mo^{th}.	2868.
Fox. Everell.	John Fox hath put himselfe App'ntise to James Evrell, for 6 yeares, from this p'sent day.	2869.

Preface. XXIX

At a Quarter Co't at Boston ye 1st of the 1st Moth 1641/1642.
Present. Mr Governo^r Mr Winthrop.
Mr Dudley. Increase Nowell. Mr Bradstreet.

2870. Mr Timothy Tomlins. & Thomas Elington were graunted administration of the estate of Mr Ballard, & they are to dispose of the Children, & their estates. — Mr Ballards estate.

2871. George Story vpon his miscarriage was comitted, & after vpon his submission, & ackowledgement of his fault, hee was discharged. — Story comitted. &c.

2872. Charlestowne delivered in a transcript of their Lands. Sudbury dd in a transcript of their Lands. Dedham delivered in a transcript of their Lands. — Charlestowne. Sudbury. Dedham Lands.

2873. Malachy Browne had six shillings 8. pence Costs graunted against Francis Perry, for warning him to appeare, & not prosecuting him. — Browne. Perry.

2873. Mr Nicholas Trerice | his fine | [*interlined*] of forty shillings is remitted him. — Mr Trerice fine rem.

2874. Peter Thatcher for plotting Piracy was comitted, & to bee whipt; Matthew Collaine, Robert Allen, & Marmaduke Barton, were whipped for conceiling the plot of Piracy. — Thatcher, Collaine, Allen, Barton, whipt.

2875. Samuel Sherman is remitted his fine of 20^s. — Shermans fine remit.

2876. Henry Singleman is bound in 20^{lb} to bee of good behavio^r & to appeare at the Quarter Co't in the 7th Moth 1642. & Samuel Fuell is bound in 10^{lb} for the good behavio^r & appearance of Singleman. — Singleman, Fuell, bound.

2877. James Hawkins for prophaining the Sabbath hee was censured to bee whipt, & bound with his Brother Thomas Hawkins in 40^{lb} to appeare at the Generall Co't. & answer for venting his corrupt Opinions, & to bee of good behavio^r till then. — Hawkins whipt.

2878. Elizabeth Sedgwicke for hir many theftes, & lyes was censured to bee severely whipt, & condemned to slavery, till shee have recompenced double for all hir thefts. — Sedgwicke for theft, whipt. &c.

2879. Pesons, or George the Indian, was banished not to come among the English after a weeke. — Pesons banished.

2880. Minearry, the blackmore was admonished, & dismissed. — Minearry admonisht. &c.
2881. John Smith was admonished & dismissed. — Smith admonisht.
2882. Susan Cole was enjoyned to make double restitution. — Coles Restitution.

At a Co't at Boston 28th 2^d Moth 1642.
Present. The Governo^r Mr Winthrop.
Mr Dudley. Mr Staughten. Increase Nowell.

2883. Marmaduke Barton for his theft, & running away, was comitted to the keeper, as a slave, till the next Generall Co't. — Barton comitted.

2884. Thomas Briant for conceeling Thatchers Plott, & consenting to it, was censured to bee severely whipped. — Briant whipt.

2885. Elisha Jackson was with his owne consent turned over for his time, from George Barrell, to John Millam. — Jackson.

The 12th 3^d Moth 1642.
Present, The Governo^r.
Mr Winthrop. Increase Nowell.

2886. John Woodcooke for his many miscarriages was censured to bee whipped. — Woodcooke whipt.

At a Co't at Boston 20th 12th Mo'h 1642.
Present. The Governo' Mr Dudley.
Mr Bellingham. Increase Nowell.

Chadwickes fine discharged. Whittney fined. Charles Chadwicke is discharged of his fine of 3ˢ 4ᵈ & John Whit- ney the Constable is fined 2ᵈ for not warning him.

Story discharged. George Story appearing is discharged of his Bond for appearance to answer Capteine Keayne this Co't.

Charlestownes Constables allowed. It was ordered that the Constables of Charlestowne should bee allowed 9ˡᵇ 12ˢ 8ᵈ for the charge of

Mr. Ruck, Stow. Mr Thomas Rucke, & John Stow appearing, were appointed to appeare at the next Generall Co't, to give in their finall answer about the 50ˡᵇ comitted into their hands.

Davies, Kempe. [279] It was Ordered James Davies should have 3ˡᵇ 12ˢ for keeping of John Kempe for 12 weekes, at six shillings p weeke.

Hoare, Read. Mary Hoare was Ordered to pay John Read 10ˢ for hir theft, & trouble of him.

Chapman. payd. It was Ordered that Jacob Chapman should bee allowed 15ˢ for 9 dayes travell, & 2ˢ 6ᵈ layd out of purse.

Mrs Strainge Hingha. Order was sent to the Constables of Hingham, that Mrs Strainge & hir child should bee supplied according to their necessity that they may bee comfortablie mainteined by the helpe of such worke, as shee is able to doe, & hereof not to faile, as they will answer it.

Stiles allowance. It is conceived John Stiles should be allowed nine pound per annum for the time hee hath served, & twenty shilings, for being turned away in winter, vnprovided.

Marvin allowance. It is conceived that Thomas Marvin should bee allowed nine pound p annum for the time he served, & twenty shillings, for being turned away in winter, vnprovided, & 40ˢ for the 8 wolves killed.

The 16th of the 12th Mo'h 1642.
Present The Governo'.
Mr Bellingham. Increase Nowell.

Owles Willoughby fined. Daniel Owles comeing before vs, for drinking part of severall pints of wine, with William Willoughby was fined ten shillings.

Willoughby comitted. William Willoughby for beeing distempered with wine, & misspending his time, & neglecting both publique, & private Ordinances, was comitted to Prison to bee kept to worke there.

At a Quarter Co't at Boston 7th 1st Moth 1642/1643.
p'sent The Governo'.
The Dep'tie Gov' Mr Dudley.
Mr Bellingham. Mr Bradstreet.
Mr Flint. Increase Nowell.

Briscoe fined. Mr Nathaniel Briscoe for certeine mutinous speeches, & writings was fined 10ˡᵇ.

Pescot, Winter dism. John Pescot was dismissed with an admontion. John Winter is discharged wᵗʰ an admonition.

Mr Collecot payd. Mr Richard Collecot his bill of 21ˡᵇ 8ˢ 10ᵈ was assigned to bee paid him, & for himselfe for 18 days, 2ˡᵇ 14ˢ & for Mr Holeman, for 18 dayes, 2ˡᵇ 14ˢ.

2902.	M{r} Richard Browne beeing questioned for vnmeete & filthy dalliance, with Sarah now wife of Thomas Boylston, for want of full evidence, they were dismissed with an admontion.	Browne, Boylston's wife dis-missed.
2903.	Will{m} Bull, & Blith now his wife, were fined 20{s} for fornication comitted before marriage.	Bulls, Bliths fornic. fined.
2904.	John Stowers for reading to divers offensive passages (before comp{n}) out of a booke, against the Officers, & Church of Watertowne, & for making disturbance there, was fined forty shillings.	Stowers fined.
2905.	Sarah Bell for hir theft, stealing money from hir master, was censured to bee whipped, except shee behave hir selfe well, betwixt this, & the next Co{r}t, & soe as the Co{r}t see cause to remit it.	Bells theft.
2906.	John Cornish was comitted, & after was ordered to bee released vpon his owne bond, for his good behavio{r}, & appearance, & the next Co{r}t.	Cornish comitted &c.
2907.	Susan Hewet, & others which sold Sarah Pell goods were Ordered to take their goods backe, & repay the money to M{r} Newgate.	Hewet repay.
2908.	T[eagu] Ocrimi for a foule, & divilish attempt to bugger a cow of M{r} Makepeaces, was censured to bee carried to the place of execution, & there to stand with an halter about his necke, & to bee severely whipped.	Ocrimi punished.
2909.	Robert Wyar, & John Garland beeing indited for ravishing two yong girles, the fact confessed by the girles, & the girles both vpon search found to have bin defloured, & filthy dalliance confessed by the boyes; the Jury found them, not guilty, w{th} reference to the Capitall Law. The Co{r}t judged the boyes to bee openly whipped at Boston, the next market day, & againe to bee whipped at Cambridge on the Lecture day, & each of them to pay 5{lb} a peece to their master in service. It was also judged that the two girls Sarah Wythes, & Ursula Odle beeing both guilty of that wickednes, shall bee severely whipped at Cambridge in the p{r}sence of the Secretary.	Wyar, Garland whipt, & fined. Wythes, Odle, whipt.
3000.	The 15{th} 2{d} M{th}, M{r} Francis Norton, & John Penteeus, beeing formerly chosen Constables of Charlestowne, by the Towne, did take their Oathes to discharge that Office.	M{r} Norton, Penteeus, Charlestowne constables.

At a Co{r}t at Boston, the 27{th} 2{d} Mo{th} 1642.
Present.
  The Governo{r} M{r} Deputie, M{r} Dudley.
  M{r} Bellingham, M{r} Flint, Increase Nowell.

3001.	An Inventory of the estate of Edward Wood deceased, was delivered in, & an account how the Children are disposed of, which the Co{r}t doth approve.	Woods inventory.
3002.	Richard Taylo{r} beeing enjoyned to appeare at the next Co{r}t to answer for his rude & vnmeete speeches, hee was dismissed with an admonition.	Taylor admonished & dismissed.
3003.	Henry Neale appearing, his servant Henry Hobson was freed from him, and put [280] to another, & Henry Neale was enjoyned to pay all the witnesses, & deliver vp all bonds, & soe all things were ended betweene them.	Hobson freed. Neale to pay witnesses.
3004.	Henry Hobson is put to Goodman Thomas Meakins for the rest of his time, for 4{lb} p annū and vpon his good behavio{r} to have 2{s} 8{d} at the end of his time.	Hobson to Meakins

Stone, Armitage costs graunted.	John Stone, & Joseph Armitage, vpon a warrant from Joshuah Hubbard had ten shillings cost graunted them, against Joshua Hubbard for not prosecuting. 3005.
Owles servant to French.	Daniel Owles is put to Serjeant William French for a yeare, & then to bee brought againe to the Co't, to have further consideration had of the case, whether Serj' French had sufficient recompense for the losse of his servant, Edward Waldo, whom Owles conceald, plotting to run away, & councelled thereto. 3006.
Smith bound.	Richard Smyth concealing his knowledge of Edward Waldo his intent of running away, is bound in ten pound to appeare at the next Co't. 3007.
Wyar to Bowtle.	Robert Wyer is put to Leonard Bowtle, with his Masters consent for the rest of his time. 3008.
Browne whipt.	William Browne for running away, deriding an Ordinance of God, refusing to give account what hee had learned, & refusing to obey his master, was censured to be severely whipped. 3009.
Mindam discharged.	Robert Mindam appearing haveing bin imprisoned vpon an attachment by M' Campian, vpon pretence of a debt of 35^{lb} to M' Trerice, he was discharged, because noe action is entered, nor none appeareth to prosecute. 3010.
Quick whipt.	The 16th 3^d Moth Richard Quick for beeing distempered by drinking wine, & for his idlenes, stubbornes, & dalliance, was censured to bee whipped. 3011.
Roberts fined 12^d.	Edward Roberts was appointed to pay 12^d for drinking to Richard Quick. 3012.
Perry Whipt.	John Perry for running away was censured to bee whipped 17th 3^d Moth. 3013.
Harding, Hollister, Weymouth Constables.	John Harding, & John Hollister beeing chosen Constable of Weymouth, did take their oath to that place apperteining. 23. 3^d Moth. 3014.
Baker Ordinary keep.	M' Baker of Ipswich is allowed to *allowed to* keepe an Ordinary instead of Goodm. Andrews. 3015.
Goodnow Clarke of ye Band.	Edward Goodnow beeing chosen Clearke of the Band did take his Oath 5th 4th Moth. 3016.
M' Tomlins Ensigne.	M' Edward Tomlins beeing chosen is allowed Ensigne at Linn. 3017.
M' Tory Ensigne.	M' William Tory is appointed Ensigne at Weymouth. 3018.
Johnson.	Edward Johnson is appointed to traine the Company at Wooborne. 3019.

The 7th day of the 4th Moth 1642.
p'sent

The Govern'o' The Deputie. M' Dudley. M' Bellingham.

M' Bradstreet. M' Stoughton. M' Flint. Increase Nowell.

Dedham Lands.	Dedham delivering in a transcript of their lands, the Co't gave M' Allen leave to have the transcript backe againe. 3020.
Forbearance.	The other Townes, to wit Boston, Dorchester, Braintree, & Water-towne, had time graunted them till the 4th Moth 1643. 3021.
M' Paine discharged. Costs graunted.	M' Edward Paine vpon his appearance was discharged there beeing noe Action entered by Clement Campion, and M' Paine was graunted 6' 6^d costs against Clement Campion. 3022.
Wood fined.	Edward Wood was fined 8^s for baking wheat meale contrary to order. 3023.

Preface. XXXIII

3024. Thomas Scot, & his wife for coitting fornication before marriage, were enjoyned to stand an ho'e vpon the 16th p'sent, in the market place, with each of them a paper with great letters, on their hatts. — *Scott, & his wives punishment for fornicacon.*

3025. Thomas Morrice his will was delivered & vpon oath testified by Edward Woolastone, & William Hudson. — *Morrice will delivered, &c.*

3026. Thomas Whittamore because of his sore leg was dismissed with an admonition. — *Whitmore dismissed.*

3027. Concord delivered in a transcript of their Lands, but vnsubscribed, which not beeing according to Order, was delivered backe againe to them to perfect. — *Concord transcript imperfect.*

3028. Anne Keayne for hir grosse failing in not testifying the truth, when shee was called vpon oath shee was coitted to the Keeper, & vpon hir petition, & confession of hir fault, she was released. — *Keayne Comitted, &c.*

3029. Jonathan Bosworth for discountenancing a wittnesse, was coitted till hee find sureties; Samuel Ward, & Nicholas Jacobs were bound in 10lb a peece for Jonathan Bosworth his good behavio', & appearance at the next Quarter Co't, & Jonathan Bosworth himselfe was bound in 20lb. — *Bosworth bound, & to find suretyes.*

3030. Eliz: Strainge vpon acknowledgment of hir sincere —, with an injunction to acknowledge hir sin publiquely at Hingham, & that to bee certified by the Constable, shee was dismissed with an admonition. — *Eliz: Strainge dism.*

3031. William Jones vpon his acknowledgment here, beeing enjoyned to acknowledge the like Publiquely at Hingham, with an admonition, & an injunction to pay the witnesses 5ˢ a peece, he was dismissed. — *Jones dismissed.*

3032. M' Richards is abated twenty shillings of his fine. — *Richards fine abated.*

3033. [281] John Long Gent. for his misdemeano', distemper in drinke, swearing & cursing was fined twenty pound, & to put in sureties before his departure. — *Mr. Long fined.*

3034. Thomas Wilson his fine is respited till the end of the second Moneth 1643. and Anthony Staniard is bound in twenty pounds for the payment of Thomas Wilsons fine. — *Wilsons fine respited.*

3035. Isaac Morrell was fined 5ˢ for his absence, which hee is to pay to the rest of the Jury. — *Morrell fined.*

3036. Nicholas Powell is appointed Surveyo' of the Armes for Dedham. — *Powell Surveyo' of Armes.*

3037. It was Ordered that M' Stodder should have three pound of M' John Long, for himselfe, & ten shillings for the rest of his Company, for the trouble, & danger they sustained by M' Long. — *M' Longs damage.*

At a Small Co't at Boston, the 28th of the 5th Mo'h 1642.
p'sent
The Governo', M' Dudley. Mr. Stoughton. Increase Nowell.

3038. Henry Smith not appearing (beeing warned by the Governo'). — *Smith.*

3039. Margeret Stephenson is judged at liberty to be married to Benjamin Scott. — *Stephenson liberty graunted.*

3040. The Constable of Roxbury was Ordered to take care of John Kempe, servant formerly to Isaac Morrell, both for his maintenance, & cure, till the next Quarter Co't, and then further order should bee setled. — *Kempe cared for.*

3041. The Co't thought meet Dermondt Matthew should bee set to worke by such, as have occasion to imploy him, vntill his M' shall appeare, & take co'se about him. — *Matthew to worke.*

Bradley Administracon &c.	Katherin Bradley is graunted administration of hir husbands estate, who gave hir all his estate, only some cloathes, & tooles to his brother.	3042.

At a Quarter Co't the 6th of the 7th Mo^th 1642.

p'sent

The Governo' The Deputie Gov' M'. Dudley. M'. Bellingham. M' Saltonstall. M' Stoughton. M' Bradstreet. M' Flint. Increase Nowell.

Roberts comitted.	George Roberts was comitted to the keeper for his ill carriage, but after had leave, to goe take care of his corne, beeing it lay vpon spoyling.	3043.
Cooper, Hubbard, Converse constable. Bosworth discharged. Sever fined.	Thomas Cooper, & Joshua Hubbard Constables of Hingham.	3044.
	Edward Converse Constable of Wooborne.	3045.
	Jonathan Bosworth is discharged from his bond.	3046.
	Robert Sever for his miscarriage in neglecting the watch, is fined twenty pound which the Co't doth respite.	3047.
The Elders advice desired.	Severall of the Members of Hingham, vpon admonition of the Co't, did refer it to the Co't, to speake to the Elders to consider the case, & to send some of themselves to see, if it may please the Lord by advise to helpe to reconsile their differences, and settle them in a way of Christ.	3048.
Wooldrige fined.	M' John Wooldrige was fined 3^lb, & enjoyned vpon paine of 5^lb to acknowledge his offence, at Boston, Charlestowne, & Cambridge, reading an acknowledgment, written for his drunkenesse, & swearing.	3049.
Batter costs graunted.	M' Edmund Batter had six shillings, eight pence cost graunted him, against M' John Humphrey for serving him to appeare, & not prosecuting.	3050.
Lewis whipt.	John Lewis for running away, and breaking an house, was censured to bee whipped, & sent home to his Master.	3051.
Cole to worke.	Richard Cole was comitted to worke for his liveing, till a master bee found for him.	3052.
Walcot Whipt.	William Walcot was censured to bee whipped, & kept in Prison, till further Order, for his idlenesse, & abuse of his friends.	3053.
White comitted. releas.	Richard White beeing comitted for refusing to watch, vpon his submission he was released.	3054.
Het. Whipt, &c.	Anne Hett for attempting to droune hir child was censured to bee whipped, and kept to hard labo', & spare diet.	3055.
Coteree whipt.	Thomas Coteree was censured to bee severly whipped, for his vnmeet dalliance with two or three girles.	3056.
Juryes verdict returned.	The Jury returned verdict about the death of Richard Silvester his child.	3057.
Part of Mo. Thyeryes estate.	The Governo' hath in his hands about 4^lb of the estate of one Mountsier Thyery, a French man, that dyed here.	3058.
Watt's fined.	[282] George Watts is appointed to give ten shillings in cotton woole for swearing.	3059.
Cole put to Haward.	Richard Cole is put to William Haward for a yeare, vpon such wages as shall bee suteable to his yearnings.	3060.

At a Co't at Boston the 27th 8th Mo^th 1642.

p'sent

The Governo' M' Dudley. M' Bellingham. Increase Nowell.

3061. Samuel Finch, & John Gorton, for not appearing vpon the Alarme, their excuses were accepted, and they freed. Robert Vnion not appearing vpon the Alarme, his fine of 5lb is respited, till the Generall Co't. French Gorton excused. Vnions fine respited.

3062. Widdow Merriam is graunted administration of hir late husband Merriam his estate. Widdow Merriam administracon graunted.

3063. William Web for his neglect, in not carefully attending the Order of Co't about his bread, is fined ten shillings. Web fined.

3064. Vpon Consideration (severall Petitions p'ferred to this Co't) It was Ordered that Mr John Smith, Mr William Bacon, togeather with Mr John Oliver, Lervt Lusher, & Anthony Fisher, these, or any three of them whereof the said Mr John Smith, & Mr John Oliver to bee two, shall have power to take into their custody all the bookes, & writings of the said Edward Allen, to cast vp, & to cleare the accounts, for devideing of the interests of the severall Parties, & to pay, & receive all debts and to certify the Co't with what speed they may. Comitted appointed.

3065. The Treasuro' had order to pay Mr Oliver the summe of 12lb for his paines about Mansfield. Mr Oliver's summe.

3066. John Newton, & Edward Allen are graunted the Administracon of the estate of Mr Edward Allen. Administracon graunted.

3067. Davyd Conway servant to Wm Beamsley, for resisting his master was censured to be whipped. Conway whipt.

3068. John Neale servant to Mr Cockram was comitted vpon suspition of felony. Neale comitted.

3069. William Hudson was graunted six shillings, eight pence against Symon Kempthorne, for attaching, & causing him to attend, & not prosecuting. Hudson costs graunted.

3070. Frances Pembroke tooke hir oath, that Mr Allen, vpon his death bed gave his estate to John Newton, & Edward Allen his kinsman, & that he was then, & after in good memory, & vnderstanding. Mr Allens gift testified.

3071. The 14th of the 9th Moth 1642. Daniel Mansfeild is put to William Denux for five yeares from this p'sent day. Mansfeild to Denux.

At a Quarter Co't at Boston, the 6th of the 10th Moth 1642.
p'sent.
The Governo' Mr Dudley. Mr Bellingham. Mr Flint. Increase Nowell.

3072. Charles Cadwicke, & Robert Holmes, are fined three shillings, foure pence a peece, for beeing absent, being warned. Chadwicke. Holmes fined.

3073. Edward Lewis, Williams, John Shearman, & George Munnings, are appointed to view the leather which is tanned in Watertowne, & to certify vpon their oathes, (& in perticular leather tanned by John Winter, for which hee was p'sented, which John Warren can testify) at the next Quarter Co't. Searchers appointed.

3074. William Shepheard for covenanting for 15lb wages p annum, is fined two pound. Shepheard fined.

Laurence Copeland for covenanting for 15lb wages p annum is fined 2lb, beeing both released one halfe of the time, which was ordered to bee stayed in John Mowers hand, and by him, to bee payd two shillings to Martin Saunders, & 3lb 18s to the Treasuro'. Copeland fined.

3075. Watertowne p'sentment is referred to the next Quarter Co't. Watertowne p'sentm'.

Mr Hibbins allowed.	It was ordered that Mr Hibbins should bee allowed twenty pounds 3076. for his horse killed in Pubique service.
Mr Bartholomew cause refered.	Mr Bartholomew his cause, vpon his brothers vndertaking to bee 3077. surety to answer for his brother, at the next Quarter Co't, it was referred to the next Quarter Co't: And Capteine Keaynes Action is
Capt. Keaynes Action defer.	deferred by consent, till Mr Bartholomew doe come.
Weane to Gunnison.	David Weane by consent put himselfe to Hugh Gunnison for 3lb 3078. 15s till that bee wrought out.
Addington deposition.	Isaac Addington did depose that Timothy Higgenson had 6. gallons 3079. of Mr Eldreds wine, Robert Gillam had 5. gallons, William Pearce as hee thinketh had 5. gallons, & himselfe had 5. gallons.
Matthew to Dexter.	Dearmant Matthew is put to Thomas Dexter for the rest of his 3080. time, Dexter promiseth to pay what wages Dearmant proveth to bee due, and all is referred to Mr Sadler, & goodman Armitage to heare, & end all businesses, & the 3 attachments are discharged.
Walton have his goods againe.	It was Ordered that Mr Walton should have his goods againe, 3081. which were vnjustly taken and the Arbitrato" to end the businesse of the sow, if they can.
Lee costs graunted.	[283] John Lee is graunted six shillings 8. pence against 3082. Richard Lettin, for somoning him to appeare, causing him to attend, & not prosecuting.
Braintree fined.	Martin Saunders vndertooke the Bridges, p'sented, should bee re- 3083. paired, soe Braintree was fined three shillings, foure pence, & discharged.
Mr Ruck, Stow called.	It was Ordered that Mr Ruck, & Goodman Stow, should bee sent 3084. vnto, to come in at the next Co't, & should shew how they have disposed of the 50lb, or bring it in, or shew why they should not.
Davies fined.	William Davies was fined 5lb for his contempt, in keeping victu- 3085. alling against Order of Co't.
Hingham discharged. Boston discharged. p'sentments respited.	Hingham vpon oath given, that the way is made out, is discharged. 3086. Boston is discharged, the way to Charlestowne being made good. 3087. The other p'sentments are respited till the next Quarter Co't 3088. because of the weather.
El. Hasnet put to Wilson.	The 11th Moth 1642. 5. day. Elizabeth Hasnet is put to William 3089. Wilson, for 50s wages, for the yeare.
Wicks Constable.	The 12th day. George Wicks beeing chosen Constable of Dorchester 3090. tooke his Oath.

At a Quarter Co' at Boston the 10th of the 4th Moth 1643.
p'sent

The Governo'	The Deputie.	Mr Dudley.
Mr Bellingham.	Mr Saltonstall.	Mr Bradstreet.
Mr Hibbens.	Mr Flint.	Increase Nowell.

Ridway payd.	It was Ordered that forty five shillings of the estate of Mr William 3092. Bladen, should bee payd to James Riddway, who was his servant for his yeares provision.
Boston p'sented.	The Towne of Boston beeing p'sented for defect of their high- 3093. waies, they had bin p'sented for
Mr Oliver payd.	It was Ordered that Mr Oliver should have for his paines, &.charge 3094. about the Saylo' three pound, about Mansfeild twenty shillings, about Kemp seaven pounds; togeather eleven pounds.

Preface.

3095. Robert Heathersby appearing is discharged of his bond, & graunted 10ˢ costs against. — *Hethersby discharged.*

3096. James Brittaine beeing p'sented, & traversing the p'sentment was respited to the next Co't, and bound himselfe in twenty pounds to appeare then, & answer. William Brandon to appeare for a witnesse. — *Brittaine respited &c.*

3097. Thomas Layton appearing was discharged. — *Layton dis. charged.*

3098. Richard Smyth beeing convented, for beeing privy to Edward Waldo his intent to run away, which was wittnessed by Blith Bull, hee was comitted to. — *Smith comitted.*

3099. George Mills for a Battery is fined ten shillings. — *Mills fined.*

3100. Richard Willis for a foule Battery is fined 2ᵗᵇ 10ˢ, & comitted till hee pay or give sufficient security. — *Willis fined com.*

3101. William Chadborne, senio', John Low, Robert Butcher, William Affeild, John Woodward, Ambrose Leach & Sacheas Bosworth were fined 10ˢ apeece, for drinking too much. — *Chadborne, Low, Butcher, Affeild, Woodward &c. fined.*

3102. Ralph Golthrope is fined 10ˢ for beeing distempered with wine. — *Golthrope fined.*

3103. William Filpot was admonished to take heed of suffering drinking in his house. — *Filpot admonished.*

3104. Anker Ainsworth beeing p'sented for taking excessive wages, it did not appeare, & soe hee was discharged. — *Ainsworth discharged.*

3105. Mr Draytons Cause against Mr Wannerton is transmitted to the Co't at Piscataq. — *Mr Draintons cause transm.*

3106. Mr Stodder beeing p'sented for selling cloth at an excessive rate, it appeared noe excesse in him, soe hee promising to satisfy Mr Paine was discharged. — *Mr Stodder p'sented, disch.*

3107. Henry Leake, & his wife for fornication were enjoyned to appeare the next Lecture day, at Dorchester after the Lecture, and to acknowledge their fault. — *Leake & his wife, for fornication to acknowledge.*

3108. John Smyth Clarke of the Band at Dorchester. — *Smyth Clarke of the Band.*

3109. Francis Pemble bound him in 20ᵗᵇ to appeare at the next Co't, to answer for his lewd, & reproachfull speaches. — *Pemble bound.*

The 27ᵗʰ of the 5ᵗʰ Moᵗʰ 1643.
p'sent

Mr Governo' Mr Dudley. Mr Bellingham. Mr Hibbens. Increase Nowell.

3110. Nicholas Rogers for beeing distempered with wine, or strong drinke, was fined 2ᵗᵇ who being imprisoned is remitted to ten shillings. — *Rogers fined.*

3111. William Scutt for selling powder, & shot to the Indians was fined 10ᵗᵇ to pay the halfe, when come is payable, & the other halfe a 12. Moᵗʰ after, & Thomas Spaule is surety. — *Scutt selling powder to Indians, fined.*

3112. Samuel Bacon for stealing wine, & other thinges, was censured to be severely whipped, & to make double restitution, to Mʳˢ Hull, & his Dame. — *Bacon stealing, whipt. &c.*

3113. Robert Rogers was, for receiving stollen wine, being consenting in it, enjoyned to pay Mr Manning 32ˢ & fined to the Countrey 40ˢ. — *Rogers consenting to theft, fined &c.*

3114. Miles Tompson for drinking with them, & beeing privy, was to pay Mr Manning 16ˢ. — *Tompson.*

Toby Davies beeing privy, & drinking with them was to pay Mr Manning 10ˢ. — *Davies.*

Wyar.	[284] Robert Wyar for drinking with Bacon, beeing privy to the
Cooper.	taking of it, was enjoyned to pay Mr Manning 4^s Thomas Cooper for drinking, beeing privy to the manner of taking it, to pay Mr Manning 4^s.
Tapping for theft, whipt.	Nathaniel Tappin for breaking, & *breaking* into severall houses, 3115. and stealing severall thinges, was censured to be whipped, & put to Goodman Gillam.
Langley Lin Constable.	William Langley beeing chosen Constable of Linn, tooke his Oath. 3116.

At a Quarter Co't at Boston the 5th of the 7th Moth 1643. p'sent

Mr Deputie Govr Mr Dudley. Mr Bellingham. Mr Saltonstall. Mr Pinchon. Mr Bradstreet. Mr Flint. Mr Symons. Mr Hibbens. Increase Nowell.

Clough fined.	John Clough is fined 6^s 8^d for his absence when the Jury was called. 3117.
Colthrop fined.	Ralph Colthrop was fined 3^s for his distem*p* in drinke, & if he fayle 3118. in that againe, to have Corporall punishment.
Legacyes payd.	It is Ordered that vpon the Letter of Atturney shewed heare in 3119. Co't, the Legacyes should bee payd by Mr Smyth of Springfeild to John Porter.
Wilson fornication fined.	Gawen Wilson is fined twenty shillings for fornication, which M^r 3120. Bozoon Allen vndertooke to satisfy in cotton-woole by Mr Coitmore.
Napper discharged.	George Napper was discharged, & comitted to his Master, and to 3121. stay with him, soe much longer for the time hee hath bin absent.
Bairstow discharged.	William Bairstowe appearing was discharged. 3122.
Eliz. Vane comitt. relens.	Elizabeth Vane, for hir miscarriage in abuseing one of the Magistrates, & Mrs Newgate, was comitted at the pleasure of the Co't, & vpon hir humble Petition, & acknowledgment, was released. 3123.
Jeames Ilingham Const.	Francis James chosen Constable of Hingham, tooke his Oath. 3124.
Gell whipt. runing away.	Richard Gell servant to Francis Fellingham of Salem, for runing 3125. away was censured to bee whipped, & sent to his Master, whom hee is to serve for the time hee hath lost.
Bartlet whipt. fined.	John Bartlet for his swearing, theft, & drunkenes was comitted to 3126. Prison, & censured to bee whipped, & fined twenty shillings. Stephen
Day comitted. Gammage whipt.	Day for his defrauding severall men was comitted. John Gammage for his swearing, drunkenes, & other prophanes, & disorder, was censured to bee well whipped.
Arbitrato^{rs}.	Mr Symons, Mr Fowle, Mr Smyth, Mr Dan, & Goodman Bendall, 3127. are appointed by consent to arbitrate betweene Mr Humphrey & Mr Robert Saltonstall.
Anker fined.	Thomas Anker payd 5^s for his destem*p* in drinke which 3128.
M^r. Pendleton Sudbury.	Mr Briant Pendleton is appointed to exercise the Company at Sudbury. 3129.
Watts fined.	George Watts for his destem*p* in drinke, swearing, & abusing the 3130. watch was fined 10^{lb} & to pay *to pay*, or give sufficient security before hee bee released.
Serj^t. Wardall Exeter.	Serjt. Wardall is appointed to traine the Company at Exeter. 3131.
Lewis enjoyned. Lewis freed.	Lewis is enjoyned not to strike his servant John Lowe, & to set the 3132. said John Low free the 24th of the 4th Moneth 1644.
Administration graunted.	Andrew Allen is graunted administration of his Brother Edward 3133. Allen his estate, who was killed the fourth of this p'sent Moneth.

3134.	The eighth Moth twelfth. Nicholas Rogers for his drunkenes, and makeing others drunke with his strong-water, was censured to bee whipped.	Rogers whipt.
	Swiniard Lewis for his beeing drunke, was fined ten shillings, which hee paid.	Lewis fined.
3135.	The 19. day. Israel Hart is fined twenty shillings for neglecting the watch, and enjoyned allsoe to pay the two witnesses, and the officer.	Hart fined.
3136.	The 20. day. Richard Wood is allowed to keepe an Ordinary at Roxbury.	Wood Ordinary keep.
3137.	Thomas Burges for his distemper, was dismissed with an admonition to take heed of the like fayling.	Burges admonisht.
3138.	Thom. White is graunted 13^s 4^d against Andrew Belcher, for the 5^{lb} of powder, & trouble he hath put him to.	White costs graunted.
3139.	Thomas Bauldwin for his miscarriage to his master, and striking him was committed to prison.	Bauldwin committed.
3140.	Robert Wright is fined twenty shillings for beeing twice distempered in drinke, or to sit an houre in the stocks, the next Market day at Boston.	Wright fined.
3141.	William Barnes for swearing is fined ten shillings.	Barnes fined.
3142.	James Kinloah appearing for want of proofe hee was discharged.	Kinloah discharged.
3143.	It was Ordered that Francis Lightfoot should have paid him, by Mr Edward Gately ten shillings, and by Joseph Armitage foure shillings, for the trouble, & attendance they caused to him.	Lightfoot payd.

[285] At a Co^rt at Boston the 26 of the 8th 1643.
p'sent
The Deputie Governo^r Mr Thomas Flint. Increase Nowell.

3144.	Leonard Fryar was fined 10^s Leonard Fryar, James Nelme, & David Wayne, all 3. are bound in 40^s apeece to appeare at the next Quarter Co^rt to answer for excessive drinking, & distemper.	Fryar fined. Fryar, Nelme, Wayne, bound to appeare.
3145.	John Garland for stealing severall thinges to the value of 3^s 6^d was enjoyned to make double restitution.	Garland to make restitution.
3146.	Thomas Arnold beeing chosen Constable of Watertowne, tooke the Constables Oath.	Arnold Watertowne Const.
3147.	The will, & Inventory of William Fry, to the Recorder was delivered the ninth of the ninth Moneth, the widow beeing Executrix, and the wittnesses Thomas Bayly, & John Burges tooke their Oaths.	Fryes will recorded.
3148.	David Dauling, Mary Andley, & Jane Jeffrey, for their filthy, & vncleane practise, were censured to bee severely whipped.	Dauling, Audley, Jeffrey, whipt.

At a Co^rt at Boston the 5th of the 10th Moth 1643.
p'sent The Governo^r Mr Dudley. Mr Winthrop Junr.
Mr Stoughton. Mr Hibbens. Mr Flint. Increase Nowell.

3149.	Capteine John Chadwicke for swearing many oathes, and other disorder is fined twenty pounds.	Capt. Chadwicke fined.
3149.	Capteine Aaron Williams for distemp in drinke, is fined ten shillings, which hee paid.	Capt. Williams fined.
3150.	It was Ordered that John Johnson the Surveyo^r should take out of the Cattell which came from Providence, the money disbursed for that Company, & vndertaking, which is twenty five pounds three shillings, & nine pence, as p pticulers.	Souldiers charges disbursed.

Sudbury Mill fined.	The owners of Sudbury Mill are fined 3ˢ 4ᵈ for want of Scales, & 3151. Weights, and they are to provide them, by the next Quarter Co't in paine of twenty shillings.
Dedham transcript accepted.	Dedham delivered in a transcript of their Lands, and was discharged; and for the way betweene Dedham and Cambridge, they have time till the fourth moneth next. 3152.
Painter stockt.	Thomas Painter for disturbing the Church of Hingham, was censured to bee sett in stocks a Lecture day, at Lecture time, except hee humble himselfe, and give the Church satisfaction. 3153.
Ardway accused, dismissed.	Abner Ardway beeing accused for dallying with Mary Giles for want of proofe he was dismissed with an admonition. 3154.
Read dismissed. Williams whipt.	John Read for refusing to watch hee was dismissed, and the thing to bee considered. David Williams for assaulting the watch was censured to be whipped at Braintree, and warrant to George Read, to stop 3155.
Porter considered of.	out of the wages, to pay the witnesses. William Porter for refusing to watch to bee considered of.
Archers whipping respited.	John Archer for resisting his Master was censured to bee whipped, which is respited. 3156.
Too much wages considered of.	James Loranson, John Callwell, Thomas Danfort, John Gill, and his wife, with John Pope beeing p'sented, for taking too much wages, to bee considered of. 3157.
Johnson chosen Leivtenant.	Edward Johnson beeing chosen Leivt' of Wooborne is allowed of. 3158.
Merryfeild respited. Beamis fined.	Henry Merryfeild beeing p'sented for lewd speeches, is respited. John Beamis for freeing his servant against Order, was fined ten shillings. M' Broughton is dismissed, hee beeing not respondent for it. 3159.
Mr. Broughton dismissed. Barnard fined.	John Barnard for his daingerous well, is fined 10ˢ and enjoyned to make it safe with 28 dayes, vpon paine of 40ˢ.
Adams Braintree Coustab. Golthrop whipt, or fined.	Henry Adams beeing chosen Coustable of Braintree, tooke his Oath. Ralph Golthrop for beeing againe distempered with drinke, was censured to bee whipped, which if hee bring sureties for his good behavio' and pay twenty shillings, hee is discharged. 3160. 3161.
Campion costs graunted.	Clement Campion is graunted three pounds 6. shillings, & 8. pence against John Rogers, for attaching him, & not prosecuting. 3162.
Killmaster fined. Betts discharged. Weatherly fined.	John Killmaster for beeing twice distempered with drinke was fined twenty shillings. John Betts appearing, for want of proofe was discharged. Thomas Weatherly for swearing, & quarrelling was fined twenty shillings, and to pay the wittnesses five shillings. 3163.
Hudson Ordinary Keep.	William Hudson Junio' is allowed to keepe an house of entertein-ment. 3164.
M' Stileman discharged.	M' Stileman appearing about the way, for want of wittnesses, was discharged. 3165.
Fryar. Nelme. Waine. forfeit.	Leonard Fryar, Jasp Nelme, & David Wayne forfeited forty shillings a peece for not appearing. 3166.
Wright bound.	George Wright for his attempt to vncleanes with a married woman, is bound to his good behavio' in forty pound, & to appeare at yᵉ Quarter Co't the first Moneth, and to pay the wittnesses. 3167.
Knop ordinary keep. Osborne costs graunted.	William Knops wife is allowed to keepe an house of enterteinment. Richard Osborne was graunted six shillings, 8. pence, against Thomas Turner for warning him to appeare, & not prosecuting. 3168. 3169.
Capt. W'' discharged from Capteine Chadwicke.	Capteine Aaron Williams is discharged from Capteine John Chadwicke, in regard hee swore hee would kill him, as was testifyed. 3170.

Preface. XLI

3171. Attachments were graunted against such as beeing warned did not   Attachm'ts graunted. appeare, as, Carew Latham. Richard Quick, Samuel Finch his wife &c.

3172. Mr Dunsters Petition is graunted him, & any two of the Feofees to   Mr Dunsters Petition graunted. have power to dispose of thinges, and to receive, & pay the debts.

       At a Co^rt at Boston the 25th of the 11th Mo^th 1643.
       p^rsent
       The Governo^r Mr Dudley. Mr Hibbens. Mr Flint. Increase Nowell.

3173. The Constable of Boston is fined ten shillings for not returning his   Boston Const. fined. warrant. Thomas Grub not appearing upon the Jury is fined 5^s this is   Grubs fine discharged. discharged. Thomas Moulton for his light carriage, is bound in ten   Moulton bound. pound to bee of good carriage, and to appeare at the next Co^rt.

3173. [286] Bridget Barnard for stealing from Mr Stodder   yards   Barnard stealing. of ribben 3^s 24. douzen of buttons, 4^s from William Knop senior ½ yard of bayes 1^s 6^d from Goodw. Button a peece of callico, 8^d & from John Trotman 2. paire of shooes 6^s.

3174. William Flint beeing a married man haveing gotten a slutt with child   Flint fornication fined. is fined 20^lb whereof 10^lb is left to the Toune of Salem to bring vp the child with, and the other ten pound to the Publique, and to lye in Prison till hee pay it. or give security.

3175. Mr Treasuro^r was desired to cast vp Goodm. Turners bill, & if it be   Co^rt Charges. found right 53^lb 15^s 6^d to allow it.

3176. David Weane is remitted 20^s of the 40^s forfeited for non appearance,   Weanes, Nelmes fine in part remitted. to pay the other 20^s which George Burden vndertook to pay. within a Month. Jasp Nelme is remitted 20^s of his forty shillings forfeited, to pay the other twenty shillings.

3177. William Chadborne appearing to answer John Shaw is discharged   Chadborne Shaw. for the p^rsent.

3178. The transcript of Watertowne Lands is respited till the Quarter   Watertowne Lands. transcript respited. Co^rt in the 4th Mo^th next.

3179. Mary Bentley for stealing *for stealing* Mr Waltons jewell of 11^s   Bentley stealing. Restitution. price, hee haveing the jewell againe and 9^s 6^d of hir wages shee is to pay 18^d more.

3180. John Parker appearing vpon sumons from John Kendall, &   Parker Kendall. Kendall not prosecuting John Parker is graunted six shillings, eight pence against Kendall.

3181. The 2^d of the 12th Mo^th Hugh Mason, and George Munnings, beeing   Mason, Munnings, sealers. Bayly to Hill. p^rsented for sealers, & searchers of leather. Richard Bayly put himselfe for 4. yeares to Abramim Hill, from the 13. of ye 11 Mo^th past.

       At a Quarter Co^rt at Boston the 5th of ye 1st Mo^th 1643/44.
       p^rsent.
       The Governo^r The Deputie Govr Mr Dudley. Mr Bellingham. Mr Winthrop jun^r. Mr Bradstreet. Mr Hibbens. Mr Flint. Mr Symonds. Increase Nowell.

3182. George Frost beeing distempered with wine was fined ten shillings.   Frost distempered fined.
3183. John Hart beeing distempered with wine was fined twenty shillings.   Hart distempered fine.
3184. Thomas Cooper beeing absent from the Grand Jury, when it was   Cooper Gillam fined. called, is fined six shillings, eight pence. Benjamin Gillam beeing absent from the Jury of Tryalls is fined five shillings.

Halsteeds Inventory, his eldest son Administrator.	The Inventory of Nathaniel Halsteed amounting to 213^{lb} 13^s 2^d was p'sented, & it was ordered the eldest son should have 106^{lb} 10^s & the other 2. children, 106^{lb} 10^s, & the eldest son William is graunted to bee administrato'.
Fryars forfeiture remitted, for distemp' fined. Latham, Johnson, Bauldwin, fined.	Leonard Fryar his forfeiture is remitted, & hee is fined 15^s for distemper in drinke, & disorder. Carew Latham is fined 10^s for his disorder, & dismissed. Edward Johnson jun' for imoderate drinking was fined 5^s, & dismissed. John Bauldwin for excessive drinking, was fined 5^s, & dismissed.
Anne Clarke divorced.	Anne Clarke beeing deserted by Denis Clarke hir husband, & hee refusing to accompany with hir, she is graunted to bee divorced, his refusall was vnder his hand, & seale, which hee gave before Mr John Winthrop jun^r Mr Emanuel Downing, Mr Nehemiah Bo'ne, & Richard Babington, alsoe hee confesseth hee liveth in adultry with one, by whom hee hath had 2. & refuseth hir which hee had 2 children by.
Wright discharged.	George Wright appearing & testimony of his good carriage hee was discharged.
Milam discharged.	John Milam appearing, & declaring hee had the cloth of Mr Stoughton for 9^s hee was discharged.
Mr Dutchfeild fined.	Mr Thomas Dutchfeild for distemper in drinke is fined 10^s & admonished, & dismissed.
Amedowne, Harris.	Roger Amedowne was enjoyned to pay 2^s 6^d fees, admonished, & discharged. John Harris to pay two^s 6^d fees, was admonished, & discharged.
Brittaine, Latham for adultery condemned.	James Brittaine beeing found guilty of adultery with Mary Latham, he was condemned to death. Mary Latham beeing found guilty of adultery with James Brittaine, she was condemned to death.
Taylor	Rebecka the wife of John Taylor.
Betson.	Stephen Betson for his sinfull attempt hee was bound to his good behavio^r, & enjoyned to appeare y^e next Co^{rt}.
Smith theft fined.	Nathaniel Smith for his theft was ordered to pay Capt. Sedgwicke 49^s & fined 20^s for his intem_pate drinking.
Stow, Concord 222 acres.	Vpon releasment of John Stow, Concord men are graunted Power to seize the 222. acres of Land, & hay, & debts due by any rent of the said Land.
Moulton discharged. Richardson sequestred from Fryar.	Thomas Moulton appearing was discharged. It was Ordered that John Richardson should be sequestred from Elizabeth Fryar, to whom he was married, ye 12th of the 8th Moth, & neither to meddle with hir Person, nor estate, till thinges bee cleared by advice from England, & Christop. Lawson is to keepe 5^s p weeke out of his yearnings, when his debts are paid.
Co^{rt} Charges.	Francis Smith is graunted his bill of 2^{lb} 3^s 11^d for ferridge, & horse pasture, of Magistrates, & Deputies horses from the 25th of y^e 2^d Moth 1642. to the 5th of the 1st Moth $\frac{1642}{1643}$.
Merrickes fined. Orton, Sheepe, fined.	[287] James, & John Merricke for drinking intemperately, and suffering others to drinke at their house, & selling wine, are fined 10^s apeece, & to pay 2^s 6^d apeece, fees. Thomas Orton for intem_pate drinking is fined 5^s & 2^s 6^d fees. Thomas Sheepe for intem_pate drinking is fined 5^s & 2^s 6^d fees.

Right margin numbers: 3185. 3186. 3187. 3188. 3189. 3190. 3191. 3192. 3193. 3194. 3195. 3196. 3197. 3198. 3199. 3200. 3201.

3202. The 23. of the 3ᵈ Moᵗʰ Barnabas Fawer tooke the oath for Constable for Dorchester for the yeare ensueing. *Fawer. Dorchester Constable.*

The 30ᵗʰ day. Thomas Richards, & William Read beeing chosen Constables of the Toune of Waymouth did take their oathes. *Richards. Read Waymouth Cō.*

3203. John Johnson, & William Parks are appointed a Comittee to examine, by the former Comissionoʳˢ or otherwise, to find out, gather vp, & receive into their custody, which hereby they are Authorized to doe, & to certify how they find thinges about Mʳ Samuel Cooke his estate. *Johnson. Parks. Comittee Mʳ Cookes estate.*

INTRODUCTION.

The history of the published Laws of the Colony of Massachusetts is naturally divided into four periods. First, the publication of the Body of Liberties in 1641; secondly, the issue of the first collection of Laws, in 1649; thirdly, the revision of 1660; fourthly, the further revision of 1672, with its supplements through 1686.

Having already been able to reprint the edition of the Laws of 1672, with its supplements, I now have the satisfaction of presenting in this volume two of the other earlier documents, namely, the Body of Liberties of 1641 and the revision of the Laws as printed in 1660. The other edition, that of 1649, is doubtless hopelessly lost, no copy being now known. We may, however, conclude that its title was the same as the first part of that prefixed to the edition of 1660; and we are assured by the preface to the last-named book that the edition of 1649 was arranged "in an alphabetical order," that it had a preface or "epistle" telling "there would be need of alterations and additions." It is also clear that the editions of 1660 varied from that of 1649 by the omission of such laws as had been repealed and the addition of such laws as had since been enacted. Those which were omitted cannot be recovered, but by comparing the Body of Liberties with the edition of 1660, and by striking out of the latter also all the laws dated after 1649, it would still be possible to reconstruct the edition of 1649 in almost perfect form.

It is perhaps as well to state here that for a long time a spurious Code of Laws has been cited as the genuine Body of Liberties of 1641. I refer to the pamphlet issued in 1641 in London, which was undoubtedly the work of Rev. John Cotton. It was reprinted there in 1655 under the care of William Aspinwall, and has in later years been reprinted, in 1798, in the fifth volume of the first Series of the Collection of the Massachusetts Historical Society, and, in 1844, in the third volume of Force's Tracts. It was also printed in Hutchinson's Collections of Papers (Boston, 1769), and reprinted with notes in the re-issue of that book by the Prince Society (Albany, 1865).

Although, as will be shown, the evidence is conclusive that Cotton's Code was only *proposed* and never accepted, while a totally different set of laws was actually enacted in 1641, this error has obtained in many quarters, and needs to be authoritatively denied and disproved.

Reverting therefore to the facts which can be ascertained, it is well to remember that our system of making laws by a representative body was not coincident with the settlement of the colony of Massachusetts. The Charter of March 4, 1629, provided for a governor, a deputy-governor, and eighteen[1] assistants to be chosen from time to time out of the freemen of the company, whereof seven assistants, together with the two officers, were to be a quorum. They were to meet once a month or oftener at their pleasure, and four times in each year, viz., upon every last Wednesday in Hilary, Easter, Trinity, and Michaelmas terms, were to hold a Great and General Court. In the General Court new members could be admitted, and at that time they could " make laws and ordinances for the good and welfare of the said Company, and for the government and ordering of the said lands and plantation and the people inhabiting and to inhabit the same, as to them from time to time shall be thought meet. So as such laws and ordinances be not contrary or repugnant to the laws and statutes of this our realm of England." (Records, p. 12.)

In fact, for several years after the settlement here the powers of the General Court were allowed to lie dormant. The Court of Assistants met from time to time, as seemed necessary, but the General Court met only as follows: —

1630.	October 19.	(Records,	i. p. 79, printed edition.[2])
1631.	May 18.	"	i. p. 86.
1632.	May 9.	"	i. p. 95.
1633.	May 29.	"	i. p. 104.
1634.	May 14.	"	i. p. 116.

The Records as preserved show both the extent of the powers exercised by the Assistants, and the insignificance of the action of

---

[1] This number was not observed until 1680. Before this twelve was the highest number actually serving, and eight or nine more usual. — W. H. W.

[2] I cite Savage's edition of Winthrop, Boston, 1853; and in all cases the printed edition of the Records, issued by the State. — W. H. W.

the body of freemen assembled in the annual General Court. The Assistants acting as a Court had during these three years inflicted fines, whippings, and imprisonments, had levied taxes and granted lands. In fact, at the first General Court on Oct. 19, 1630, it was voted " by the general vote of the people and the erection of hands," that the Governor and Deputy Governor with the Assistants, " should have the power of making laws and choosing officers to execute the same." (Records, p. 79.)

Winthrop indeed records (Hist. i. 81) that in February, 1631-2, the settlers at Watertown objected to paying £8 as their part of a rate for £60 for fortifying the new town, on the ground that the government was like that of a mayor and aldermen. But they were convinced by the Governor and Council " that this government was rather in the nature of a Parliament."

In 1634, however, the freemen of the colony showed a desire to take a part in the government. Winthrop (i. 152-3) thus introduces the matter: —

" Notice being sent out of the General Court to be held the 14th day of the third month called May, the freemen deputed two of each town to meet and consider of such matters as they were to take order in at the same General Court ; who having met, desired a sight of the patent, and, conceiving thereby that all their laws should be made at the General Court, repaired to the Governor to advise with him about it, and about the abrogating of some orders formerly made, as for killing of swine in corn, &c. He told them, that when the patent was granted, the number of freemen was supposed to be (as in like corporations) so few, as they might well join in making laws ; but now they were grown to so great a body, as it was not possible for them to make or execute laws, but they must choose others for that purpose : and that howsoever it would be necessary hereafter to have a select company to intend that work, yet for the present they were not furnished with a sufficient number of men qualified for that business, neither could the company bear the loss of time of so many as must intend it. Yet this they might do at present, viz. they might at the General Court make an order, that once in the year, a certain number should be appointed (upon summons from the Governor) to revise all laws, &c. and to reform what they found amiss therein ; but not to make any new laws, but prefer their grievances to the Court of Assistants ; and that no assessment should be laid upon the country without the consent of such a committee, nor any lands disposed of."

At the meeting of the General Court, May 14, 1634, there were present, besides the Governor, Deputy, and six other assistants, twenty-four deputies, undoubtedly sent by Newtown (*i.e.*, Cambridge), Watertown, Charlestown, Boston, Roxbury, Dorchester, Saugus (*i.e.*, Lynn), and Salem; three from each place.³

This regular Legislature proceeded to vote (Records, i. 117), that none but the General Court had power to choose and admit freemen, nor to make and establish laws, to appoint or remove officers and fix their duties, nor to raise money and taxes, nor to dispose of lands. It was also ordered (p. 118), that there should be four General Courts yearly, to be summoned by the Governor, and not to be dissolved without the consent of the major part of the Court. Lastly, they ordered that the freemen of every town might choose two or three men to prepare business to be submitted to each Court, — a provision which was soon neglected, — and also the following system which has continued ever since.

"Such persons as shall be hereafter so deputed⁴ by the freemen of the several plantations, to deal in their behalf in the public affairs of the commonwealth, shall have the full power and voices of all the said freemen, derived to them for the making and establishing of laws, granting of lands, &c., and to deal in all other affairs of the commonwealth wherein the freemen have to do, the matter of election of magistrates and other officers only excepted, wherein every freeman is to give his own voice."

From this time on, the records of the General Court show that this body exercised its powers vigorously and extensively, but at the beginning without much idea of theoretical legislation. General laws were often passed, but they related to special subjects, often to trivial ones. No constitution and no general code of system of laws was enacted, though of course the laws of England were supposed to be the authority on which all orders or sentences were founded.

In 1635 a step was taken as follows: At a General Court held at New Town, May 6, 1635, it was voted (Records, i. 147): —

"The Governor [John Haynes], the Deputy Governor [Richard Bellingham], John Winthrop and Thomas Dudley, Esquires, are deputed by the Court to make a draught of such laws, as they shall judge useful for the well ordering of this Plantation, and to present the same to the Court."

---

³ Savage (Winthrop, i. 154) writes that he identified the residences of all but one or two. He adds, that Ipswich sent deputies on March 4, 1635, Weymouth in September, 1635, Hingham in May, 1636, Newbury in September, 1636, and Concord in April, 1637. — W. H. W.

⁴ "At first the deputies were chosen for each General Court; from 1639 to 1640 they were chosen semiannually; and in 1642 and ever since that time they have been elected once a year." — F. C. Gray.

Winthrop (History, i. 191) confirms this as follows:—

"6th of 3d month (May) 1635. The deputies having conceived great danger to our state in regard that our magistrates, for want of positive laws, in many cases, might proceed according to their discretions, it was agreed, that some men should be appointed to frame a body of grounds of laws, in resemblance to a Magna Charta, which being allowed by some of the ministers and the general court, should be received for fundamental laws."

At the General Court for March 3d, 1635–6 (Records, i. 169, 170), the system of Courts to be held by the magistrate was settled; and it was ordered that only two General Courts should be held annually, one in May for elections and other affairs, and one in October for making laws and other public occasions. It was also provided that, since there might be differences in the General Courts between the magistrates and the deputies,

"No law, order, or sentence shall pass as an Act of the Court, without the consent of the greater part of the magistrates on the one part, and the greater number of the deputies on the other part; and for want of such accord, the cause or order shall be suspended, and if either party think it so material, there shall be forthwith a committee chosen, one-half by the magistrates, and the other half by the deputies, and the committee so chosen to elect an umpire, who together shall have power to hear and determine the cause in question."

At the General Court, May 25, 1636, it was ordered as follows (Records, i. 174–5):—

"The Governor [Henry Vane], the Deputy Governor [John Winthrop], Thomas Dudley, John Haynes, Richard Bellingham, Esquires, Mr. Cotton, Mr. Peters and Mr. Shepherd are entreated to make a draught of laws agreeable to the word of God, which may be the Fundamentals of this Commonwealth, and to present the same to the next General Court. And it is ordered that in the mean time the magistrates and their associates shall proceed in the Courts to hear and determine all causes, according to the laws now established, and where there is no law, then as near the law of God as they can; and for all business out of Court for which there is no certain rule yet set down, those of the standing council [5] or some two of them, shall take order by

---

[5] This refers to a curious experiment made in 1636, in the form of a council for life. March 3, 1635–6 it was voted that the General Court should, from time to time, elect a certain number of the magistrates for the term of their lives as a Standing Council, to be removed only for crime, insufficiency, or other weighty cause; the Governor always to be president of the body, and the power to be such as the General Court might indue them with. May 25, 1636, Gov. Winthrop and Thomas Dudley were so chosen; May 17, 1637, John Endicott was elected; but none others were ever added. The scheme was connected with certain proposals by Lord Say and

their best discretion, that they may be ordered and ended according to the rule of God's word, and to take care for all military affairs until the next General Court."

We have seen that in May, 1636, Mr. Cotton, Mr. Peters, and Mr. Shepherd were asked to assist in preparing a code, and Winthrop gives this further information (Hist., i. 240), under date of Oct. 25, 1636:—

"Mr. Cotton being requested by the General Court, with some other ministers, to assist some of the magistrates in compiling a body of fundamental laws, did, this Court, present a copy of Moses his judicials, compiled in an exact method, which were taken into further consideration till the next General Court."

There is nothing to show that any action was taken on Mr. Cotton's draft of laws, nor, indeed, that anything was done by the committee of 1635 and 1636.

At the General Court, begun March 12, 1637–8, however, a vigorous show of work was made. The following order was then passed (Records, i. 222):—

"For the well ordering of these Plantations now in the beginning thereof, it having been found by the little time of experience we have here had, that the want of written laws hath put the Court into many doubts and much trouble in many particular cases, this Court hath therefore ordered, that the freemen of every town (or some part thereof chosen by the rest) within this jurisdiction, shall assemble together in their several towns, and collect the heads of such necessary and fundamental laws, as may be suitable to the times and places, where God in his providence hath cast us, and the heads of such laws to deliver in writing to the Governor for the time being before the 5th day of the 4th month, called June, next, to the intent that the same Governor [John Winthrop] together with the rest of the standing council, and Richard Bellingham Esquire, Mr. Bulkeley, Mr. Phillips, Mr. Peters and Mr. Shepherd, elders of several churches, Mr. Nathaniel Ward, Mr. William Spencer, and Mr. William Hawthorne, or the major part of them, may, upon the survey of such heads of laws, make a compendious abridgement of the same by the General Court in Autumn next, adding yet to the same or detracting therefrom what in their wisdoms shall seem meet, that so the whole work being perfected to the best of their skill, it may be presented to the General Court for confirmation or

---

Sele and others in England to join the colony, if hereditary rank and privileges were conceded. Hutchinson (History, i. 501) copies a letter from Rev. John Cotton to Lord Say, in 1636, wherein he cites this establishment of a council for life, as intended as a concession to him. But the popular feeling was opposed to the plan, and it was dropped informally, though for a year or two some duties were imposed on these three members. — W. H. W.

rejection, as the Court shall adjudge. And it is also ordered, that the said persons shall survey all the orders already made, and reduce them into as few heads as they may, and present them unto the General Court for approbation or refusal as aforesaid."

The next step is shown by the order passed by the General Court, Nov. 5, 1639 (Records, i. 279), viz.: —

"It is ordered that the Governor [J. Winthrop], Deputy Governor [Thomas Dudley], Treasurer and Mr. Stoughton or any three of them, with two or more of the deputies of Boston, Charlestown or Roxbury, shall peruse all those models which have been or shall be further presented to this Court, or themselves, concerning a form of government and laws to be established, and shall draw them up into one body, (altering, adding or omitting what they shall think fit,) and shall take order, that the same shall be copied out and sent to the several towns, that the elders of the churches and freemen may consider of them against the next General Court, and the charges to be defrayed by the Treasurer."

The full meaning of this order and the cause of the endless delays are explained by Winthrop's memorandum under the date of November, 1639. It is as follows (History, i. 388–389) : —

"The people had long desired a body of laws, and thought their condition very unsafe, while so much power rested in the discretion of magistrates. Divers attempts had been made at former courts, and the matter referred to some of the magistrates and some of the elders; but still it came to no effect; for, being committed to the care of many, whatsoever was done by some, was still disliked or neglected by others. At last it was referred to Mr. Cotton and Mr. Nathaniel Warde, &c., and each of them framed a model, which were presented to this General Court, and by them committed to the Governor and Deputy and some others, to consider of, and so prepare it for the Court in the third month next. Two great reasons there were, which caused most of the magistrates and some of the elders not to be very forward in this matter. One was, want of sufficient experience of the nature and disposition of the people, considered with the condition of the country and other circumstances, which made them conceive, that such laws would be fittest for us, which should arise *pro re nata* upon occasions, &c., and so the laws of England and other states grew, and therefore the fundamental laws of England are called customs, *consuetudines*. 2. For that it would professedly transgress the limits of our charter, which provide, we shall make no laws repugnant to the laws of England, and that we were assured we must do. But to raise up laws by practice and custom had been no transgression; as in our church discipline, and in matters of marriage, to make a law that marriages shall not be solemnized by ministers, is repugnant to the laws of England; but to bring it to a custom by practice for the magistrates to perform it, is no law made repugnant, &c. At length (to satisfy the people) it proceeded, and the two models were digested with divers alterations and additions, and abbreviated^g and sent to every town, (12) to be considered of first by the magistrates and elders, and then to be published by the constables to all the people, that if any man should think fit, that any thing therein ought to be altered, he might acquaint some of the deputies therewith against the next Court."

We have here the evidence of a most competent witness, that the delay in framing a code of laws was intentional on the part of the magistrates and elders. It is also clear that two schemes were framed, one by Rev. John Cotton and the other by Rev. Nathaniel Ward, and, fortunately, both documents are extant. As already stated, Cotton's scheme was rejected; and yet, having been put in print under a false title, it has long enjoyed an undeserved credit. The plan proposed by Ward, possibly amended by the towns or the General Court, was adopted in 1641, was known as the Body of Liberties, and is the foundation of the legislation of Massachusetts.

This fact, herein fully set forth and verified, ought to restore this inestimable document to its proper place, to serve as the basis for all future citations of our laws.

The few remaining entries in regard to Ward's Body of Liberties may now be cited. At the General Court, May 13, 1640 (Records, i. 292–293), it was voted: —

"Whereas a Breviate of Laws was formerly sent forth to be considered by the elders of the churches and other freemen of the Commonwealth, it is now desired, that they will endeavour to ripen their thoughts and counsels about the same by the general court in the next 8th month."

At the General Court, June 2, 1641 (Records, i. 320) : —

"The Governor [Richard Bellingham] is appointed to peruse all the laws, and take notice what may be fit to be repealed, what to be certified, what to stand, and make return to the next General Court."

---

^g These manuscript copies were made by Thomas Lechford, as appears by his "Note-Book" (Boston, 1885, pp. 237-8). He enters. "I writt 5 copies more of the Lawes for the Country by the direction of our Governor, 11. 8, 1639. Seven of them and the former had 3 lawes added. A Coppie of the Abstract of the Lawes of New England delivered to the Governor, 11. 15. 1639. And 12 coppies of the said Lawes first delivered, vizt., in 10 last. For writing a Coppy of the breviat of the body of Lawes for the Country, 12. 5. 39. The 3 lawes added to the Copie of Lawes for Dorchester, delivered to the Constable, 12. 6. 1639. The 3 lawes added to 4 more of the said Coppies brought by the marshall. 12. 11. 39. Three Copyes of the said breviat delivered to the Governor besides the first, 12. 12. 1639 ..... One coppy of the said breviate delivered to Mr. Bellingham, with one coppy of the originall Institution and limitation of the Councell, 12. 17. 1639. Seven coppyes more of the said breviate. — W. H. W,

At the General Court October 7, 1641 (Records, i. 340): —

"The Governor [Bellingham] and Mr. Hawthorne were desired to speak to Mr. Ward for a Copy of the Liberties and of the Capital laws to be transcribed and sent to the several towns."

Subsequently at the same Court, under the date of December 10, 1641, is the following entry (Records, i. 344): —

"Mr. Deputy Endicot, Mr. Downing, and Mr. Hawthorne are authorized to get nineteen Copies of the Laws, Liberties and the forms of oaths transcribed and subscribed by their several hands, and none to be authentic but such as they subscribe, and to be paid for by the Constable of each Town, ten shillings a piece for each copy, and to be prepared within six weeks."

Finally, at the end of this session of December 10, 1641, on the original record is the written attestation of Gov. Winthrop as follows: —

"At this Court, the bodye of laws formerly sent forth among the Freemen, etc., was voted to stand in force, etc."

Winthrop (History, ii. 66) writes in regard to the General Court of December, 1641, as follows: —

"This session continued three weeks, and established one hundred laws, which were called the Body of Liberties. They had been composed by Mr. Nathaniel Ward (some time pastor of the church of Ipswich: he had been a minister in England and formerly a student and a practiser in the course of the common law) and had been revised and altered by the Court and sent forth into every town to be further considered of, and now again in this Court, they were revised, amended and presented, and so established for three years, by that experience to have them fully amended and established to be perpetual."

We have thus, following the exhaustive selections of authorities made by Mr. F. C. Gray, arrived at a few certain conclusions. First, that John Cotton and Nathaniel Ward each prepared a code of laws; secondly, that Mr. Ward's code was adopted in 1641 and was the Body of Liberties; thirdly, that his code consisted of one hundred laws; and, lastly, that the Athenæum manuscript is a true copy, containing 98 numbered sections, which, with the Preamble and concluding paragraph, make out the requisite one hundred.

That a copy of the manuscript Body of Liberties should have survived is one of the fortunate accidents of literature. In the

Boston Athenæum there is preserved a volume which was formerly owned by Elisha Hutchinson, who was the grandfather of Gov. Thomas Hutchinson, and who died, in 1717, at the age of 77. It is evident from this collection that Hutchinson gave a careful attention to the question of the laws. He had the printed edition of 1672, to which he added the Supplements, making the collection so nearly complete that it was used for our recent reproduction. He copied some laws in manuscript, he corrected errors of pagination, and in fact did everything possible to perfect his copy.

Prefixed to the Laws is a collection of manuscripts, as follows: —

1. King Charles' Letter from Hampton Court, June 28, 1662.
    Printed in Hutchinson's Collection, p. 377.
2. Declaration of the General Court, 23 May, 1665.
3. Commissioners' Reply, May 24, 1665.
    Both printed in Hutchinson, Hist., i. 246, &c.
4.* King Charles' Letter, Whitehall, April 23, 1664.
    Printed in 2d Hazard, 634.
5. Colony Charter March 4, 1629.
    Printed in Hutchinson, Coll. 1.
6.* Copy of the Liberties of the Massachusetts.
7. Parallel between the Fundamental Laws of England & Massachusetts. A part only, the whole is printed in Hutchinson, Coll., 196.
8. Answer of a Committee of the General Court to matters proposed touching their Liberties, June 10, 1661.
    Printed in Hutchinson, Hist., i. 529.
9. King Charles' Commission to Col. Nichols.
    Printed in Hutchinson, Hist., i. 535.
10.* Order in Council, Whitehall July 20, 1677.
11. King Charles' Letter, Newmarket, Sept. 30, 1680.
    Printed in Hutchinson, Coll., 522.

All these documents are on uniform paper with a ruled border, but the first nine seem to be in one handwriting, not that of Elisha Hutchinson. Numbers 10 and 11 seem to be written by the collector and transcriber of the Laws. The pagination is 1–47, covering only the articles Nos. 5, 6, and 7, and the book is in its original sheep binding. On the inside of the last cover is the autograph "Elisha Hutchinson," and on the inside of the first cover that of William S. Shaw, Jan., 1816. Mr. Shaw was Librarian of the Boston Athenæum from 1813 to 1822, and this book

---

* These three articles were not used by Gov. Hutchinson. — W. H. W.

was doubtless acquired through him, although there is no record of the early accessions to this library.

From the fact that eight out of the eleven manuscripts were printed by Gov. Hutchinson, it must be conceded that he probably used this volume. It seems strange that he did not recognize the value of this copy of the Body of Liberties, and that he should have assigned any hand in the compilation to Rev. John Cotton. In his note to his reprint of Cotton's book, Hutchinson writes:—

" It should rather be entitled An Abstract of a Code or System of Laws prepared for the Commonwealth of the Massachusetts Bay; for although when they compiled their laws, they made this abstract their plan in general, yet they departed from it in many instances, and in some which were very material." Again, Hutchinson writes (Hist., i. 442), " In the first draught of the laws by Mr. Cotton, which I have seen corrected with Mr. Winthrop's hand, divers other offences were made capital, viz. —" (Here he cites Nos. X., XIII., XVIII., XIX., XX., XXI., of Chapter VII. of Cotton's book) —" The punishment by death is erased from all these offences by Mr. Winthrop, and they are left to the discretion of the court to inflict other punishment short of death."

This statement occurs in the fifth chapter of Hutchinson's History, wherein he is explaining "The System or Body of Laws established in the Colony." He adds (Hist., i. 437):—

" In the year 1634 the plantation was greatly increased, settlements were extended more than 30 miles from the capital town, and it was thought high time to have known established laws, that the inhabitants might no longer be subject to the varying uncertain judgments which otherwise would be made concerning their actions. The ministers, and some of the principal laymen, were consulted with, about a body of laws suited to the circumstances of the colony civil and religious. Committees, consisting of magistrates and elders, were appointed almost every year, for 12 or 14 years together, and whilst they were thus fitting a code, particular laws, which were of greatest necessity, from time to time were enacted; and in the year 1648 the whole collected together were ratified by the court and then first printed. Mr. Bellingham of the magistrates, and Mr. Cotton of the clergy had the greatest share in this work."

In reply to these general remarks by Hutchinson, I would urge the fact that he seems never to have used, even if he possessed, a copy of the printed laws of 1660 or of 1649. As will be noted he says the laws were first printed in 1648; but the title of the edition of 1660 says that they were published in the General Court held in May, 1649, and this seems to be the true date. Now, the volume owned by Elisha Hutchinson not only contains merely the edition of 1672, but the manuscript references made in his copy of the Body of Liberties refer entirely to this later edition. It is reasonable to suppose that if Elisha Hutchinson had possessed a copy of the earlier editions, the text of which more nearly conformed to the Liberties, he would have cited one of them.

It does not seem necessary to reprint John Cotton's book, as it has been so often republished. It is to be noted that its first publication, in 1641, was anonymously, in London. The title is, "An Abstract of the Lawes of New England, as they are now established. London, Printed for F. Coules and W. Ley at Paules Chain, 1641." Pp. 1–15 and two pages of the Table. Any one sending this book to the press from Boston, would have known that there was no colony named New England. These laws at most could only relate to the colony of Massachusetts Bay. It was doubtless the work of some English friend of Cotton's, who had a copy of his manuscript, and who, hearing that a code of laws had been established, jumped to the conclusion that this was the one.

But in 1655 William Aspinwall, who had lived here and in Rhode Island, reprinted Cotton's book in London, increasing the bulk by printing at length the citations from the Bible and even adding some that were lacking. A full comparison of the two editions is given in the reprint of Hutchinson's Collection of Papers by the Prince Society of Boston, 1865, i. 181–205.

In his preface, Aspinwall makes the following plain disclaimers of any idea that Cotton's work ever became law. He says these laws were

"Acommodated to the Colonie of the Massachusets in New England, and commended to the General Court there, which had they then had the heart to have received, it might have been better both with them there, and us here, than it now is. . . . . These are not properly Laws, but prudentiall [7] Rules, which he recommended to that Colonie,

---

[7] This word "prudential" is one which has had a great significance in our legislation. Liberty 66 says: "The freemen of every township shall have power to make such by-laws and constitutions as may concern the welfare of their town, provided that they be not of a criminal, but only of a *prudential* nature, and that their penalties exceed not twenty shillings for one offence; and that they be not repugnant to the public laws and orders of the country. And if any inhabitant shall neglect or refuse to observe them, they shall have power to levy the appointed penalties by distress."

The foundation of the law, but not the term, is in a vote of the General Court, March 3, 1635-6 (Records, i. 172), where it is ordered that "the freemen of every town, or the major part of them, shall only have power to dispose of their own lands and woods, with all the privileges and appurtenances of the said towns, to grant lots, and make such orders as may concern the well ordering of their own towns, not repugnant to the laws and orders here established by

to be ratified with the common assent of the freemen in each Towne, or by their Representatives in the General Court, as publique Contracts. Which being once made and assented to for their owne conveniencce, do binde as Covenants do, untill by like publique consent they be abrogated and made voyd. For though the Author attribute the word [Law] unto some of them; yet that it was not his meaning that they should be enacted as Lawes (if you take the word *Law* in a proper sense), appears by his conclusion taken out of *Isa.* 33:22. Hee knew full well that it would be an intrenchment upon the Royall power of Jesus Christ, for them or any other of the sonnes of Adam to ordain Lawes.

"It is not my purpose to perswade this or any other nation (were they willing to heare) to enact or ratifie these by any power of their own (in a solemn convention of their Representatives) as Laws : Neither do I believe it was the Authors intention so to do, when he drew up this modell. For alas, what energie or vertue can such an act of poore sinfull creatures adde unto the most perfect and wholesome lawes of God? It is enough for us, and indeed it is all that can be done by any people upon earth : 1. To declare by their Representatives, their voluntary subjection unto them, as unto the lawes of the Lord their God. 2. After such professed subjection to fall unto the practice thereof, in the name and strength of Christ their King and Law-giver."

"This Abstract may serve for this use principally (which I conceive was the main scope of that good man, who was the author of it) to shew the com-

---

the General Court; as also to lay mulcts and penalties for the breach of these orders, and to levy and distrain the same, not exceeding the sum of twenty shillings; also to choose their own particular officers, as constables, surveyors for the highways, and the like."

June 14, 1642, the General Court (Records, ii. 6) passed a law for the proper training and employment of children, and state "that in every town the chosen men appointed for managing the *prudential affairs* of the same shall henceforth stand charged with the care of the redress of this evil."

Again, Oct. 7, 1646 (Records, ii. 162-163) the Court passed this order : "Whereas there is no order made appointing who shall end causes in towns under the value of 20 shillings, where one only magistrate dwells, and the cause concerns himself, it is therefore hereby ordered, that in such cases the 5 or 7 or more men in every such town, which are selected for *prudential affairs*, shall have power to hear and determine such cases," etc., etc.

Nov. 4, 1646, the General Court (Records, ii. 180) passed certain orders entitled Prudentiall Laws, though it is not clear that more than the first section was so designated. That one reads : "Every township, or such as are deputed to order the *prudentialls* thereof, shall have power to present to the Quarter Court all idle and unprofitable persons, and all children who are not diligently employed by their parents, which Court shall have power to dispose of them, for their own welfare and improvement of the common good."

So again an order of the General Court, May 26, 1647 (Records, ii. 19), declares that "henceforth it shall and may be lawful for the freemen within any of the said towns to make choice of such inhabitants, though non-freemen, who have taken or shall take the oath of fidelity to this government, to be jury men, and to have their vote in the choice of selectmen for town affairs, assessment of rates, *and other prudentials*, proper to the selectment of the several towns."

May 26, 1658 (Records, iv. part 1, pp. 335-336) the Court speaks of two laws in the printed book, title Township, about the right of all Englishmen who have taken the oath of fidelity to be chosen jury men or constables, and to have their vote in the choice of the selectmen for the town affairs, assessments of rates, and other *prudentials* proper to the selectmen of the several towns. These laws are all repeated in the edition of 1660, pp. 75-76.

plete sufficiency of the word of God alone, to direct his people in judgment of all causes, both civil and criminal, as we are wonted to distinguish them. Which being by him done, and with all sweetness and amiableness of spirit tendered, but not accepted, he surceased to press it any further at that season, knowing full well that the Lord's people shall be a willing people in the day of his power. But the truth is, both they and we, and the other Gentile nations, are loth to be persuaded to dwell in the tents of Shem, and to lay aside our old earthly forms of government, to submit to the government of Christ."

It seems, therefore, to be certain that any claim that Cotton prepared the Body of Liberties, rests upon an unauthorized title-page and the vague and unsupported opinions of Gov. Hutchinson. The evidence to the contrary is found in Aspinwall's positive statements above cited, and in the very nature of Cotton's book. It is a treatise in ten chapters, stating powers, duties, rights, and penalties, fortified throughout by references to the Old Testament. The sections are not framed as laws are, and the only wonder is that any one could suppose for a moment that any legislature ever enacted them.

The same words are again used in the edition of Laws in 1672, pp. 147, 148.

Under the new Charter, in the session of 1692-3, chap. 28 (Province Laws, Goodell's edition, i. 66) the freeholders and inhabitants in a town meeting could pass "necessary rules, orders and by-laws for the directing, managing and ordering the *prudential affairs* of such town," with penalties not exceeding twenty shillings, etc., to be approved by the justices in Quarter Sessions. In 1696 (Ibid., i. 218) the clause requiring the consent of the justices was repealed, and an appeal to them was granted to any one punished under such by-laws.

Again, after the establishment of the State, chap. 75 of Acts of 1785 repeated the powers of towns to make "rules, orders and by-laws for the directing, managing and ordering the *prudential affairs* of the town," with penalties not exceeding thirty shillings, and provided the laws are approved by the Court of General Sessions of the Peace in the same county.

The Revised Statutes of 1836, chap. 15, § 13, continues the same words, with twenty dollars penalty, and the approval of the Court of Common Pleas.

The General Statutes of 1860, chap. 18, § 11, retains the phrase, "directing and managing the *prudential affairs*" of the town; as does the Public Statutes of 1882, chap. 27, § 15, which, in defining the powers of towns to pass by-laws, allows them "for directing and managing the *prudential affairs*, preserving the peace and good order, and maintaining the internal police thereof."

I have thus briefly traced this phrase, "prudential affairs," from the Body of Liberties in 1641 to the present time, and can only say that the earliest definition is the clearest and best. All matters, not reserved for state jurisdiction, but affecting the welfare of the town in its corporate capacity, and evidently susceptible of proper regulation under the penalty of a moderate fine, have been, and still are, suitable subjects for control in towns by by-laws, and in cities by ordinance. The origin of the term is obscure. One would expect to find it in the contemporary theological literature, but it was certainly not in common use. Perhaps Ward invented it, as his "Cobler" is full of strange words. In 1653 (Records, Vol. iv., part i., p. 145) a matter is said to be " safe and prudential," and there the word is equivalent to "prudent." A similar use of a word is "economy" and "economical." A man is economical, but we speak of political economy, and towns regulate their domestic or internal economy. — W. H. W.

Introduction. 15

But equally strong evidence remains to show what the Body of Liberties actually contained. The Laws of 1660 as well as those of 1672 contain numerous citations of laws under the date of 1641. These laws, with very few exceptions, are not entered on the Records of the General Court, as passed in that year. Hence these must have been comprehended in some general enactment, to wit, the Body of Liberties. An analysis of these laws is given later on. In the meantime I would cite the following evidence: First, on October 17, 1643 (Records, ii. 48), the General Court declared "that whereas in the Book of Liberties, No. 23, it was ordered none should take above 8.6 per cent., — bills of exchange are excepted." This reference is to our No. 23. Secondly, March 7, 1643–4 (Records, ii. 61), the Governor [Winthrop], Mr. Dudley, and Mr. Hibbens, or any two of them, were made " a committee to consider of the Body of Liberties against the next General Court." Third, the General Court voted May 26, 1647 (Records, ii. 194), " for explanation of the order in the Liberties about 6 days warning to be given to the defendant in every action, &c., it is hereby declared that the day of the summons or attachment served and the day of appearance shall be taken inclusively as part of the six days." Here the reference is to Liberty No. 21, as printed herein, amended in Laws of 1660, p. 4, title Attachments, § 2, line 5, by adding the word " inclusively " after the words " six days." Of course our copy of the Liberties is the earlier form, prior to May, 1647.

Lastly and most conclusive of all, the General Court in 1646 had to consider a Remonstrance and Petition from Robert Child and others who were dissatisfied with the government. The Court empowered Governor Winthrop, Deputy Governor Dudley, Richard Bellingham, and the Auditor General (Lieut. Nathaniel Duncan) to draw up a reply to be forwarded to England by Mr. Winslow. This document is printed in Hutchinson's Collection of papers (Prince Soc. edition, i. 223–247). One of their chief arguments, to prove that the laws here are conformable to those of England, is an elaborate parallel of items printed face to face.

"In this they set forth forty-four fundamental propositions, annexing to each the authorities for it. Six times they refer for authority to their Charter; seven times to custom; eight times to laws of specified dates; once to the Bible; and twenty-seven times to the Liberties, citing each by its appropriate number." — *F. C. Gray.*

Not one of these citations of the Liberties conforms to any item in Cotton's book; but every one of them, by specific number, refers to and agrees with a section of the manuscript copy preserved by Elisha Hutchinson. The separate sections (one or two being cited more than once) are Nos. 1, 2, 3, 10, 14, 17, 18, 29, 31, 36, 37, 42, 48, 53, 59, 63, 65, 81, 82, 94, and 95; in all twenty-one out of one hundred, and scattered from number one to number ninety-five. It is impossible to present stronger evidence that this manuscript copy of the Body of Liberties is identical with the one used by the Committee of the General Court in 1646.

As the original book containing these citations is quite rare, and in order that there may be no question of the identification, the following extracts are given of such paragraphs, as they occur in order, which are said to be taken from the Body of Liberties: —

"FUNDAMENTALLS OF THE MASSACHUSETTS.

Compared with Magna Charta.

1. All persons orthodoxe in judgment and not scandalous in life may gather into a church estate according to the rules of the gospell of Jesus Christ. Liberty 1.[8]

Such may choose and ordaine their owne officers, and exercise all the Ordinances of Christ, without any injunction in doctrine, worship or discipline. Liberty 2 & 38.[9]

2. No mans life, honor, liberty, wife, children, goods or estate shall be taken away, punished or endamaged, under colour of lawe, or countenance of authoritie, but by an expresse lawe of the general court, or in defect of such lawe, by the word of God &c. Liberty, 1.

Every person within the jurisdiction &c shall enjoy the same justice and lawe &c without partiality or delay. Liberty 2.

All lands and hereditaments shall be free from all fines, forfeitures &c. Liberty 10.

Every man may remove himselfe and his familie &c if there be no legal impediment. Liberty 17.

6. Difficult cases are finally determinable in the court of assistants or in the generall court by appeale or petition, or by reference from the inferiour court. Liberty 31 & 36.

7. Upon unjust suites the plaintiff shall be fined proportionable to his offence. Liberty 37.

No man's goods shall be taken away but by a due course of justice.

---

[8] This is the clerical error for Item 1 of Liberty 95. — W. H. W.

[9] This is the similar error for Items 2, 3, and 8 of Liberty 95. — W. H. W.

Liberty 1. In criminal causes it shall be at the liberty of the accused partie to be tryed by the bench or by a jury. Liberty 23.[10]

Compared with the Common Laws of England.

7. In our own court of judication all causes civill and criminall are determinable, either by the judges and jury, or by the judges alone &c as in England. This is done both by custome and by divers laws established according to our charter, as Liberty 29, &c.

12. In all criminall offences, where the law hath prescribed no certaine penaltie, the judges have power to inflict penalties, according to the rule of God's word. Liberty 1, and by Charter, &c.

15. All publicke charges are defrayed out of the publicke stocke. Custome and Liberty 63.

19. No mans person shall be restrained or imprisoned &c. before the lawe hath sentenced him thereto, if he can put in sufficient baile, &c. except in crimes capitall, &c. Liberty 18.

20. The full age, for passing lands, giving votes, &c. is twenty one yeares. Liberty 53.

21. Married women cannot dispose of any estate, &c. nor can sue or be sued, without the husband. Custome and Liberty 14.

22-1. The eldest sonne is preferred before the younger in the ancestors inheritance. Liberty 81.

2. Daughters shall inherit as coparceners. Liberty 82.

3. No custome or prescription shall ever prevail &c to maintaine anything morally sinnfull. Liberty 65.

4. Civill authority may deale with any church member or officer, in a way of civill justice. Liberty 59.

5. No man shall be twice sentenced by civill justice for the same offence. Liberty 42.

6. No man shall be urged to take any oath or subscribe any articles, covenant, or remonstrance of a publick and civill nature, but such as the generall court hath considered, allowed and required. Liberty 3.

7. Publick records are open to all inhabitants. Liberty 48.

They also cite under the Common Law.

13. Treason, murther, witchcraft, sodomie and other notorious crimes are punished with death; But theft &c is not so punished, because we read otherwise in the scripture. Capitalls &c.

---

[10] This is the third clerical error; it should be Liberty 29. A comparison with the fragmentary copy contained in Elisha Hutchinson's book shows that the first citation was Libr. 1; the second was "Libr. 3 & 5 in Eccles." meaning of course Liberty 95 concerning Churches; and the third is plainly Libr. 29. Evidently the errors of the text are simply clerical ones, and not citations from any other arrangement of the Liberties. I have put in an Appendix a facsimile of the manuscript copy of this article, as the larger draft, printed by Gov. Hutchinson, seems to be lost. It is complete as far as it goes. — W. H. W.

14. Adultery is punished according to the canon of the spirituall law, viz. the scripture. Capitalls &c.

These two references are plainly to Liberty 94, which is entitled "Capitall Laws."

The absolute certainty of the identification of our manuscript copy being thus shown, it may be well to say a few words about the author or authors of the drafts. Hutchinson says, as before cited, that Mr. Bellingham of the magistrates and Mr. Cotton of the clergy had the greatest share in this work. We have seen that he was wrong as to Cotton; but Bellingham undoubtedly served on nearly all the committees, as did Winthrop and Dudley. Bellingham was bred a lawyer and was Recorder of Boston in Lincolnshire from 1625 to 1633; hence his connection with the compilation of our code is extremely natural and may well have been of considerable influence. It is to be noted that in the controversies between the Assistants and the Deputies he took sides with the latter, and may thus be claimed as likely to favor popular rights in the establishment of this Magna Charta of New England.

But, after all, the contemporary evidence of Governor Winthrop assigns the main work of compiling the code to one man, namely, Rev. Nathaniel Ward, of Ipswich. From an interesting memoir, prepared by a descendant, John Ward Dean, and published at Albany, 1868, we learn that Ward had special qualifications for this work. He was born about A.D. 1578 at Haverhill, England, and was the son of Rev. John Ward, an eminent minister there. He was graduated at Emmanuel College, Cambridge, A.M., in 1603. He studied and practised law, and Candler says that he was at Utter Barrister. He was admitted to Lincoln's Inn, May 15, 1607, and nominated a barrister, 17 Oct. 1615. (N. E. Hist. and Gen. Register, vol. 43, p. 326.)

He then travelled on the continent and stayed some time at Heidelberg. He entered the ministry about 1618, and was probably chaplain at Elbing, in Prussia. Returning to England he became rector of Stondon-Massey in Essex, but was suspended by Laud for Puritanism. In 1634 he came to New England, and settled at Ipswich, where he was pastor and Rev. Thomas Parker was teacher. He resigned his charge in about two years, owing to illness. In the winter of 1646–7 he returned to England, leaving his family here; and in June, 1647, he preached before the

House of Commons. In May, 1648, he was appointed minister at Shenfield, about five miles from his former home at Stondon-Massey. Here he ended his days in 1652 or 1653, aged some seventy-five years. He wrote various books,[11] of which the most famous was his "Simple Cobler of Agawam," written here and published in London in January, 1646-7. He was a witty as well as an earnest writer; a conservative, and yet forced by events to stand with the Parliament against the King. There is printed in Mass. Soc. Coll. 4th S. vol. vii. pp. 26-27, a letter from Ward to Governor Winthrop, in 1639, concerning the new laws, wherein he doubts the expediency of "sending the Court business to the common consideration of the freemen." He says, "I see the spirits of the people runne high, and what they gett they hould. They may not be denyed their proper and lawfull liberties; but I question whether it be of God to interest the inferiour sort in that which should be reserved *inter optimates penes quos est sancire leges*. If Mr. Lachford have writ them out, I would be glad to peruse one of his copies, if I may receive them. . . . . . . There is a necessity that the Covenant, if it be agreed upon, should be considered and celebrated by the several congregations and towns, and happily the tenure, but I dare not determyne concerning the latter. I mean of putting it to the suffrage of the people."

Without overrating the influence of any one man in the preparation of this admirable code, and believing firmly that it embodied the best judgment of Winthrop and other leaders, there seems to be no reason to doubt that the main literary work, at least, was due to Nathaniel Ward, and that his legal abilities and training were at least equal to those of any of his associates. In his "Simple Cobler" (edit. of 1843, p. 68) he writes, "I have read almost all the Common Law of England, and some Statutes." It may well be that the Common Law of England was the source from which these wise provisions were extracted, for in the Reply of the Colony in 1646, already cited, (*ante*, pp. 16, 17,) our laws are compared only with Magna Charta and the Common Laws of England.

We know of one instance in which a change was made in the first draft. Thomas Lechford, of whom we have before spoken as a copyist employed on the work, has recorded the fact that his remonstrance changed one item. In his "Plain Dealing, or News

[11] Among the strange words used by Ward, I note, pudder, exulcerations, colluvies, sedulity, jadish, interturbe, corrive, quidanye, prestigiated, ignotions, mundicidious, dedolent, exadverse, per-peracute, nugiperous, nudiustertian, futilous, perquisquilian, indenominable, precellency, surquedryes, prodromies, digladiations, prosult, bivious, awke; besides many, almost innumerable, oddities of combination. — W. W. H.

from New England," London, 1642 (Trumbull's edition, Boston, 1867, pp. 72–74), he prints a paper delivered by him to the Governor, etc., March 4, 1639–40. We cite as follows:—

Whereas you have been pleased to cause me to transcribe certain Breviats of Propositions delivered to the generall Court, for the establishing a body of Lawes, as is intended, for the glory of God, and the welfare of this People and Country; and published the same, to the intent that any man may acquaint you or the Deputies for the next Court, what he conceives fit to be altered or added, in or unto the said lawes; I conceive it to be my duty to give you timely notice of some things of great moment, about the same Lawes, in discharge of my conscience, which I shall, as *Amicus curiæ*, pray you to present with all faithfulnesse, as is proposed, to the next generall Court, by it, and the reverend Elders, to be further considered of, as followeth:—

1. It is propounded to be one chiefe part of the charge, or office of the Councell intended, to take care that the *conversion* of the *Natives* be endeavoured.

2. It is proposed, as a liberty, that a convenient number of Orthodox Christians, allowed to plant together in this Jurisdiction, may gather themselves into a Church, and elect and ordaine their Officers, men fit for their places, giving notice to seven of the next Churches, one month before thereof, and of their names, and that they may exercise all the ordinances of God according to his Word, and so they proceede according to the rule of God, and shall not be hindered by any Civill power: nor will this Court allow of any Church otherwise gathered.

This clause (*nor will the Court allow of any Church otherwise gathered*) doth as I conceive contradict the first proposition.

He then argues, briefly but clearly, that to convert the Indians they must send evangelists, and that the converts must be gathered into churches. But these churches are not made up, as the law requires, of " a convenient number of orthodox Christians," planting together and gathering themselves into a church; and therefore are prohibited from any recognition under the law. The point seems sound, though very small; and the remonstrance apparently had its effect. The law of March 3, 1635–6 (Records, i, 168), said "it is ordered that all persons are to take notice that this Court doth not, nor will hereafter, approve of any such companies of men as shall henceforth join in any pretended way of church fellowship, without they shall first acquaint the magistrates and the elders of the greater part of the churches in their jurisdiction, with their intentions, and have their approbation herein." Liberty 95, § 1, as enacted, allows that "All the people of God within this jurisdiction who are not in a church way, and be orthodox in judgment, and not scandalous in life, shall have full liberty to gather themselves into a Church estate: provided they do it in a Christian way, with due observance of the rules of Christ revealed in his word."

We see from Lechford's report, the rough draft of a law which was proposed, and in the published Liberty we see the amended statute. How many other cases there were is necessarily unknown. But in this example two things are noteworthy. First, Lechford himself was not a favorite with those in authority. He differed on various topics, he argued with the magistrates and the clergy. He was silenced by order of the rulers, and he was finally starved into returning to England. Yet his comments seem to have been fairly considered, and being found valid, they influenced the form of the law as passed. Secondly, it seems very strange that he, one of the few lawyers in the colony, should have found nothing else to which to object, in view of the great amount of legislation thus put into force, for which the English statutes gave no precedent.

The Body of Liberties as established in 1641 can be traced with only trifling changes in the edition of Laws of 1660. It is not cited in that book by that name, but as nearly all of the sections have the date of their enactment appended, we can easily trace the laws assigned to 1641.

The following table and notes will enable the reader to see that the legislation of 1641, so incorporated into the collected Laws of 1660, is not to be found on the records of the Legislature. It must, therefore, be sought in some other collective body of enactments of that date, and we have already seen that such was the Body of Liberties.

Laws dated 1641.

Acts of 1660.	Acts of 1672.	Title.	Body of Liberties. Number.
P. 1	P. 1	Preamble.	Preamble.
1	1	Ability, Age.	11, 53.
2	3	Actions, § 7, 8.	22, 28, 37.
2	3	Appeal.[12]	36.
3	4	Appearance.	4.

[12] This law is cited as 1642 in both editions of the Laws; but Hutchinson notes that it was founded on Liberty No. 36. — W. H. W.

Laws dated 1641. — Continued.

Acts of 1660.	Acts of 1672.	Title.	Body of Liberties. Number.
P. 4	P. 6	Arrests.	33.
4	8	Attachments, § 1, 2.	39, 21, 25.
5	9	Barratry.	34.
5	9	Benevolences.	See Notes, 1.
5	10	Bond-slavery.	91.
6	10	Bounds of Towns.	See Notes, 2.
8	14, 15	Capital Laws.[13]	94.
10	17	Cask, Cooper.	See Notes, 3.
11	18	Cattle, § 3.[14]	24.
14	22	Charges, Public.	63.
15	25	" § 3.[15]	13.
17	28	Children and Youth, §§ 5 and 6.	83, 84.
18	29	Clerk of the Writs.	See Notes, 4.
19	30	Condemned.	44.

[13] The Capital Laws as printed in 1660 are those contained in Liberty 94, for the first twelve laws, with slight changes in Nos. 3 and 4. The General Court, June 14, 1642 (Records, ii, 22), added three more capital crimes, viz.: criminal connection with a child under ten years of age, ravishing a married woman or betrothed maid, or ravishing a single woman aged over ten years. It was also ordered that all these capital laws be printed. Accordingly, in Major John Child's book, printed in London in 1647, entitled "New England's Jonas cast up at London," etc. (Marvin's edition, Boston, 1869), will be found a reprint of these fifteen Capital Laws, arranged somewhat differently in order. Nos. 3 and 4 are, however, the same as in the Body of Liberties.

But the General Court on November 4, 1646 (Records, ii, 177), passed a preamble and law about Blasphemy, which superseded Law No. 3 of the Liberties, and is the form followed in the Revision of 1660. At the same time (Records, ii, 179) they passed the two capital laws against wicked children, which are Nos. 13 and 14 in the Laws of 1660; and also (Records, ii, 182) the section punishing those accused of capital crimes who did not stand a trial.

The Laws of 1660 contain but one section about Rape, thereby ignoring two of the laws passed, as we have seen, in 1642. These punished fornication with a female child under ten years of age, and ravishing a married woman or a betrothed maid. The citation for this section is 1649, but I fail to find any express legislation on that subject in that year. I am therefore inclined to believe that the change was made in the revision of 1649, under the powers given the revisers.

It is evident that the revision was not satisfactory, for the General Court, Oct. 12, 1669, on a flagrant case, finding that there was then no law, re-enacted (Records, vol. iv, part ii, pp. 437–8) the punishment for abusing a child under ten years, as death. Laws of 1672, p. 15, § 17.

Still there seems to have been no punishment provided for ravishing a married woman. Under the New Charter (Goodell's Province Laws, i, 56), an Act was passed defining capital crimes, including ravishing *any* woman. It was passed in 1693, but disallowed by the Crown. In 1697 (Ibid., i, 296) an Act was passed punishing the rape of *any* woman or the abuse of a woman child under ten years of age. — W. H. W.

[14] Cited as 1646, but referred by Hutchinson to this Liberty. — W. H. W.

[15] This law is dated 1646, 47, 51, 57; but Hutchinson notes that the last paragraph of § 3 is based on Liberty No. 13. — W. H. W.

Laws dated 1641. — Continued.

Acts of 1660.	Acts of 1672.	Title.	Body of Liberties. Number.
P. 20	P. 32	Conveyance, § 3.	40, 15.
21	33	do § 4.	See Notes, 5.
22	35	Courts, § 4.	72, 73.
23	"	do § 6.	69, 71.
"	36	do § 6.	19, 20.
24	38	do § 10.	41.
"	"	do § 12.	See Notes, 6.
24	39	Cruelty.	92.
25	39	Death untimely.	57.
25	41	Deputies, § 2.	62, 68.
26	41	Distress.	35.
26	42	Dowries.	See Notes, 7.
26	43	Drovers.[16]	93.
27	"	Ecclesiastical, § 3–12.	95, §§ 1–10, 58, 59, 60. [§ 2 is new, and the numeration is thereby changed.]
29	48	Elections, § 4.	67.
30	49	Farms.	See Notes, 8.
31	50	Ferries.	See Notes, 9.
40	73	Impresses.	5, 6, 7, 8.
40	74	Imprisonment.	18.
43	77	Indians.	See Notes, 10.
47	86, 87	Jurors, § 1, 2, 3, 5.	50, 61, 31, 76, 49.
48	88	Lands, Free.	10.
50	90, 91	Liberties, Common.	12, 16, 17.
51	101	Marriage, &c.	80.
54	105	Masters & Servants, § 6, 7, 8, 9.	85, 86, 87, 88.

[16] It is worth while to note that in Liberty 93, the word "lambe" is used, and in the Laws of 1660, the word is "lame." — W. H. W.

Laws dated 1641. — Concluded.

Acts of 1660.	Acts of 1672.	Title.	Body of Liberties. Number.
P. 61	P. 116	Mines.	See Notes, 11.
62	119	Monopolies.	9.
62	119	Oaths.[17]	3.
66	126	Prescriptions.	65.
67	128, 129	Protests.	75.
67	129	Punishment, Torture.[18]	42, 43, 45, 46.
68	129–131	Records, &c., § 1, 3.	64, 38, 48.
69	132	Replevin.	32.
72	139	Ships, § 1.	See Notes, 12.
73	143	Strangers.	2, 89.
75	147, 148	Township.[19]	56, 66, 74.
76	150	Treasurer.[20]	78.
77	152	Trials.	29, 30, 52.
78	153	Usury.	23.
78	153	Votes.[21]	54, 70, 77.
81	158	Wills.	81, 82.
81	158	Witnesses.	47.
83	161	Wrecks.	90.

[17] By Hutchinson wrongly marked as p. 219. — W. H. W.
[18] This chapter is undated in the Laws, but Hutchinson refers it to Liberties 42, 43, 45 and 46. — W. H. W.
[19] This chapter is dated 1630, 1642, 47, 53, 58; yet there are three sections taken from the Body of Liberties. The omission of 1641 is clearly a clerical error. — W. H. W.
[20] This chapter has no citation in the Laws under date of 1641, but Hutchinson rightly assigns part of it to Liberty 78. — W. H. W.
[21] This is erroneously dated 1651, yet Hutchinson properly refers it to Liberties nos. 54, 70, and 77. — W. H. W.

The following explanatory notes will, perhaps, make the matter plainer: —

First. Laws of 1660, p. 5, Title "Benevolence." This law is dated 1641, but is not in the Body of Liberties. It was passed June 2, 1641 (Records, i, 327), and therefore probably after the Body of Liberties had been compiled.

Second. Edition of 1660, p. 6, Title " Bounds of Towns." Citation 1641, though in the edition of 1672 cited as 1651. A short law was passed June 2, 1641 (Records, i, 319), but the main part of this act was passed Nov. 11, 1647 (Records, ii, 210).

Third. Laws of 1660, p. 9–10, Title " Cask & Cooper." The laws are dated 1641, 1647, 1651, 1652. I find no law on the subject in 1641, but there was one passed Sept. 27, 1642 (Records, ii, 29), the terms of which are incorporated in the Laws of 1660. Evidently the date is a misprint, by no means the only one.

Fourth. Laws of 1660, p. 18, Title " Clerk of the Writs." This law was passed Dec. 10, 1641 (Records, i, 345), and, of course, after the Body of Liberties was already in form.

Fifth. Laws of 1660, p. 20–21, Title " Conveyances," &c. § 4 is assigned to 1641 and 1642. This law was passed October 7, 1640, and this date is incorporated into the law as printed. Evidently 1341 is a misprint for 1640.

Sixth. Laws of 1660, p. 24, Title " Courts," § 12. This is a law that " every Court in this jurisdiction where two magistrates are present, may admit any church members that are fit, to be freemen; giving them the oath: and the Clerk of each Court shall certify their names to the Secretary at the next General Court." 1641.

This date of 1641 is clearly a misprint. May 20, 1642 (Rec. vol. ii, pp. 2–8 *of the second edition only*) the following order was passed : " There is power given to every Court within our jurisdiction, that hath two magistrates, to admit any church members that are fit to be free, and to give them the freeman's oath, and to certify their names to the Secretary at the next General Court." May 10, 1643 (Records, ii, 38), it was ordered " concerning members that refuse to take their freedom, the churches should be writ unto, to deal with them." In the list of Freemen (Records, ii, 291) all seem to have been made free in May of the respective years, except a few at Salem in Dec., 1642, and February, 1642–3, and some at Springfield, in April, 1648. As to these last, it was ordered Nov. 11, 1647 (Records, ii, 224) that "Mr. Pinchin is authorised to make freemen in the town of Springfeild, of those that are in covenant and live according to their profession."

Again, Nov. 11, 1647 (Records, ii, 208), it was voted that " there being in this jurisdiction many members of churches, who to exempt themselves from all public service in the commonwealth, will not come in to be made freemen," . . . . it is ordered that they be not exempt from serving in town offices, if elected.

June 19, 1650 (Records, iv, pt. 1, p. 19), Robert Clements, at the request of the town of Haverhill, was empowered to give the oath of fidelity. In 1653 (Ibid., p. 127, 129) special commissioners were sent to establish jurisdiction at Kittery and at Saco, and they admitted freemen there. Other special cases may be found on the records.

May 31, 1660 (Records, iv. pt. 1, p. 420) the General Court declared "that no man whatsoever shall be admitted to the freedom of this body politic, but such as are members of some church of Christ, and in full communion; which they declare to be the true intent of the ancient law, page the 8th of the second book, anno g^r 1631."

June 28, 1662, Charles II. sent a letter to the Colony ordering the redress of grievances. It is printed in Hutchinson's Collections, Prince Soc. edit. ii, 100–104. He especially ordered a change in the law concerning freemen. Accordingly on Aug. 3, 1664 (Records, iv, part ii, p. 117), the General Court declared, "that the law prohibiting all persons except members of churches, *and also that for allowance of them in any County Courts*, are hereby repealed."

See my preface for an explanation of the differences between the two editions of the printed Records.

Seventh. In the edition of 1672, p. 42, Title "Dowries," the date is given as 1641. But in the laws of 1660 it is dated 1647, which is somewhat confusing. The reference to 1641 may refer to Liberty No. 79; but it looks more like a misprint. The records do not contain any law of 1647, but May 2, 1649 (Records, ii, 281), reference is made to "the printed law concerning dowries," and amends it by striking out the clause giving the widow "a third part of her husband's money, goods, and chattels, real and personal;" and also by ordering in the 14th line of said order the insertion of the words "then by act or consent of such wife."

Both these changes are incorporated in the text in 1660, and the proviso is made that the law shall not affect houses, lands, etc., sold before the last of November, 1647. Hence, it would seem that there was a law passed and printed in that year, though not entered in the legislative records.

Eighth. Laws of 1660, p. 30, Title "Farms." The order that all farms in a town shall belong therein, except Medford, is dated 1641, and is not in the Liberties. It was passed June 2, 1641 (Records, i, 331), and may have been too late for insertion, or, more probably, was not of a nature to be placed there.

Ninth. Laws of 1660, p. 31, Title "Ferries." Reference is made to law of 1641. Much of § 1 will be found in orders passed

Oct. 7, 1641 (Records, i. 338, 341), explaining this reference. But the law is not in the Body of Liberties for the reasons given in the preceding example.

Tenth. Laws of 1660, p. 43, Title "Indians." At the end of section 10, the citation is 1633, 37, 40, 41, etc. I find nothing passed in 1641 relating to this section; but § 7, cited as passed in 1640, 48, in the last clause does contain a law passed June 2, 1641 (Records, i, 329), that if harm be done by the Indians to the English in their cattle any three magistrates may order satisfaction. Hence I infer the general citations under section 10 cover all the preceding sections, and this is the law of 1641, which is not in the Body of Liberties.

Eleventh. Laws of 1660, p. 61, Title "Mines." Citation of law of 1641, which is not in Body of Liberties. The law was passed June 2, 1641 (Records, i, 327).

Twelfth. Laws of 1660, Title "Ships," p. 72, citation of 1641. The law was passed Oct. 7, 1641 (Records, i, 337-338).

It will be noted that of these twelve laws dated in 1641, and not in the Body of Liberties, Numbers 1, 2, 8, 10 and 11 were passed in June, 1641, Nos. 9 and 12 in October, 1641, and No. 4 in December, 1641. These were all passed too late to be placed in that document. Nos. 3, 5, 6, and 7 are wrongly dated.

The result, however, is to show that nearly all of the acts ascribed to the year 1641 in the late revisions are simply sections of the Body of Liberties.

One other point remains to be considered. A few of the Liberties were not incorporated into the Statutes in 1660, and are not checked by E. Hutchinson on the margin of his manuscript. These are numbered 14, 26, 27, 51, 55, 79, and 95, § 11.

No. 14 is to the effect that a conveyance made by a married woman, a child, an idiot, or distracted person shall be good, if ratified by the General Court.

This may have been dropped on consideration as contrary to English law at that time.

No. 26 empowered any man unable to plead his own case to have any unpaid attorney. The prohibition to employ a paid lawyer was in force in 1641, as Winthrop records (History, ii, p. 43). May 2, 1649 (Records ii, 279), it is ordered that appeals shall be made by the party, or his attorney, in writing. Also, it was ordered that after one month's publication hereof, no one should ask council or advice of any magistrate in regard to a case to be tried. We may infer from these two citations that the necessity of paid attorneys had become so evident that this Liberty was quietly dropped.

No. 27 relates to the defendant's right to answer in writing if the plaintiff put in his case in that form.

No. 51 provides that associates to aid the assistants in the Inferior Courts shall be chosen by the towns.

No. 55 provides and gives the widest liberty to both plaintiffs and defendants in making claims and pleas.

These details in regard to the courts were naturally modified from time to time, between 1641 and 1660, as the records show. There seems to have been a great amount of experimenting in arranging the inferior courts, and hence we cannot find the exact equivalents of these Liberties, though they were preserved in spirit.

No. 79 provides that if a man did not provide for his widow out of his estate, the General Court should relieve her. This idea is carried out in the law of Dowries, as printed in 1660, to which reference has already been made. See also Wills, § 3.

It is evident, therefore, that the Body of Liberties was virtually incorporated into the earliest system of laws, and that no part of it was found to be superfluous. Both in regard to its extent and its phraseology it is a noble monument to the compilers, and to the community which so promptly accepted it. In its present form it will be easily examined, and the most thorough study will confirm the impression of its importance in any investigation of the growth of the Commonwealth, through original processes worked out on the spot, from a trading company to a free state, the parent and exemplar of so many later communities. —W. H. W.

THE BODY OF LIBERTIES.

1641.

IN FAC-SIMILE FROM THE HUTCHINSON MANUSCRIPT, WITH A
LINE-FOR-LINE PRINTED VERSION.

TABLE OF CONTENTS.[1]

PREAMBLE:

Liberty 1. Persons and property inviolable except by law.
2. Equal justice to all.
3. The Legislature alone to impose oaths.
4. Unavoidable absences not punishable.
5. Public service required only by law.
6. Exemptions from public service.
7. Limit of military service.
8. Property taken for public use to be paid for.
9. Monopolies forbidden but patents allowed.
10. Fines on alienations, heriots, &c., forbidden.
11. Wills and alienations allowed.
12. Freedom of speech and action in public meetings permitted.
13. Property abroad not taxable here.
14. Conveyances by married women, children, or insane persons legalized by the Legislature.
15. Fraudulent deeds invalid against just claims.
16. Free fishing and fowling defined.
17. Free emigration allowed.
18. Provision made for bail.
19. Assistants punished for misconduct.
20. Judges punished for misconduct.
21. Summons served not over six days before the Court, and the cause to be specified therein.
22. False claims to excessive debts or damages punishable.
23. Legal rate of interest fixed at 8% per annum.
24. Contributory negligence a good defence.
25. Technical errors not allowed if the Court understand the person and the cause.
26. Unpaid attorneys allowed.
27. Written pleas and answers permitted.
28. Suits may be discontinued before a verdict and renewed in another court.
29. Trials may be either by the bench or by a jury.
30. Jurors may be challenged.
31. Special verdict allowed, and appeals to the Legislature.
32. Cattle or goods may be replevined.
33. Imprisonment for debt regulated.
34. Common barrators punished.

Liberty 35. Distress of perishable goods regulated.
36. Appeals from inferior courts provided.
37. Malicious suits punished.
38. Evidence to be recorded on court rolls.
39. Courts may respite executions in all actions.
40. Deeds or promises given under duress are invalid.
41. Persons accused of crime shall be tried at the next Court.
42. No one shall be tried twice for the same offence.
43. Punishment by whipping regulated.
44. Time for executing criminals regulated.
45. Torture forbidden.
46. Barbarous or cruel punishments forbidden.
47. Death inflicted only on the evidence of two of three witnesses, or the equivalent.
48. Public records open to inspection.
49. Jury service regulated.
50. Towns to choose jurymen.
51. Towns to elect associates in inferior courts.
52. Children, strangers, and others to be protected in all suits.
53. Age of discretion fixed at twenty-one.
54. Powers and duties of moderators defined.
55. The fullest liberty allowed in pleas and answers.
56. Town-meetings protected from disturbance.
57. Inquests in case of sudden deaths.
58. Church regulations may be enforced by civil courts.
59. Church officers and members amenable to civil law.
60. Church censure inoperative upon civil officers.
61. Silence on conscientious grounds allowable.
62. Qualifications of deputies to the Legislature.
63. The expenses of certain officials to be a public charge.
64. Court records to be fully kept by the clerk.
65. The Word of God to overrule any custom or prescription.
66. Freemen in each town to manage their prudential affairs.

---

[1] This Table is put in modern form, and the term Legislature is used for the General Court. W. H. W.

Liberty 67. The chief officers to be elected annually by the freemen, and may be discharged for cause at other meetings of the General Court.
68. Deputies need not reside in the towns choosing them. The number of deputies to be fixed only from year to year.
69. Consent of a majority required to dissolve or adjourn the Legislature.
70. Freedom of speech and vote ordained.
71. Casting-vote allowed to presiding officers.
72. Reprieves and pardons regulated.
73. Messengers may be sent abroad on public affairs.
74. Selectmen allowed.
75. Protests in all meetings shall be allowed and recorded.
76. Jurors may consult bystanders in open court.
77. Voting not compulsory.
78. Public money to be spent only with the consent of the taxpayers.
79. Provision for widows in case of intestacy.

Liberty 80. Wives not subject to conjugal correction.
81. Gavelkind regulated.
82. Daughters as copartners.
83. Appeal from parental tyranny.
84. Protection for orphans.
85. Runaway servants protected.
86. Transfers of indentures of servants.
87. Servants recompensed for bodily injuries.
88. Servants to be rewarded.
89. Christian immigrants welcome.
90. Shipwrecked vessels to be assisted.
91. Slavery prohibited.
92. Cruelty to animals forbidden.
93. Travelling drovers assisted.
94. Death penalty for certain crimes.
95. Relations between church and civil authority defined.
96. These Liberties to have the force of law.
97. Suits allowed to give effect to these Liberties.
98. Liberties to be revised annually for three years.

Penalty if the Legislature in the next three years neglect Liberty 98.

82

A Coppie of ȳ Liberties of ȳ Massachusetts Colonie in New England

The free fruition of such liberties Immunities & priviledges as humanitie, Civilitie, & Christianitie call for as due to every man in his place & proportion; without impeachment & Infringement hath ever bene & ever will be the tranquillitie & stabilitie of Churches & Comon wealths. And ȳ deniall or deperverall thereof, the disturbance if not ȳ ruine of both.

We hould it therefore o'duty & safetie whilest we are about the further establishing of this Governament to collect & expresse all such freedomes as for present we forsee may concerne us, & our posteritie after us, And to ratify them with our sollemne consent.

Wee doe therefore this day religiously & unanimously decree & confirme these following Rites, liberties, & priviledges, concerneing o'churches, & Civill State to be respectivelye impartiallie & inviolablie enioyed & observed through out o'Iurisdiction for ever.

1. No mans life shall be taken away, no mans honour or good name shall be stayned, no mans person shall be arested, restrayned, banished, dismembred, nor any wayes punished, no man shall be deprived of his wife or children, no mans goods or estate shall be taken away from him, nor any way indamaged under colour of law, or Countenance of Authoritie, unlesse it be by vertue or equitie of some expresse law of ȳ Country warrantinge ȳ same, established by a generall Court & sufficiently published, or in case of ȳ defect of a law in any perticuler case by ȳ word of god. And in Capitall cases, or in cases concerning dismembringe or banishment, according to ȳ word to be iudged by ȳ Generall Court.

2. Every person w'th in this Iurisdiction, whether Inhabitant or forrainer shall enioy ȳ same Iustice & law, ȳ is generall for ȳ plantation, w'ch we constitute & execute one towards an other, w'thout partialitie or delay.

3. No man shall be urged to take any oath or subscribe any articles, Covenant, or remonstrance, of a publique and Civill nature, but such as ȳ Generall Court hath considered, allowed, & required.

4. No man shall be punished for not appearing at or before any Civill Assembly, Court, Councell, magistrate, or officer, nor for the omission of any office or service, if he shall be necessarily hindered, by any apparent Act or providence of god, w'ch he could neither foresee nor avoid, Provided ȳ this law shall not prejudice any person of his iust cost or damage in any civill action.

5. No man shall be compelled to any publique worke or service unlesse ȳ presse be grounded upon some act of ȳ generall Court, & have reasonable allowance therefore.

6. No man

88

A COPPIE OF THE LIBERTIES OF THE MASSACHUSETS COLONIE IN NEW ENGLAND.

The free fruition of such liberties Immunities and priveledges as humanitie, Civilitie, and Christianitie call for as due to every man in his place and proportion without impeachment and Infringement hath ever bene and ever will be the tranquillitie and Stabilitie of Churches and Commonwealths. And the deniall or deprivall thereof, the disturbance if not the ruine of both.

We hould it therefore our dutie and safetie whilst we are about the further establishing of this Government to collect and expresse all such freedomes as for present we foresee may concerne us, and our posteritie after us, And to ratify them with our sollemne consent.

We doe therefore this day religiously and unanimously decree and confirme these following Rites, liberties and priveledges concerneing our Churches, and Civill State to be respectively impartiallie and inviolably enjoyed and observed throughout our Jurisdiction for ever.

1. No mans life shall be taken away, no mans honour or good name shall be stayned, no mans person shall be arested, restrayned, banished, dismembred, nor any wayes punished, no man shall be deprived of his wife or children, no mans goods or estaite shall be taken away from him, nor any way indammaged under coulor of law or Countenance of Authoritie, unlesse it be by vertue or equitie of some expresse law of the Country waranting the same, established by a generall Court and sufficiently published, or in case of the defect of a law in any parteculer case by the word of god. And in Capitall cases, or in cases concerning dismembring or banishment, according to that word to be judged by the Generall Court. pag. 1.

2. Every person within this Jurisdiction. whether Inhabitant or forreiner shall enjoy the same justice and law, that is generall for the plantation, which we constitute and execute one towards another without partialitie or delay. pag. 143.

3. No man shall be urged to take any oath or subscribe any articles, covenants or remonstrance, of a publique and Civill nature, but such as the Generall Court hath considered, allowed, and required. pag. 219

4. No man shall be punished for not appearing at or before any Civill Assembly, Court, Councell, Magistrate, or Officer, nor for the omission of any office or service, if he shall be necessarily hindred by any apparent Act or providence of God, which he could neither foresee nor avoid. Provided that this law shall not prejudice any person of his just cost or damage, in any civill action. pag. 4.

5. No man shall be compelled to any publique worke or service unlesse the presse be grounded upon some act of the generall Court, and have reasonable allowance therefore. pag. 73. sect. 2.

6. No man

6. No man shall be pressed in psson to any office, worke, warres, or other publique service, yt is necessarily & sufficiently exempted by any naturall or psonall impediment, as by want of yeares, greatnes of age, defect of minde, fayling of senses, or impotencie of lymbes. — pag 71

7. No man shall be compelled to goe out of yᵉ limits of this plantation vpon any offensiue warres wᶜʰ this Comon wealth or any of o͏r freinds or confederats shall voluntarily vndertake, But onely vpon such vindictiue & defensiue warres in o͏r owne behalfe, or yᵉ behalfe of o͏r freinds, & confederats as shall be enterprized by yᵉ Counsell and consent of a Court generall, or by Authority derived from yᵉ same. — pag 73

8. No mans Cattell or goods of what kinde so ever shall be pressed or taken for any publique vse or service, vnlesse it be by warrant grounded vpon some act of yᵉ generall Court, nor wthout such reasonable prices & hier as yᵉ ordinarie rates of yᵉ Countrie do afford. And if his Cattle or goods shall perish or suffer damage in such service, yᵉ owner shall be sufficiently recompensed — pag. 73

9. No monopolies shall be granted or allowed amongst vs, but of such new Inventions yt are profitable to yᵉ Countrie, & yt for a short time. — pag 119

10. All oʳ lands & heritages shall be free from all fines & licenses vpon Alienations, & from all hariotts, wardships, Liueries, Primerseisins, yeare day & wast, Escheates, & forfeitures, vpon yᵉ deaths of parents, or Ancestors, be they naturall, vnnaturall, or Iudiciall. — pag 8

11. All psons wᶜʰ are of yᵉ age of 21 yeares, & of right vnderstanding & meamories, whither excommunicate or condemned shall haue full power & libertie to make there wills & testaments, & other lawfull alienations of their lands & Estates. — pag 1

12. Every man whether Inhabitant or forreiner, free or not free shall haue libertie to come to any publique Court, Councell, or Towne meeting, & either by speech or writing to moue any lawfull, seasonable, & materiall question, or to present any necessary motion, complaint, petition, Bill or information, whereof yᵗ meeting hath proper cognizance, so it be done in convenient time, due order, & respectiue manner. — pag 9

No man shall be rated here for any estate or revenue he hath in England or in any forreine partes till it be transported hither. — pag 75

Any Conueyance or Alienation of land or other estate what so ever, made by any woman yᵗ is married, any childe vnder age, Idyott, or distracted pson, shall be good, if it be passed & ratified by yᵉ consent of a generall Court.

15 All Courts

6	No man shall be pressed in person to any office, worke, warres or other publique service, that is necessarily and suffitiently exempted by any naturall or personall impediment, as by want of yeares, greatnes of age, defect of minde, fayling of sences, or impotencie of Lymbes.	pag. 73. sect. 2
7	No man shall be compelled to goe out of the limits of this plantation uppon any offensive warres which this Commonwealth or any of our freinds or confederats shall volentarily undertake. But onely upon such vindictive and defensive warres in our owne behalfe or the behalfe of our freinds and confederats as shall be enterprized by the Counsell and consent of a Court generall, or by Authority derived from the same.	pag. 73.
8	No mans Cattel or goods of what kinde soever shall be pressed or taken for any publique use or service, unlesse it be by warrant grounded upon some act of the generall Court, nor without such reasonable prices and hire as the ordinarie rates of the Countrie do afford. And if his Cattle or goods shall perish or suffer damage in such service, the owner shall be suffitiently recompenced.	pag. 73.
9	No monopolies shall be granted or allowed amongst us, but of such new Inventions that are profitable to the Countrie, and that for a short time.	pag. 119.
10	All our lands and heritages shall be free from all fines and licences upon Alienations, and from all hariotts, wardships, Liveries, Primerseisins, yeare day and wast, Escheates, and forfeitures, upon the deaths of parents or Ancestors, be they naturall, casuall or Juditiall.	pag. 88.
11	All persons which are of the age of 21 yeares, and of right understanding and meamories, whether excommunicate or condemned shall have full power and libertie to make there wills and testaments, and other lawfull alienations of theire lands and estates.	pag. 1.
12	Every man whether Inhabitant or fforreiner, free or not free shall have libertie to come to any publique Court, Councel, or Towne meeting, and either by speech or writing to move any lawfull, seasonable, and materiall question, or to present any necessary motion, complaint, petition, Bill or information, whereof that meeting hath proper cognizance, so it be done in convenient time, due order, and respective manner.	pag. 90.
13	No man shall be rated here for any estaite or revenue he hath in England, or in any forreine partes till it be transported hither.	pag. 25. sect. 2.
14	Any Conveyance or Alienation of land or other estaite what so ever, made by any woman that is married, any childe under age, Ideott or distracted person, shall be good if it be passed and ratified by the consent of a generall Court.	

15. All Coven^ts

15. All Countie or fraudulent alienations or Conveyances of Lands, tenem̄t, or any hereditaments, shall be of no validitie to defeate any man from due debts, or legacies, or from any just title, clame or possession, of y̆ w̆ch is so fraudulently conveyed.   *pag. 3. sec. 3*

16. Every Inhabitant y̆t is an house holder shall have free fishing & fowling in any great ponds & Bayes, Coves & Rivers, so farre as y̆e sea ebbes & flowes w̆th in y̆e lymits of y̆e towne where they dwell, unlesse y̆e free men of y̆e same Towne or y̆e Generall Court have otherwise appropriated them, provided y̆t this shall not be extended to give leave to any man to come upon others proprietie without there leave.   *pag. 9. sec. 2*

17. Every man of or w̆thin this Jurisdiction shall have free libertie notw̆thstanding any Civill power to remove both himselfe & his familie at their pleasure out of y̆e same, provided there be no legall impediment to y̆e contrarie.   *pag. 91 sec. 3*

Rites Rules & Liberties concerning Judiciall proceedings.

18. No mans p̆son shall be arrestained or imprisoned by any Authoritie whatsoever, before y̆e law hath sentenced him thereto, If he can put in sufficient securitie, bayle, or mainprise, for his appearance, & good behavior in y̆e meane time, unlesse it be in Crimes Capitall, & Contempts in open Court, & in such cases where some expresse act of Court doth allow it.   *pag. 71*

19. If in a generall Court any miscariage shall be amongst y̆e Assistants when they are by them selves y̆t may deserve an Admonition or fine under 20s, it shall be examined & sentenced amongst y̆em selves, If amongst y̆e Deputies when they are by themselves, it shall be examined & sentenced amongst themselves, If it be when y̆e whole Court is together, it shall be judged by y̆e whole Court, & not severallie as before.   *pag. 36 sec. 6*

20. If any who are to sit as Judges in any other Court shall demeane themselves offensively in y̆e Court, the rest of y̆e Judges p̆sent shall have power to censure him for it, if y̆e cause be of a high nature it shall be p̆sented to & censured at y̆e next Superior Court.   *pag. 76 sec. 6*

21. In all cases where y̆e first Sumons are not served six dayes before y̆e Court, & y̆e cause briefly specified in y̆e warrant, where appearance is to be made by y̆e ptie sumoned, it shall be at his libertie whether he will appeare or no, Except all cases y̆t are to be handled in Courts suddainly called, or, upon extraordinary occasions, In all cases where there appeares p̆sent & urgent cause, Any Assistant or officer apointed, shall have power to make out attachments for y̆e first sumons.

15. All Covenous or fraudulent Alienations or Conveyances of lands, tenements, or any hereditaments, shall be of no validitie to defeate any man from due debts or legacies, or from any just title, clame or possession, of that which is so fraudulently conveyed.   pag. 32. sec. 3.

16. Every Inhabitant that is an howse holder shall have free fishing and fowling in any great ponds and Bayes, Coves and Rivers, so farre as the sea ebbes and flowes within the presincts of the towne where they dwell, unlesse the free men of the same Towne or the Generall Court have otherwise appropriated them, provided that this shall not be extended to give leave to any man to come upon others proprietie without there leave.   pag. 90. sec. 2.

17. Every man of or within this Jurisdiction shall have free libertie, notwithstanding any Civill power to remove both himselfe, and his familie at their pleasure out of the same, provided there be no legall impediment to the contrarie.   pag. 91. sec. 3.

Rites Rules and Liberties concerning Juditiall proceedings.

18. No mans person shall be restrained or imprisoned by any Authority whatsoever, before the law hath sentenced him thereto, If he can put in sufficient securitie, bayle or mainprise, for his appearance, and good behaviour in the meane time, unlesse it be in Crimes Capital, and Contempts in open Court, and in such cases where some expresse act of Court doth allow it.   pag. 74.

19. If in a generall Court any miscariage shall be amongst the Assistants when they are by themselves that may deserve an Admonition or fine under 20 sh. it shall be examined and sentenced among themselves, If amongst the Deputies when they are by themselves, It shall be examined and sentenced amongst themselves, If it be when the whole Court is togeather, it shall be judged by the whole Court, and not severallie as before.   pag. 36. sec. 6.

20. If any which are to sit as Judges in any other Court shall demeane themselves offensively in the Court, the rest of the Judges present shall have power to censure him for it, if the cause be of a high nature it shall be presented to and censured at the next superior Court.   pag. 36. sec. 6.

21. In all cases where the first summons are not served six dayes before the Court, and the cause breifly specified in the warrant, where appearance is to be made by the partie summoned, it shall be at his libertie whether he will appeare or no, except all cases that are to be handled in Courts suddainly called, upon extraordinary occasions, In all cases where there appeares present and urgent cause Any Assistant or officer apointed shal have power to make out Attaichments for the first summons.   pag. 7. sec. 2.

22. No man

22. No man in any suit or action agt an other shall falsely pretend great
debts or damages to vex his Adversary, if it shall appeare any doth
so, the Court shall have power to set a reasonable fine on his head. pag. 3 sec. 8

23. No man shall be adjudged to pay for detayning any debt from any
Creditor above eight pounds in y hundred for one yeare, And not
above y rate pporsionable for all somes what so ever, neither
shall it be a coulour or countenance to allow any usurie amongst
us contrarie to y law of god. p. 153

24. In all trespasses or damages done to any man or men, if it can
be proved to be done by y meere default of him or them to whom y
trespasse is done, it shall be judged no trespasse, nor any damage
given for it. pag. 18 sec. 3

25. No summons pleading judgement, or any kinde of proceeding in
Court or course of Justice shall be abated, arested, or reversed, upon any kinde of circumstantiall errors or mistakes, if y pson &
cause be rightly understood & intended by y Court. pag. 7 sec. 2

26. Every man y findeth him selfe unfit to plead his owne cause in
any Court, shall have libertie to imploy any man agt whom the
Court doth not except, to helpe him, provided he give him no
fee, or reward for his paines. This shall not exempt y ptie him
selfe from Answering such questions in pson as y Court shall
think meete to demand of him.

27. If any plantife shall give into any Court a declaration of his cause
in writeing, the defendant shall also have libertie & time to
give in his answer in writeing. And so in all further pceedings
betweene ptie & ptie, so it doth not further hinder y dispatch of
Justice then y Court shall be willing unto.

28. The plantife in all Actions brought in any Court shall have libertie
to withdraw his Action, or to be non suit before y Jurie hath given
in y verdict, in wch case he shall alwaies pay full cost & chardges
to y defend, & may afterwards renew his suite at an other Court
if he please pag. 3 sec. 7

29. In all Actions at law it shall be y libertie of y plant & defen. by mut-
uall consent to choose whither they will be tryed by y Bench, or by
a Jurie, unlesse it be where y law upon just reason hath otherwise
determined. The like libertie shall be granted to all psons in Criminall cases. pag. 15 sec. 2

30. It shall be in y libertie both of plantife & defen, & likewise every
Delinquent (to be judged by a Jurie) to challenge any of y Jurors.
And if his challenge be found just & reasonable by y Bench, or
y rest of y Jurie, as y challenge shall choose it shall be allowed
him, & tales de circumstantib; impanelled in y roomes. p. 142 s. 3

31. Jurors

22. No man in any suit or action against an other shall falsely pretend great debts or damages to vex his Adversary, if it shall appeare any doth so, The Court shall have power to set a reasonable fine on his head.   pag. 3. sec. 8.

23. No man shall be adjudged to pay for detaining any debt from any Crediter above eight pounds in the hundred for one yeare, And not above that rate proportionable for all somes what so ever, neither shall this be a coulour or countenance to allow any usurie amongst us contrarie to the law of god.   pag. 155

24. In all Trespasses or damages done to any man or men, If it can be proved to be done by the meere default of him or them to whome the trespasse is done, It shall be judged no trespasse, nor any damage given for it.   pag. 18 sec. 3.

25. No Summons pleading Judgement, or any kinde of proceeding in Court or course of Justice shall be abated, arested or reversed upon any kinde of cercumstantiall errors or mistakes, If the person and cause be rightly understood and intended by the Court.   pag. 7. sec. 2.

26. Every man that findeth himselfe unfit to plead his owne cause in any Court shall have Libertie to imploy any man against whom the Court doth not except, to helpe him, Provided he give him noe fee or reward for his paines. This shall not exempt the partie him selfe from Answering such Questions in person as the Court shall thinke meete to demand of him.

27. If any plantife shall give into any Court a declaration of his cause in writing, The defendant shall also have libertie and time to give in his answer in writing, And so in all further proceedings betwene partie and partie, So it doth not further hinder the dispach of Justice then the Court shall be willing unto.

28. The plantife in all Actions brought in any Court shall have libertie to withdraw his Action, or to be nonsuited before the Jurie hath given in their verdict, in which case he shall alwaies pay full cost and chardges to the defendant, and may afterwards renew his suite at an other Court if he please.   pag. 3. sec. 7.

29. In all Actions at law it shall be the libertie of the plantife and defendant by mutnal consent to choose whether they will be tryed by the Bench or by a Jurie, unless it be where the law upon just reason hath otherwise determined. The like libertie shall be granted to all persons in Criminall cases.   pag. 152 sec. 2.

30. It shall be in the libertie both of plantife and defendant, and likewise every delinquent (to be judged by a Jurie) to challenge any of the Jurors. And if his challenge be found just and reasonable by the Bench, or the rest of the Jurie, as the challenger shall choose it shall be allowed him, and tales de cercumstantibus impaneled in their room.   pag 152 S. 3.

31. In all

31. In all cases where evidence is so obscure or defective that the Jurie cann not clearely & safely give a positive verdict, whether it be a grand or petit Jurie, It shall have libertie to give a non Liquit, or a speciall verdict in which, if a speciall verdict, the judgement of the cause shall be left to the Court. And all Jurors shall have libertie in matters of fact if they cannot finde the maine issue, yet to finde & present in their verdict so much as they can, If the peticioner Jurors shall goe differ at any time about their verdict if either of them cannot proceede for feare of non consience the case shall be referred to the Generall Court, who shall take the question from both & determine it.

32. Every man shall have libertie to replevy his Cattell or goods impounded, distreined, seised, or extended, unlesse it be upon execution after judgement, & in paiet of fines. Provided he puts in good securitie to prosecute his replevin, and to satisfie such demaundes as his Adversarie shall recover agt him in Law.

33. No mans person shall be Arrested, or imprisoned upon execution or judgement for any debt or fine, If the law can finde competent meanes of satisfaction otherwise from his estate. And if not his person may be arested & imprisoned where he shall be kept at his owne charge not the plts, till satisfaction be made; unlesse the Court that had cognizance of the cause or some Superior Court shall otherwise provide.

34. If any man shall be proved & judged a common Barrator vexing others with frequent & endlesse suites, It shall be in the power of Courts both to denie him the benefit of the law, and to punish him for his Barratry.

35. No mans Corne nor hay that is in the feild or upon the Cart, nor his garden stuffe, nor any thing subject to present decay shall be taken in any distresse, unles he that takes it doth presently bestow it where it may not be imbeseled nor suffer spoile or decay, or gives securitie to satisfie the woorth thereof if it comes to any harme.

36. It shall be in the libertie of every man cast to be condemned or sentenced in any cause in any Inferior Court, to make their Appeale to the Court of Assistants, provided they tender their appeale & put in securitie to prosecute it before the Court be ended where the sentence was given. And if in six dayes next ensuing put in good securitie before some Assistant to satisfie what his Adversarie shall recover agt him; And if the cause be of a criminall nature, for his good behaviour, and appearance. And everie man shall have libertie to complaine to the Generall Court of any injustice done him in any Court of Assistants or other.

37 In all

31. In all cases where evidence is so obscure or defective that the Jurie cannot clearely and safely give a positive verdict, whether it be a grand or petit Jurie, It shall have libertie to give a non Liquit, or a speciall verdict, in which last, that is in a speciall verdict, the Judgement of the cause shall be left to the Court, and all Jurors shall have libertie in matters of fact if they cannot finde the maine issue, yet to finde and present in their verdict so much as they can, If the Bench and Jurors shall so differ at any time about their verdict that either of them cannot proceede with peace of conscience the case shall be referred to the Generall Court, who shall take the question from both and determine it.   P. 87. S. 3, part of it.

32. Every man shall have libertie to replevy his Cattell or goods impounded, distreined, seised, or extended, unlesse it be upon execution after Judgement, and in paiment of fines. Provided he puts in good securitie to prosecute his replevin, And to satisfie such demands as his Adversary shall recover against him in Law.   P. 132.

33. No mans person shall be Arrested, or imprisoned upon execution or judgment for any debt or fine, If the law can finde competent meanes of satisfaction otherwise from his estaite, and if not his person may be arrested and imprisoned where he shall be kept at his owne charge, not the plantifes till satisfaction be made: unlesse the Court that had cognizance of the cause or some superior Court shall otherwise provide.   P. 6.

34. If any man shall be proved and Judged a commen Barrator vexing others with unjust frequent and endlesse suites, It shall be in the power of Courts both to denie him the benefit of the law, and to punish him for his Barratry.   P. 9.

35. No mans Corne nor hay that is in the feild or upon the Cart, nor his garden stuffe, nor any thing subject to present decay, shall be taken in any distresse, unles he that takes it doth presently bestow it where it may not be imbesled nor suffer spoile or decay, or give securitie to satisfie the worth thereof if it comes to any harme.   P. 41.

36. It shall be in the libertie of every man cast condemned or sentenced in any cause in any Inferior Court, to make their Appeale to the Court of Assistants, provided they tender their appeale and put in securitie to prosecute it before the Court be ended wherein they were condemned, And within six dayes next ensuing put in good securitie before some Assistant to satisfie what his Adversarie shall recover against him; And if the cause be of a Criminall nature, for his good behaviour, and appearance, And everie man shall have libertie to complaine to the Generall Court of any Injustice done him in any Court of Assistants or other.   P. 3. part of it.

37. In all

37. In all cases where it appeares to ye Court yt ye plant hath wittingly and wittingly done wrong to ye deft in comencing & prosecuting any action or complaint agt him, they shall have power to impose upon him a pro- portionable fine to ye use of ye deft, or arrived pson, for his false complaint, or clamor.

38. Everie man shall have libertie to Record in ye publique Rolles of any Court any testimony given upon oath in ye same Court, or before two Assistants, or any deede or evidence legally confirmed ye to remaine in perpetuam rei memoriam, yt is for perpetuall memoriall or evidence upon occasion.

39. In all Actions both reall & psonall betweene ptie & ptie, ye Court shall have power to respite execution for a convenient time, when in their prudence they see just cause so to doe.

40. No Conveyance, Deede, or promise what so ever shall be of validi- tie if it be gotten by illegall violence, imprisonmt, threatenings, or any kinde of forcible compulsion called Duresse.

41. Everie man yt is to answere for any Criminall cause, whether he be in prison or under bayle, his cause shall be heard & determined at ye next Court yt hath proper Cognizance thereof, And may be done wth out prejudice of Justice.

42. No man shall be twise sentenced by Civill Justice for one & the same Crime, offence, or trespasse.

43. No man shall be beaten wth above 40 stripes, nor shall any true Gentleman, nor any man Equall to a gentleman be punished wth whipping, unles his crime be very shamefull, & his course of life vitious and profligate.

44. No man condemned to dye shall be put to death wthin fower dayes next after his condemnation, unles ye Court see speciall cause to ye contrary, or in case of martiall law, nor shall ye body of any man so put to death be unburied 12 howers, unlesse it be in case of Anatomie.

45. No man shall be forced by torture to confesse any Crime agt himselfe nor any other unlesse it be in some Capitall case, where he is first fullie convicted by cleere & sufficient evidence to be guilty, After wch if ye cause be of yt nature, that it is very apparent yt be other conspiratours, or confederates wth him, then he may be tor- tured, yet not wth such tortures as be Barbarous & inhumane.

46. ffor bodilie punishments we allow amongst us none yt are inhumane Barbarous or cruell.

47. No man shall be put to death wthout ye testimony of two or three witnesses, or yt wch is equivalent thereunto.

48. Every Inhabitant

37	In all cases where it appeares to the Court that the plantife hath wilingly and witingly done wronge to the defendant in commenceing and prosecuting any action or complaint against him. They shall have power to impose upon him a proportionable fine to the use of the defendant, or accused person, for his false complaint or clamor.	P. 3. S. 8.
38	Everie man shall have libertie to Record in the publique Rolles of any Court any Testimony given upon oath in the same Court, or before two Assistants, or any deede or evidence legally confirmed there to remaine in perpetuam rei memoriam, that is for perpetuall memoriall or evidence upon occasion.	P. 132.
39	In all actions both reall and personall betweene partie and partie, the Court shall have power to respite execution for a convenient time, when in their prudence they see just cause so to doe.	P. 7. S. 1.
40	No Conveyance, Deede, or promise whatsoever shall be of validitie, If it be gotten by Illegal violence, imprisonment, threatenings, or any kinde of forcible compulsion called Dures.	P. 32. S. 3.
41	Everie man that is to Answere for any Criminall cause, whether he be in prison or under bayle, his cause shall be heard and determined at the next Court that hath proper Cognizance thereof, And may be done without prejudice of Justice.	P. 38 S. 10.
42	No man shall be twise sentenced by Civill Justice for one and the same Crime, offence, or Trespasse.	P. 123
43	No man shall be beaten with above 40 stripes, nor shall any true gentleman, nor any man equall to a gentleman be punished with whipping, unles his crime be very shamefull, and his course of life vitious and profligate.	P. 124
44	No man condemned to dye shall be put to death within fower dayes next after his condemnation, unles the Court see speciall cause to the contrary, or in case of martiall law, nor shall the body of any man so put to death be unburied 12 howers, unlesse it be in case of Anatomie.	P. 30.
45	No man shall be forced by Torture to confesse any Crime against himselfe nor any other unlesse it be in some Capitall case where he is first fullie convicted by cleare and sufficient evidence to be guilty. After which if the cause be of that nature, That it is very apparent there be other conspiratours, or confederates with him, Then he may be tortured, yet not with such Tortures as be Barbarous and inhumane.	P. 129.
46	For bodilie punishments we allow amongst us none that are inhumane Barbarous or cruel.	P. 125.
47	No man shall be put to death without the testimony of two or three witnesses or that which is equivalent thereunto. 48. Every Inhabitant	P. 155.

48	Every Inhabitant of y Countrie shall have free libertie to search and veiw any Bookes, Records, or Registers of any Court or office except y Councells, And to have a transcript or exemplification thereof written, examined, & signed by y hand of y officer of y office paying y appointed fees therefore.	p. 138 S. 3
49	No free man shall be compelled to serve upon Juries above two Courts in a yeare, except grand Jurie men, who shall hould two Courts together at y least.	p. 87 S. 5
50	All Jurors shall be chosen continually by y freemen of y towne where they dwell.	p. 86 S. 6
51	All Associates selected at any time to assist y Assistants in Inferior Courts, shall be nominated by y Townes belonging to y Court, by orderly agreement amonge them selues.	
52	Children, Idiots, distracted psons, & all f are strangers, or new comers to o plantation, shall haue such allowances and dispensations in any cause whether Criminall or other as religion & reason require.	p. 152 S. 9
53	The age of discretion for passing away of lands or such kinde of hereditments, or for giuing of votes, verdicts, or sentence in any Ciuill Courts or causes, shall be one & twentie yeares.	p. 6
54	When so euer any thing is to be put to vote, any sentence to be pronounced, or any other matter to be proposed, or read in any Court or Assembly, If y president or moderator thereof shall refuse to pforme it, y maior pte of y members of y Court or Assembly shall haue power to appoint any other meete man of them to do it, And if y be iust cause to punish him y should & would not.	p. 153
55	In all suites or Actions in any Court, the plant shall haue libertie to make all y titles & claims to y suite for his case. And y defent shall haue libertie to plead all y pleas hereon in answere to them, & y Court shall judge according to y intire euidence of all.	
56	If any man shall behaue in selfe offensiuely at any Towne meeting, y rest of y freemen then present, shall haue power to sentence him for his offence, soe be it y mulct or penaltie exceede not twentie shilings.	p. 147 S. 6
57	When so ever any pson shall come to any very suddaine untimely & unnaturall death, Some Assistant, or y Constables of y towne, shall forth wth summon a Jury of twelue free men to inquire of y cause & manner of their death, & shall present their verdict thereof to some next Assistant, or y next Court to be helde for y towne upon their oath.	p. 39

Liberties more.

48	Every Inhabitant of the Country shall have free libertie to search and veewe any Rooles, Records, or Regesters of any Court or office except the Councell, And to have a transcript or exemplification thereof written examined, and signed by the hand of the officer of the office paying the appointed fees therefore.	P. 131. S. 3.
49	No free man shall be compelled to serve upon Juries above two Courts in a yeare, except grand Jurie men, who shall hould two Courts together at the least.	P. 87. S. 5.
50	All Jurors shall be chosen continuallie by the freemen of the Towne where they dwell.	P. 86. S. 1.
51	All Associates selected at any time to Assist the Assistants in Inferior Courts shall be nominated by the Townes belonging to that Court, by orderly agreement amonge themselves.	
52	Children, Idiots, Distracted persons, and all that are strangers, or new commers to our plantation, shall have such allowances and dispensations in any Cause whether Criminall or other as religion and reason require.	P. 152. S. 4.
53	The age of discretion for passing away of lands or such kinde of herediments, or for giveing of votes, verdicts or Sentence in any Civill Courts or causes, shall be one and twentie yeares.	P. 1.
54	Whensoever anything is to be put to vote, any sentence to be pronounced, or any other matter to be proposed, or read in any Court or Assembly, If the president or moderator thereof shall refuse to performe it, the Major parte of the members of that Court or Assembly shall have power to appoint any other meete man of them to do it, And if there be just cause to punish him that should and would not.	P. 153.
55	In all suites or Actions in any Court, the plaintife shall have libertie to make all the titles and claims to that he sues for he can. And the Defendant shall have libertie to plead all the pleas he can in answere to them, and the Court shall judge according to the entire evidence of all.	
56	If any man shall behave himselfe offensively at any Towne meeting, the rest of the freemen then present, shall have power to sentence him for his offence. So be it the mulct or penaltie exceede not twentie shilings.	P. 145. S. 1.
57	Whensoever any person shall come to any very suddaine untimely and unnaturall death, Some assistant, or the Constables of that Towne shall forthwith sumon a Jury of twelve free men to inquire of the cause and manner of their death, and shall present a true verdict thereof to some neere Assistant, or the next Court to be helde for that Towne upon their oath.	P. 39.

39. Liberties more

Liberties more peculiarlie concerning the
free men.

58. Ciuill Authoritie hath power & libertie to see ye peace, ordinances &
Rules of Christ obserued in every church according to his word. so it be
done in a Ciuill & not in an Ecclesiasticall way.

59. Ciuill Authoritie hath power & libertie to deale wth any Church member in a way of Ciuill Justice, notwth standing any Church relation, office
or interest.

60. No church censure shall degrade or depose any man from any Ciuill dignitie, office, or Authoritie he shall haue in ye Comon wealth.

61. No magistrate, Juror, officer, or other man shall be bound to informe, present
or reveale any private crime or offence, wherein there is no peril or danger to this plantation or any member thereof: when any necessarie tye
of conscience binds him to secresie, grounded upon ye word of god, unlesse
it be in case of testimony lawfully required.

62. Any shire or Towne shall haue libertie to chose their deputies whom
& where they please for ye Generall Court, so be it they be free men
& haue taken theire oath of fealtie, & Inhabiting in this Jurisdiction.

63. No Gouernor, Dept Gouerr, Assistant, Associate, or grand Jury men at any
Court, nor any Deputie for ye Generall Court, shall at any time beare their
owne chardges at any Court, but ye necessary expences shall be defrayed
either by ye Towne, or Shire on whose service they are, or by ye Country in generall.

64. Everie Action betweene ptie & ptie, & proceedings agt delinquents in
Criminall causes shall be briefly & distinctly entered in ye Rolles of
every Court by ye Recorder thereof. That such actions be not afterwards brought againe to ye vexation of any man.

65. No custom or prescription shall ever prevaile amongst us in any morall
cause. or meaning is maintaine any thinge yt can be proved to bee
morally sinfull by ye word of god.

66. The freemen of every Towneship shall have power to make such
by lawes & constitutions as may concerne ye well fare of ye Towne. pr
uided they be not of a Criminall, but onely of a prudentiall nature.
And yt ye penalties exceede not 20ʃ for one offence. And yt they be
not repugnant to ye publique laws & orders of ye Country. And if any
Inhabitant shall neglect or refuse to observe them, they shall haue
power to levy ye appointed penalties by distresse.

67. It is ye constant libertie of ye free men of this plantation to chose
yearly at ye Court of Election out of ye free men all ye generall officers
of this Jurisdiction. If they please so discharge ym at ye day of election by
way of vote. They may doe it without shewing cause. But if at any other
Generall Court, we hould it due Justice, yt ye reasons therof be alled-
ged & proved. By generall officers we meane, or Gouerr, Dept Gouerr, Assistants, Treasurer, Generall of or warres. And or Admirall at Sea, &
such as are or heere after may be of ye like generall nature.

68. It is the

Liberties more peculiarlie concerninig the free men.

58. Civill Authoritie hath power and libertie to see the peace, ordinances and Rules of Christ observed in every church according to his word. so it be done in a Civill and not in an Ecclesiastical way. P. 44. S. 11.

59. Civill Authoritie hath power and libertie to deale with any Church member in a way of Civill Justice, notwithstanding any Church relation, office or interest. P. 44. S. 11.

60. No church censure shall degrad or depose any man from any Civill dignitie, office, or Authoritie he shall have in the Commonwealth. P. 44. S. 10.

61. No Magestrate, Juror, Officer, or other man shall be bound to informe present or reveale any private crim or offence, wherein there is no perill or danger to this plantation or any member thereof, when any necessarie tye of conscience binds him to secresie grounded upon the word of god, unlesse it be in case of testimony lawfully required. P. 86. S. 2.

62. Any Shire or Towne shall have libertie to choose their Deputies whom and where they please for the Generall Court. So be it they be free men, and have taken there oath of fealtie, and Inhabiting in this Jurisdiction. P. 40. S. 2.

63. No Governor, Deputy Governor, Assistant, Associate, or grand Jury man at any Court, nor any Deputie for the Generall Court shall at any time beare his owne chardges at any Court, but their necessary expences shall be defrayed either by the Towne or Shire on whose service they are, or by the Country in generall. P. 22. S. 1.

64. Everie Action betweene partie and partie, and proceedings against delinquents in Criminall causes shall be briefly and destinctly entered on the Rolles of every Court by the Recorder thereof. That such actions be not afterwards brought againe to the vexation of any man. P. 129. S. 1.

65. No custome or prescription shall ever prevaile amongst us in any morall cause, our meaneing is maintaine anythinge that can be proved to bee morrallie sinfull by the word of god. P. 126.

66. The Freemen of every Towneship shall have power to make such by laws and constitutions as may concerne the wellfare of their Towne, provided they be not of a Criminall, but onely of a prudentiall nature, And that their penalties exceede not 20 sh. for one offence. And that they be not repugnant to the publique laws and orders of the Countrie. And if any Inhabitant shall neglect or refuse to observe them, they shall have power to levy the appointed penalties by distresse. P. 147. S. 1.

67. It is the constant libertie of the free men of this plantation to choose yearly at the Court of Election out of the freemen all the General officers of this Jurisdiction. If they please to dischardge them at the day of Election by way of vote. They may do it without shewing cause. But if at any other generall Court, we hould it due justice, that the reasons thereof be allendged and proved. By Generall officers we meane, our Governor, Deputy Governor, Assistants, Treasurer, Generall of our warres. And our Admirall at Sea, and such as are or hereafter may be of the like genrall nature. P. 48. S. 4.

68. It is the

68. It is y liberty of y freemen to chuse such deputies for y Generall Court out of them selues, either in y owne townes or else where as they iudge fittest. And because wee cannot foresee what varieties & waight of occasions may fall into future consideration, And what councelles wee may stand in neede of, wee decree, That y deputies (to attend y Generall Court in y behalfe of y Countrie) shall not any time be stated or inacted, but from Court to Court, or at y most but for one yeare. y y Countries may haue an Annuall libertie to do in y case what is most behoofefull for y best welfaire there of.

69. No Generall Court shall be disolued or adiourned without y consent of y maj. pte there of.

70. All freemen called to giue any advise, vote, verdict, or sentence, in any Court, Councell, or Ciuill Assembly, shall haue full freedome to doe it according to y true Iudgments & Consciences, so it be done orderly & inoffensiuely for y manner.

71. The gour shall haue a casting voice when so ever an Equi vote shall fall out in y Court of Assistants, or generall assembly, so shall y President or Moderator haue in all Ciuill Courts or Assemblies.

72. The Gour & Dept Gour Ioyntly consenting or any three Assistants concurring in consent shall haue power out of Court to reprieue a condemned malefactour, till y next quarter or generall Court. y generall Court only shall haue power to pardon a condemned malefactour.

73. The Generall Court hath libertie & Authoritie to send out any member of y sd Common wealth of what qualitie, condition, or office what so ever into forreine parts about any publique message or Negotiation. Prouided y person sent be acquainted w y affaire he goeth about. & be willing to undertake y service.

74. The freemen of every Towne or Towneship, shall haue full power to choose yearly or for lesse time out of them selues a convenient number of fitt men to order y planting or prudentiall occasions of y Towne, according to instructions giuen them in writing. Provided no thing be done by them contrary to y publique lawes & orders of y Countrie. prouided also y number of such select persons be not aboue nine.

75. It is & shall be y libertie of any member or members of any Court Councell or Ciuill Assembly in cases of making or executing any order or law, y properlie concerne religion, or any cause capitall, or warres, or Subscription to any publique Articles or Remonstrance, in case they can not in iudgmt & conscience consent to y vote, the Maj: vote or suffrage goes, to make y contra Remonstrance or protestation in speech or writing, & upon request to haue y dissent recorded in y Rolles of that Court. so it be done Christianlie & respectiuely for y manner. And y dissent onely be entered w out y reasons there of, for y auoiding of tediousnes.

76. When so ever

68	It is the libertie of the freemen to choose such deputies for the Generall Court out of themselves, either in their owne Townes or elsewhere as they judge fitest. And because we cannot foresee what varietie and weight of occasions may fall into future consideration, And what counsells we may stand in neede of, we decree. That the Deputies (to attend the Generall Court in the behalfe of the Countrie) shall not any time be stated or inacted, but from Court to Court, or at the most but for one yeare, that the Countrie may have an Annuall libertie to do in that case what is most behoofefull for the best welfaire thereof.	P. 40. S. 2.
69	No Generall Court shall be desolved or adjourned without the consent of the Major parte thereof.	P. 35. S. 5.
70	All Freemen called to give any advise, vote, verdict, or sentence in any Court, Counsell, or Civill Assembly, shall have full freedome to doe it according to their true Judgements and Consciences, So it be done orderly and inofensively for the manner.	P. 153.
71	The Governor shall have a casting voice whensoever an Equi vote shall fall out in the Court of Assistants, or generall assembly, So shall the presedent or moderator have in all Civill Courts or Assemblies.	P. 35. S. 6.
72	The Governor and Deputy Governor Joyntly consenting or any three Assistants concurring in consent shall have power out of Court to reprive a condemned malefactour, till the next quarter or generall Court. The generall Court onely shall have power to pardon a condemned malefactor.	P. 35. S. 4.
73	The Generall Court hath libertie and Authoritie to send out any member of this Comanwealth of what qualitie, condition or office whatsoever into forreine parts about any publique message or Negotiation. Provided the partie sent be acquainted with the affaire he goeth about, and be willing to undertake the service.	P. 35. S. 4.
74	The freemen of every Towne or Towneship, shall have full power to choose yearly or for lesse time out of themselves a convenient number of fitt men to order the planting or prudentiall occasions of that Town, according to Instructions given them in writing, Provided nothing be done by them contrary to the publique laws and orders of the Countrie, provided also the number of such select persons be not above nine.	P. 148. S. 2.
75	It is and shall be the libertie of any member or members of any Court, Councell or Civill Assembly in cases of makeing or executing any order or law, that properlie concerne religion, or any cause capitall, or warres, or Subscription to any publique Articles or Remonstrance, in case they cannot in Judgement and conscience consent to that way the Major vote or suffrage goes, to make their contra Remonstrance or protestation in speech or writing, and upon request to have their dissent recorded in the Rolles of that Court. So it be done Christianlie and respectively for the manner. And their dissent onely be entered without the reasons thereof, for the avoiding of tediousness. 76. Whensoever	P. 128.

76	When so ever any Jurie of trialls or Jurours, are not cleare in their Judgem'ts or consciences concerning any cause wherein they are to give theire verdict, they shall have libertie in open Court to advise with any man they thinke fitt to resolve or direct them, before they give in y'e verdict.	p. 88 s. 8
77	In all cases wherein any freeman is to give his vote. be it in point of Election, making constitutions & orders or passing sentence in any case of Judicature or y'e like, if he can not see reason to give it positively any way or an other. he shall have libertie to be silent, & not pressed to a determined vote.	p. 183
78	The Generall or publique treasure or any pte y'of shall never be expended but by y'e apointm't of a Generall Court, nor any Shire treasure, but by y'e apointm't of y'e freemen there of, nor any towne treasurie but by y'e free men of y't towneship.	p. 159 s. 1. 2

Liberties of Woemen

| 79 | If any man at his death shall not leave his wife a competent portion of his estate: upon just complaint made to y'e Gen'll Court she shall be relieved. | |
| 80 | Everie marryed woeman shall be free from bodilie correction or stripes by her husband, unlesse it be in his owne defence upon her assalt. If y'r be any just cause of correction complaint shall be made to Authoritie assembled in some Court, from whom onely she shall receive it. | p. 101 s. 1 |

Liberties of Children

81	When parents dye intestate, y'e Eldie sonne shall have a doble portion of his whole estate reall & p'sonall, unlesse y'e Gen'll Court upon just cause alleadged shall judge otherwise.	p. 151 s. 3
82	When parents dye intestate, haueing noe heires males of y'r bodies y'r daughters shall inherit as Copartners, unles y'e Gen'll Court upon just reason shall iudge otherwise.	p. 153 s. 3
83	If any parents shall wilfullie & unreasonably deny any childe timely or convenient marriage, or shall exercise any unnaturall severitie towards them, such children shall have free libertie to complaine to Authoritie for redresse.	p. 28 s. 5
84	No Orphan dureing theire minoritie w'ch was not comitted to tuition or service by the parents in y'r life tyme, shall afterwards be absolutelie disposed of by any kindred, friend, Executor, Towneship or Church, nor by them sellwes w'thout y'e consent of some Court where in two Assistants at least shall be present.	p. 28 s. 6

Liberties of Servants

| 85 | If any servants shall flee from y'e tirany & crueltie of y'r masters to y'e house of any freeman of y'e same towne, they shall be ptected & sustayned till due order be taken for y'r releife. Provided due notice y'of be speedily given to y'r maisters from whom they fled. And y'e next Assistant or Constable where y'e ptie flying is harboured. | p. 105 s. 6 |

86 No servant

76	Whensoever any Jurie of trialls or Jurours are not cleare in their Judgements or consciences conserneing any cause wherein they are to give their verdict, They shall have libertie in open Court to advise with any man they thinke fitt to resolve or direct them, before they give in their verdict.	P. 87. S. 5.
77	In all cases wherein any freeman is to give his vote, be it in point of Election, makeing constitutions and orders, or passing sentence in any case of Judicature or the like, if he cannot see reason to give it positively one way or an other, he shall have libertie to be silent, and not pressed to a determined vote.	P. 153.
78	The Generall or publique Treasure or any parte thereof shall never be expended but by the appointment of a Generall Court, nor any Shire Treasure, but by the appointment of the freemen thereof, nor any Towne Treasurie but by the freemen of that Towneship.	P. 150. S. 1, 2.

Liberties of Woemen.

79	If any man at his death shall not leave his wife a competent portion of his estaite, upon just complaint made to the Generall Court she shall be relieved.	
80	Everie marryed woeman shall be free from bodilie correction or stripes by her husband, unlesse it be in his owne defence upon her assult. If there be any just cause of correction complaint shall be made to Authoritie assembled in some Court, from which onely she shall receive it.	P. 101. S. 1.

Liberties of Children.

81	When parents dye intestate, the Elder sonne shall have a doble portion of his whole estate reall and personall, unlesse the Generall Court upon just cause alleadged shall Judge otherwise.	P. 158. S. 3.
82	When parents dye intestate haveing noe heires males of their bodies their Daughters shall inherit as copartners, unles the Generall Court upon just reason shall judge otherwise.	P. 158. S. 3.
83	If any parents shall wilfullie and unreasonably deny any childe timely or convenient mariage, or shall exercise any unnaturall severitie towards them, such childeren shall have free libertie to complaine to Authoritie for redresse.	P. 28. S. 5.
84	No Orphan dureing their minoritie which was not committed to tuition or service by the parents in their life time shall afterwards be absolutely disposed of by any kindred, freind, Executor, Towneship, or Church, nor by themselves without the consent of some Court, wherein two Assistants at least shall be present.	P. 28. S. 6.

Liberties of Servants

85	If any servants shall flee from the Tiranny and crueltie of their masters to the howse of any freeman of the same Towne, they shall be there protected and susteyned till due order be taken for their relife. Provided due notice thereof be speedily given to their maisters from whom they fled. And the next Assistant or Constable where the partie flying is harboured.	P. 105. S. 6.

86. No servant

86. No servant shall be put of for above a yeare to any other neither in y{e} life time of y{e} maister nor after y{e} death by y{e} Executors, or Administrators unlesse it be by consent of Authoritie assembled in some Court, or two Assistants. p. 168

87. If any man smite out y{e} eye or tooth of his man servant, or maid servant, or otherwise mayme or much disfigure him, unlesse it be by meere casualtie, he shall let them goe free from his service. And shall have such further recompence as y{e} Court shall allow him. p. 105 & 8

88. Servants y{t} have served deligentlie & faithfully to y{e} benefitt of y{ere} maisters seaven yeares, shall not be sent away emptie. And if any have bene unfaithfull, negligent, or unprofitable in their service, notwithstanding y{e} good usage of y{ere} maisters, they shall not be dismissed till they have made satisfaction according to y{e} judgement of Authoritie. p. 105 S. 9

Liberties of fforreiners & Strangers

89. If any people of other Nations professing y{e} true Christian Religion shall flee to us from y{e} Tiranny or oppression of y{ere} persecutors, or from famyne, warres, or the like necessary & compulsarie cause They shall be entertayned & succoured amongst us, according to y{t} power & prudence god shall give us. p. 143

90. If any ships or other vessels, be it friend or enemy, shall suffer shipwrack upon o{ur} Coast. y{ere} shall be no violence or wrong offered to y{ere} persons or goods. But y{ere} persons shall be harboured, & releived, & y{ere} goods p{re}served in safetie till Authoritie may be certified thereof, & shall take further order therein. p. 158

91. There shall never be any bond slaverie villinage or Captivitie amongst us unles it be lawfull Captives taken in iust warres, & such strangers as willingly selle themselves or are sold to us. And these shall have all the liberties & Christian usages w{ch} y{e} law of god established in Israell concerning such persons doeth morally require. This exempts none from serv{i}tude who shall be Judged thereto by Authoritie.

Off the Bruite Creatures

92. No man shall exercise any Tiranny or Crueltie towards any bruite Creature w{ch} are usuallie kept for mans use. p. 39

93. If any man shall have occasion to leade or drive Cattel from place to place that is far of, So y{t} they be weary, or hungry, or fall sick, or lambe, It shall be lawfull to rest or refresh them, for a competent time, in any open place that is not Corne, meadow, or inclosed for some peculiar use. p. 41

Capitall Laws

86	No servant shall be put of for above a yeare to any other neither in the life time of their maister nor after their death by their Executors or Administrators unlesse it be by consent of Authoritie assembled in some Court or two Assistants.	P. 105. S. 7.
87	If any man smite out the eye or tooth of his man-servant, or maid servant, or otherwise mayme or much disfigure him, unlesse it be by meere casualtie, he shall let them goe free from his service. And shall have such further recompense as the Court shall allow him.	P. 105. S. 8.
88	Servants that have served deligentlie and faithfully to the benefitt of their maisters seaven yeares, shall not be sent away emptie. And if any have bene unfaithfull, negligent or unprofitable in their service, notwithstanding the good usage of their maisters, they shall not be dismissed till they have made satisfaction according to the Judgement of Authoritie.	P. 105. S. 9.

Liberties of Forreiners and Strangers.

89	If any people of other Nations professing the true Christian Religion shall flee to us from the Tiranny or oppression of their persecutors, or from famyne, warres, or the like necessary and compulsarie cause, They shall be entertayned and succoured amongst us, according to that power and prudence god shall give us.	P. 143.
90	If any ships or other vessels, be it freind or enemy, shall suffer shipwrack upon our Coast, there shall be no violence or wrong offerred to their persons or goods. But their persons shall be harboured, and relieved, and their goods preserved in safety till Authoritie may be certified thereof, and shall take further order therein.	P. 161.
91	There shall never be any bond slaverie, villinage or Captivitie amongst us unles it be lawfull Captives taken in just warres, and such strangers as willingly selle themselves or are sold to us. And these shall have all the liberties and Christian usages which the law of god established in Israell concerning such persons doeth morally require. This exempts none from servitude who shall be Judged thereto by Authoritie.	P. 10.

Off the Bruite Creature.

92	No man shall exercise any Tirranny or Crueltie towards any bruite Creature which are usuallie kept for man's use.	P. 39.
93	If any man shall have occasion to leade or drive Cattel from place to place that is far of, so that they be weary, or hungry, or fall sick, or lambe, It shall be lawful to rest or refresh them, for a competent time, in any open place that is not Corne, meadow, or inclosed for some peculiar use.	P. 42.

Capitall Laws

Capitall Laws

1.
Deut. 13:6.10
Deut. 17:2.6
Ex. 22:20
If any man after legall conviction shall have or worship any other god, but ye Lord god, he shall be put to death.
p 4
S. 1.

2.
Ex. 22:18
Lev. 20:27
Deut. 18:10
If any man or woeman be a witch, (that is hath or consulteth wth a familiar spirit, they shall be put to death.
S. 2.

3.
Lev. 24:15.16
If any pson shall blaspheme ye name of god, the father, sonne or Holie ghost, wth direct, expresse, psumptuous or high handed blasphemie, or shall curse god in ye like manner, he shall be put to death.
S. 3.

4.
Ex. 21:12
Numb. 35:13
14. 30. 31.
If any pson comitt any wilfull murther, wch is manslaughter, comitted vpon premeditated mallice, hatred, or Crueltie, not in a mans necessarie & iust defence, nor by meere casualtie against his will: he shall be put to death.
S. 4.

5.
Num. 25:20
Lev. 24:17
If any pson slayeth an other suddainely in his anger or Crueltie of passion, he shall be put to death.
S. 5.

6.
Ex. 21:14
If any pson shall slay an other through guile, either by poysoning or other such diuelish practise, he shall be put to death.
S. 6.

7.
Lev. 20:15.16
If any man or woeman shall lye wth any beast or bruite creature by Carnall Copulation, they shall surely be put to death: And ye beast shall be slaine, & buried & not eaten
S. 7.

8.
Lev. 20:13
If any man lyeth wth mankinde as he lyeth wth a woeman; both of them have comitted abhomination, they both shall surely be put to death.
S. 8.

9.
Lev. 20:19
& 18:20
Deut. 22:23
24.
If any pson comitteth Adultery wth a maried or espoused wife the Adulterer & Adulteresse shall surely be put to death.
S. 9.

10.
Ex. 21:16
If any man stealeth a man or mankinde, he shall surely be put to death.
S. 10.

11.
Deut. 19:16
18:19
If any man rise vp by false witnes, wittingly & of purpose to take away any mans life; he shall be put to death.
S. 11.

12.
If any man shall conspire & attempt any invasion, insurrection, or publique rebellion agt ye comon wealth, or shall indeavour to surprize any Towne or Townes, foort or forts ẟin, or shall treacherously & pfideously attempt ye alteration & subversion of or frame of politie or government fundamentallie, he shall be put to death.
S. 12.

A declaration

94. Capitall Laws.

1.

Dut. 13. 6, 10.
Dut. 17. 2, 6.
Ex. 22. 20.

If any man after legall conviction shall have or worship any other god, but the lord god, he shall be put to death.

P. 14.
S. 1.

2.

Ex. 22. 18.
Lev. 20. 27.
Dut. 18. 10.

If any man or woeman be a witch, (that is hath or consulteth with a familiar spirit,) They shall be put to death.

S. 2.

3.

Lev. 24. 15, 16.

If any man shall Blaspheme the name of god, the father, Sonne or Holie ghost, with direct, expresse, presumptuous or high handed blasphemie, or shall curse god in the like manner, he shall be put to death.

S. 3.

4.

Ex. 21. 12.
Numb. 35. 13, 14, 30, 31.

If any person committ any wilfull murther, which is man-slaughter, committed upon premeditated mallice, hatred, or Crueltie, not in a mans necessarie and just defence, nor by meere casualtie against his will, he shall be put to death.

S. 4.

5.

Numb. 25. 20, 21.
Lev. 24. 17.

If any person slayeth an other suddaienly in his anger or Crueltie of passion, he shall be put to death.

S. 5.

6.

Ex. 21. 14.

If any person shall slay an other through guile, either by poysoning or other such divelish practice, he shall be put to death.

S. 6.

7.

Lev. 20. 15, 16.

If any man or woeman shall lye with any beaste or bruite creature by Carnall Copulation, They shall surely be put to death. And the beast shall be slaine and buried and not eaten.

S. 7.

8.

Lev. 20. 13.

If any man lyeth with mankinde as he lyeth with a woeman, both of them have committed abhomination, they both shall surely be put to death.

S. 8.

9.

Lev. 20. 19, and 18, 20.
Dut. 22. 23, 24.

If any person committeth Adultery with a maried or espoused wife, the Adulterer and Adulteresse shall surely be put to death.

S. 9.

10.

Ex. 21. 16.

If any man stealeth a man or mankinde, he shall surely be put to death.

S. 10.

11.

Deut. 19. 16, 18, 19.

If any man rise up by false witnes, wittingly and of purpose to take away any mans life, he shall be put to death.

S. 11.

12.

If any man shall conspire and attempt any invasion, insurrection, or publique rebellion against our commonwealth, or shall indeavour to surprize any Towne or Townes, fort or forts therein, or shall treacherously and perfediouslie attempt the alteration and subversion of our frame of politie or Government fundamentallie, he shall be put to death.

S. 12.

A declaration

A Declaration of the Liberties the Lord Jesus hath given to ye Churches.

95.

1. All ye people of god wth in this Jurisdiction who are not in a church way, & be orthodox in Judgement, & not scandalous in life, shall have full libertie to gather themselues into a Church Estaite. Provided they doe it in a christian way, wth due observation of ye rules of Christ — revealed in his word.   p. 43. S. 1.

2. Every Church hath full libertie to exercise all ye ordinances of god, according to ye rules of Scripture.   S. 3

3. Every Church hath free libertie of Election & ordination of all their officers from time to time, provided they be able, pious & orthodox.   S. 4.

4. Every Church hath free libertie of Admission, Recommendation, dismission, & Expulsion, or deposall of ye officers, & members, vpon due cause: wth free exercise of ye discipline & Censures of Christ according to the rules of his word.   S. 5

5. No Jniunctions are to be put vpon any Church, Church Officers or member in point of doctrine, worship or discipline, whether for substance or circumstance besides ye Jnstitutions of ye Lord.   S. 6

6. Every Church of Christ hath freedome to celebrate dayes of fasting & prayer, & of thanksgiuing according to ye word of god   S. 7.

7. The Elders of Churches haue free libertie to meete monthly, quarterly, or otherwise, in convenient numbers & places, for conferences, & consultations about Christian & Church questions & occasions.   S. 8

8. All churches haue libertie to deale wth any of their members in a church way, & are in ye hand of Justice. So it bennot to retard, or hinder ye course y^{of}.   S. 9

9. Every Church hath libertie to deale wth any magistrate, deputie of Court or other officer what soe Ever if is a member in a church way in case of apparent & iust offence giuen in ye places. So it be done wth due observance & respect.   p. 44. S. 10

10. Wee allowe private meetings for edification in religion amongst Christians of all sortes of people. So it be w^{th}out just offence both for number, time, place, & other circumstances.   S. 12

11. for ye Granting

95. *A Declaration of the Liberties the Lord Jesus hath given to the Churches.*

1. All the people of god within this Jurisdiction who are not in a church way, and be orthodox in Judgement, and not scandalous in life, shall have full libertie to gather themselves into a Church Estaite. Provided they doe it in a Christian way, with due observation of the rules of Christ revealed in his word. P. 43
S. 1.

2. Every Church hath full libertie to exercise all the ordinances of god, according to the rules of scripture. S. 3.

3. Every Church hath free libertie of Election and ordination of all their officers from time to time, provided they be able, pious and orthodox. S. 4.

4. Every Church hath free libertie of Admission, Recommendation, Dismission, and Expulsion, or deposall of their officers and members, upon due cause, with free exercise of the Discipline and Censures of Christ according to the rules of his word. S. 5.

5. No Injunctions are to be put upon any Church, Church officers or member in point of Doctrine, worship or Discipline, whether for substance or cercumstance besides the Institutions of the lord. S. 6.

6. Every Church of Christ hath freedome to celebrate dayes of fasting and prayer, and of thanksgiveing according to the word of god. S. 7.

7. The Elders of Churches have free libertie to meete monthly, Quarterly, or otherwise, in convenient numbers and places, for conferences and consultations about Christian and Church questions and occasions. S. 8.

8. All Churches have libertie to deale with any of their members in a church way that are in the hand of Justice. So it be not to retard or hinder the course thereof. S. 9.

9. Every Church hath libertie to deale with any magestrate, Deputie of Court or other officer what soe ever that is a member in a church way in case of apparent and just offence given in their places, so it be done with due observance and respect. P. 44.
S. 10.

10. Wee allowe private meetings for edification in religion amongst Christians of all sortes of people. So it be without just offence for number, time, place, and other cercumstances. S. 12.

11. For the preventing

26. for the pr̃uenting & remoueing of Errours & offences that may grow & spread in any of y͡e Churches in this Jurisdiction. And for y͡e p͡seruing of tr̃uth & peace in y͡e seuerall churches w͡thin themselues, & for the maintenance & exercise of brotherly comunion, amongst all y͡e churches in y͡e Countrie, It is allowed & ratified, by y͡e Authoritie of this Gen͡all Court as a lawfull libertie of y͡e Churches of Christ. That once in every month of y͡e yeare (when y͡e season will beare it) It shall be lawfull for y͡e ministers & Elders, of y͡e Churches neere adioyneing together, w͡th any other of y͡e Brethren w͡th y͡e consent of y͡e churches to assemble by course in each severall Church one after another. To y͡e intent, after y͡e preaching of y͡e word by such a minister as shall be requested there to by y͡e Elders of y͡e church where y͡e Assembly is held, the rest of y͡e day may be spent in publique Christian Conference about y͡e discussing & resoluing of any such doubts & cases of conscience concerning matter of doctrine or worship or gouernm͡t of y͡e church as shall be propounded by any of y͡e Brethren of y͡e church, w͡th leaue also to any other Brother to propound his obiections or answers for further satisfaction according to y͡e word of god. Provided y͡t y͡e whole action be guided & moderated by y͡e Elders of y͡e Church where y͡e Assemblie is helde, or by such others as they shall appoint. And y͡t no thing be concluded & imposed by way of Authoritie from one or more Churches vpon another, but onely by way of Brotherly conference & consultations. That y͡e truth may be searched out to y͡e satisfying of every mans conscience in y͡e sight of god according to his worde. And because such an Assembly & y͡e worke thereof can not be duely attended to if other lectures be held in y͡e same weeke. It is therefore agreed w͡th y͡e consent of y͡e Churches. That in y͡e weeke when such an Assembly is held All y͡e lectures in all y͡e neighbouring Churches for y͡t weeke shall be forborne. That so y͡e publique service of Christ in this more solemne Assembly may be transacted w͡th greater diligence & attention.

96 Hough

11 For the preventing and removeing of errour and offence that may grow and spread in any of the Churches in this Jurisdiction, and for the preserveing of trueith and peace in the several churches within themselves, and for the maintenance and exercise of brotherly communion, amongst all the churches in the Countrie, It is allowed and ratified, by the Authoritie of this Generall Court as a lawfull libertie of the Churches of Christ. That once in every month of the yeare (when the season will beare it) It shall be lawfull for the minesters and Elders, of the Churches neere adjoyneing together, with any other of the breetheren with the consent of the churches to assemble by course in each severall Church one after an other. To the intent after the preaching of the word by such a minister as shall be requested thereto by the Elders of the church where the Assembly is held, The rest of the day may be spent in publique Christian Conference about the discussing and resolveing of any such doubts and cases of conscience concerning matter of doctrine or worship or government of the church as shall be propounded by any of the Breetheren of that church, with leave also to any other Brother to propound his objections or answeres for further satisfaction according to the word of god. Provided that the whole action be guided and moderated by the Elders of the Church where the Assemblie is helde, or by such others as they shall appoint. And that no thing be concluded and imposed by way of Authoritie from one or more Churches upon an other, but onely by way of Brotherly conference and consultations. That the trueth may be searched out to the satisfying of every mans conscience in the sight of god according his worde. And because such an Assembly and the worke theirof can not be duely attended to if other lectures be held in the same weeke. It is therefore agreed with the consent of the Churches. That in that weeke when such an Assembly is held, All the lectures in all the neighbouring Churches for that weeke shall be forborne. That so the publique service of Christ in this more solemne Assembly may be transacted with greater deligence and attention.

96. Howso-

96. How so ever these above specified rites, freedomes, Immunities, Authorities & priueledges, both Ciuill & Ecclesiasticall are expressed onely vnder ye name & title of Liberties, & not in ye exact forme of Laws, or Statutes, yet we do with one consent fullie Authorise, & earnestly intreate all yt are & shall be in due Authoritie to consider them as laws, & not to faile to inflict condigne & proportionable punishments vpon every man impartiallie, yt shall infringe or violate any of them.

97. Wee likewise giue full power & libertie to any person yt shall at any time be denyed or depriued of any of them, to commence & prosecute yr suite, Complaint, or action agt any man yt shall so doe, in any Court yt hath proper Cognizence or indicature there of.

98. Lastly because of duty & desire is to do nothing suddainlie wch fundamentally concerne vs. wee decree yt these rites & liberties, shall be audably read & deliberately weighed at every Genrll Court yt shall be held, wthin three yeares next insueing, And such of them as shall not be altered or repealed they shall stand so ratified, that no man shall infringe them wthout due punishment.

And if any Genrll Court wthin these next thre yeares shall faile or forget to reade & consider them as aboue said, the Govr & Deputy Govr for ye time being, & every Assistant present at such Courts shall forfeite 20s a man, & Everie Deputie 10s a man for each neglect, wch shall be paid out of yr proper estate, & not by ye Country or ye townes wch choose them. & when so ever yr shall arise any question in any Court amonge ye Assistants & Associates yr of about ye explanation of these rites & liberties. the Genrll Court onely shall haue power to interpret them.

96 | Howsoever these above specified rites, freedomes, Immunities, Authorities and priveledges, both Civill and Ecclesiastical are expressed onely under the name and title of Liberties, and not in the exact form of Laws or Statutes, yet we do with one consent fullie Authorise, and earnestly intreate all that are and shall be in Authoritie to consider them as laws, and not to faile to inflict condigne and proportionable punishments upon every man impartiallie, that shall infringe or violate any of them.

97 | Wee likewise give full power and libertie to any person that shall at any time be denyed or deprived of any of them, to commence and prosecute their suite, Complaint or actions against any man that shall so doe in any Court that hath proper Cognizance or judicature thereof.

98 | Lastly because our dutie and desire is to do nothing suddainlie which fundamentally concerne us, we decree that these rites and liberties, shall be Audably read and deliberately weighed at every Generall Court that shall be held, within three yeares next insueing, And such of them as shall not be altered or repealed they shall stand so ratified, That no man shall infringe them without due punishment.

And if any Generall Court within these next thre yeares shall faile or forget to reade and consider them as abovesaid. The Governor and Deputy Governor for the time being, and every Assistant present at such Courts shall forfeite 20sh. a man, and everie Deputie 10sh. a man for each neglect, which shall be paid out of their proper estate, and not by the Country or the Townes which choose them, and whensoever there shall arise any question in any Court amonge the Assistants and Associates thereof about the explanation of these Rites and liberties, The Generall Court onely shall have power to interprett them.

INDEX TO BODY OF LIBERTIES.

REFERENCES ARE TO THE NUMBER OF THE LIBERTY.

Abatements, 25.
Actions, malicious, punished, 37.
— — to be enrolled, 64.
Adjournments, 69.
Admiral, annual election of, 67.
Adultery punished by death, 94.
Age of discretion, 53.
Alienation of lands and estates allowed, 11.
—, see *Conveyances.*
Animals, cruelty to, forbidden, 92.
Answers may be in writing, 27.
Appeals, security for, to be given in six days, 36.
Assembly, presiding officer to be suspended and punished for refusing to put a vote, 54.
—— casting vote in, 71.
—— protest allowed in, 75.
Assistants, punished for misbehavior in court, 19.
—— may issue attachments, 21.
—— court of appeals, 36.
—— appeal from, to General Court, 36.
—— associates to, how chosen, 51.
Attendance, non-, before any court or officer, not punishable if unavoidable, 4.

Bail allowed, 18.
Banishment, power of, reserved to General Court, 1.
Barrator, common, punishment of, 34.
Bench, see *Judges.*
Bestiality punished by death, 94.
Blasphemy punished by death, 94.

Capital cases, reserved for General Court, 1.
—— punishment, allowed only on full evidence, 47.
—— ——, see *Executions.*
Cause, to be stated in summons, 21.
—— criminal, to be tried at next court, 41.
Children, not to convey estates, 14.
—— entitled to proper marriages, 83.
—, see *Wife.*
Churches, to be sustained by the civil power, 58.
—— members amenable to civil power, 59.
—— censure not to affect civil authority, 60.
—— privileges and rights defined, 95; especially to gather churches; to govern by Gospel rules; to elect and ordain officers; to admit and dismiss members; to be free from injunction; to appoint fasts and thanksgivings; to hold conferences; to discipline members while in the hands of civil authority; to discipline members who are church-members; to hold private religious meetings, and to hold councils of churches.
Conveyance, valid, 11.
—— invalid in certain cases, 14.
—— covenous and fraudulent, illegal, 15.
—— under duress, illegal, 40.
Court, neglect of, 4.
—— contempt of, 18.
—— errors and abatements, 25.
—— proceedings may be in writing, 27.
—— to give judgment on special verdicts, 31
—— when differing from jury may refer to the General Court, 31.

Court, to keep public records, 38.
—— may respite execution 39.
—— to enter all actions on rolls, 64.
Court, General, power in capital cases, 1.
—— —— power over life, person and property, 1.
—— —— appeal to, 31, 36.
—— —— to ratify certain conveyances, 14.
—— —— adjournment of, 69.
—— —— powers over great ponds, 16.
—— —— to revise and ratify these Liberties annually for three years, 98.
—— —— penalty for neglect of Liberty 98,— last clause.
Crime, no one to be tried twice for the same, 42.

Daughters to take as copartners, 82.
Debt, imprisonment for, 33.
Deputies, how to be chosen, 62, 67.
—— term of office, 67.
Dismembering, power of, reserved to General Court, 1.
Dissection of malefactors, 44.
Distress, perishable goods taken in, 35.
Drovers allowed privileges in travelling, 93.
Duress invalidates all conveyances or promises, 40.

Election, annual, of officers, 67.
Emigration permitted, 17.
Escheats forbidden, 10.
Estates, see *Intestate.*
Execution, criminal condemned not to be executed in less than four days from sentence, 44.
Exemptions from war or public service, 6.

Fishing, free, 16.
Foreigners to have equal protection, 2.
Forfeitures forbidden, 10.
Fowling, free, 16.
Freedom of speech and vote, 70.

General Court, see *Court, General.*
Governor to have a casting vote, 71.
—, see *Officers.*
Great ponds, fishing in, 16.

Heriots forbidden, 10.
Honor and good name protected, 1.
Householders, rights to free fishing and fowling, 16.

Idolatry punished by death, 94.
Idiots not to convey estates, 14.
Informations not to be laid, 61.
Inhabitants all to have equal justice, 2.
Inheritances free from fines, etc., 10.
Inquests provided, 57.
Interest, legal rate to be eight per cent., 23.
Intestate estates, how divided, 81, 82.

Jeofails, statute of, 25.
Judges, punished for misbehavior in court, 20.
—— may try actions without jury, 29.
—— may approve challenges of jurors, 30.
Judgments, errors in, 25.
—, may be respited, 39.
—, see *Suits.*
Jurors, right to challenge, 30.

(63)

Jurors, may allow challenges, 30.
— — may bring in a *non-liquit*, 31.
— — time of service, 49.
— — to be chosen by fellow-townsmen, 50.
— — may consult bystanders in open court, 76.
— — not compelled to vote on verdict, 77.
— — grand, to be paid, 63.

Lands free from fines, etc., 10.
Law of God to be followed in lack of statute, 1.
Laws, capital, 94; inflicting death-penalty for:
   Heresy, § 1.
   Witchcraft, § 2.
   Blasphemy, § 3.
   Murder, §§ 4, 5.
   Poisoning, § 6.
   Bestiality, § 7.
   Sodomy, § 8.
   Adultery, § 9.
   Man-stealing, § 10.
   Perjury against life, § 11.
   Treason, § 12.
Laws to be published, 1.
Liberties, to have the force of laws, 96.
— — breach of, noticed by the courts 97.
— — to be revised and ratified annually for three years, 98.
Life inviolable except by action of law, 1.
Liveries forbidden, 10.

Malefactors, after execution to be buried within twelve hours, unless dissected, 44.
Man-stealing punished by death, 94.
Marriage, parents to settle children in, 83.
Married women not to convey estates, 14.
Meetings, foreigners allowed to act in, 12.
— — moderator to have casting vote at, 71.
Monopolies forbidden, 9.
Murder punished by death, 94.

Non-liquit, see *Verdict, special.*

Oath not compulsory, 3.
Officers, general, defined, 67.
— — — elected by freemen, 67.
— — — tenure of office, 67.
— — to be repaid their expenses, 63.
Orphans to be bound out only by order of court, 84.

Patents allowed, 9.
Perjury, touching life, punished with death, 94.
Person, not to be arrested or punished except by law, 1.
— — to be free from arrest for debt or fine, if estate can be found, 33.
Pleas may be in writing, 27.
Poisoning, punished with death, 94.
Ponds, see *Great Ponds.*
Prescription not to be maintained against Gospel 65.
Presiding officer, see *Assembly.*
Press, see *Work, public.*
Primer-seisins forbidden, 10.
Property, to be taken only by law, 1.
— — not to be taken for public use without compensation, 8.
Protest allowed, 75.
Prudential affairs to be settled by towns, 66.
— — officers elected, 74.
Public expenses, see *Officers.*
— — service in foreign parts not compulsory, 73.
Punishment, of married women, 80.
— — barbarous, forbidden, 46.
— — capital, see *Laws.*
— — bodily, see *Stripes.*

Records, open to public examination, 48.
— — certified copies obtainable, 48.
— — of protests to be made, 75.
— — of courts to be kept, 38.
Removal of officers for cause, 67.
Replevin allowed, 32.
Reprieves, how granted, 72.
Rivers, see *Great Ponds.*

Security to be given in cases of replevin, 32.
Servants, to be protected, 81.
— — transfers of, regulated, 86.
— — injury to, 87.
— — to be rewarded at end of term, 88.
Slavery prohibited, 91.
Sodomy punished with death, 94.
Son, elder, to have a double portion of intestate estates, 81.
Strangers, Christian, to be received and aided, 89.
— — ship-wrecked, to be protected, 91.
— —, see *Foreigners.*
Stripes, not above forty to be given, and gentlemen to be exempt, 43.
Suits, vexatious, to be punished, 22.
— — not to be abated, arrested, or reversed for technical errors, 25.
— — may be withdrawn and renewed in another court, 28.
— — of children, idiots, strangers, etc., to be specially protected, 52.
— — parties given fullest liberty to claim and to answer, 55.
Summons to be served at least six days before trial, 21.

Taxes not to be assessed on estate outside of the colony, 15.
Testimony, to be recorded, 38.
— — *in perpetuam rei memoriam,* 38.
Torture greatly restricted, 45.
Town-meeting, disturbance at, to be punished, 56.
Towns, to choose deputies, 62.
— — to regulate their prudentials, 66.
Treason punished by death, 94.
Treasure, public, how to be disbursed, 78.
Trespass, no damages for, if party injured caused it, 24.
Trials may be by the bench alone or with a jury, 29.

Usury forbidden, 23.
— —, see *Interest.*

Verdict, suits may be withdrawn before, 28.
— — special, may be given, 31.
Vote, casting, 71.
— — must be put, 54.
Voting, freedom of, 70.
— — not compulsory, 77.

War beyond the colony, service not compulsory, 7.
Wardships forbidden, 10.
Waste, year and day, forbidden, 10.
Water-mark, high and low, limits of free fishing and fowling, 16.
Widow to receive dower, 79.
Wife and children not to be taken away, 1.
Wills allowed, 11.
Witchcraft punished by death, 94.
Women, married, free from bodily punishment by husbands, 80.
Work, public, no man to be impressed for, without due compensation, 5.
Wreck, in case of, goods to be protected, 90.
Written pleas and answers allowed, 27.

APPENDIX.

CONTAINING FAC-SIMILES OF THOSE PAGES OF THE ANSWER OF THE GENERAL COURT IN 1646, WHICH CONTAIN REFERENCES TO THE BODY OF LIBERTIES. (See *ante*, p. 16.)

(From the Elisha Hutchinson MS. in the Boston Athenæum.)

Ffoundamentall Lawes of ye Massachusetts Collonie in New England
Boston · 1(9). 1675

Ffoundamentalls of ye Massachusetts

1. All psons orthodoxe in Judgement & not scandalous in life, may gather into a Church estate, according to ye gospell of Jesus Christ. Lib. 1.
Such may choose & ordaine ye owne officers, & exercise all ye ordinances of Christ without iniunction in Doctrine, worship, or Discipline. Lib. 3. & 5. in Eccles.

2. No mans life, honour, liberty, wife, children, goods or estate, shall be taken away, punished or endamaged, under coulour of service countenance of Authoritie, but by an expresse law of ye Genrl Court, or in defect of such law, by ye word of god &c. Lib. 1.
Every pson within this Iurisdiction &c shall enjoy ye same Iustice and law &c without partiality or delay &c. Lib. 2.
All o lands & hereditaments shall be free from all fines, forfeitures &c. Lib. 10.
Every man may remove himselfe & his familie &c if ye be no legall impediment. Lib. 17.

3. The free men of everie towne may dispose of ye towne lands & may make such orders as may be for ye will ordering of ye townes &c, & may choose ye Constables & other officers. 1. (month) 1635.

4. One measure is appointed through ye Countrie according to the Kings cō standard. (3) 1631. & 1638.

5. Courts of Iudicature shall be kept at Boston for Suffolk, at Cambrige for Midlsex, at Salem & Ipswich for Esex &c upon certaine dayes yearly. (1m) 1635.

6. Difficult cases are finally determinable in ye Court of Assistants, or in ye Genrall Court, by appeale or petition, or by reference from ye Inferiour Courts. Lib. 31. & 36.

7. Upon uniust suites ye plot shall be found qportionable to his offence. Lib. 37.
No mans goods shall be taken away but by due course of Iustice. Lib. 1.
In Criminall causes it shall be at ye libertie of ye accused partie to be tryed by ye Bench or by a Iurie. Lib. 29.
We do not fine or sentence any man but upon sufficient testimony upon oath, or confession. Customie.

8. Wager of law is not allowed but according to this law, & according to, Exod. 22. 8.

9. Letters testimoniall are granted to merchants, when there is occasion. Customie.

ffundamentalls of

Fundamentalls of the Massachusetts

1. The highest Authoritie heere is in our Generall Court, both by o' Charter & o' owne positive Lawes. (3) 1639 &c.

2. In o' Gen'll Court y' people are present by theire Deputies, so as nothing can passe without theire allowance. z Charter. &(1) 1635

3. Our Deputies are chosen for all y' people, but not by all y' people, but onely by y' Company of freemen, according to o' Charter.

4. The Gov'r & Assistants being y' Aristocraticall, & y' Deputies y' Democraticall part, yet make but one Court though they sitt & act apart, & either of them hath a like Negative power. z Charter. &(1) 1635

5. The Acts of this Gen'll Court do binde all w'ch in this Jurisdiction, as well non freemen, who have no vote in Election of y' members of y' Court, as y' freemen who choose them. z Chartam

6. This Government in y' subordinate exercise thereof is either in Courts of Judicature, or out of Court, z Chartam. & many positive Lawes.

7. In o' Courts of Judicature all Causes Civill & Criminall are determinable, either by y' Judges & Juryes or by y' Judges alone & as in England. This is both Custome & by divers speciall Lawes established, according to o' Charter. as Lib. 29. &c.

8. In y' vacancy of y' Gen'll Court y' Gov'r & Assistants are y' standing counsell to take order in all such affaires. z Chartam. &(8) 1639

9. The Gov'r & Assistants out of Court have power to performe y' p'tm'rs &c. z Chartam, & Customs, y divers speciall lawes.

10. Our ministeriall officers are Martialls, Constables, Clarkes &c.

11. Our ordinary processe are Sumons, Attachments, Distresses &c. z Chartam.

12. In all Criminall offences, where y' law hath p'vided no certaine p'alty, y' Judges have power to inflict penalties according to y' rule of gods word. — Lib. 1. & by y' Charter &c

13. Treason, murther, witchcraft, Sodomie, & other such notorious Crimes are punished w'th death. but Theft &c is not so punished because we reade otherwise in y' Scripture. Capitalls &c.

14. Adultery is punished according to y' Canon of y' Spirituall Lawes. viz. y' Script. &c. Capitalls.

15. All publick charges are defrayed out of y' publick stock. Custome &c Lib. 63.

16. When we have no publick stock, we supply o' necessary publick charges, by Assessment, raised by y' Generall Court.

17. The Gen'll Court intends an Equall Assessment upon every Towne & p'son, & indeavors it, by y' best meanes they can invent, (yet in some cases y' falls out inequality) this is levied by distresse of such as are able, & yet refuse to pay. Customes & orders of Court.

18

ffundamentalls of the Massachusetts

18. The Genrll Court is not bound to give Account of ye expence of these Assessments, yet they doe sometimes, for all mens satisfaction.

19. No mans person shall be restrained or imprisoned &c (before ye law hath sentenced him there to) if he can put in sufficient baile &c. Except in Crimes Capitall. Lib. 18.

20. The full age for passing lands, giueing voates &c is 21 yeares. Lib. 53.

21. Married women can not dispose of any Estate &c nor can sue or be sued wthout their husband. Lib. 14. & Custome.

22. In Ciuill Actions a man may appeare & answere by his Attorney. Custome.

  1. The Eldest sonne is preferred before ye yonger in his Ancestors inheritance. Lib. 81.
  2. Daughters shall inherit as Copartners. Lib. 82.
  3. No Custome or prescription shall ever preuaile &c to maintaine any thing morrally sinfull. Lib. 65.
  4. Ciuill Authoritie may deale wth any Church member, or officer, in away of Ciuill Justice. Lib. 59.
  5. Publick Records are open to all Inhabitants. Lib. 48.
  6. No man shall be twise sentenced by Ciuill Justice for ye same offence. Lib. 42.
  7. No man shall be urged to take any oath, or subscribe any Articles, Covenant, or Remonstrance, of a publick & Ciuill nature, but such as ye Genrll Court hath Considered allowed & required. Lib. 3.

By this it may appeare yt or politie & foundamentalls are framed according to ye lawes of England & according to or Charter. &c

PART SECOND:

BEING

THE ACCOUNT OF THE LEGISLATION FROM 1641 TO 1672,
INCLUDING THE TWO REVISIONS OF THE
LAWS IN 1649 AND 1660.

BIBLIOGRAPHY OF THE LAWS.

WE resume the history of the publication of the Laws, at the point mentioned on page 9, *ante*, viz.: immediately after the enactment of the Body of Liberties in October, 1641.

The General Court ordered June 14, 1642 (Records, ii. 21) : —

"That the Governor [Winthrop], Mr. Bellingham and the Secretary, [Nowell] with the deputies of Boston, shall examine and survey the orders of this last Court, and perfect the same for the publishing."

Also, (Records, ii. 22) "that such laws as make any offence to be capital shall forthwith be imprinted and published, of which laws the Secretary is to send a copy to the printer, when it hath been examined by Governor or Mr. Bellingham with himself, and the Treasurer to pay for the printing of them."

September 27, 1642 (Records, ii. 28) "it is ordered, that every Court should have a copy of the laws at the public charge."

May 10, 1643 (Records, ii. 39), "the former committee of magistrates and deputies are authorized and appointed to examine and perfect the Laws."

March 7, 1643–4 (Records, ii. 58), the famous order was passed providing that the two houses should sit separately, each branch passing upon the orders forwarded from the other. This order will be found in full, *post*, p. 134.

March 7, 1643–4 (Records, ii. 61), the following vote was passed : —

"It is ordered that the Governor, [Winthrop] Mr. Dudley and Mr. Hibbens, these or any two of them, shall be a committee to consider of the Body of Liberties, against the next General Court, what is fit to be repealed or allowed, and present the same to the next Court."

"Also the Magistrates residing at Ipswich, or any two of them, are appointed a Committee for the same purpose, that so the Court conferring both together may more easily determine what to settle about the same."

"It is ordered that Richard Bellingham Esq. should finish that which was formerly committed to him about the perusing of the Book of laws, &c. and to present the same to the next Court."

May 27, 1644, the Legislature adjourned to October 30th, but the Journal of the House of Deputies contains the report of the acts of that branch during June. It appears (Records, iii. 6) that on June 7, 1644: —

"It is ordered that Lieut. Sprague, Francis Chickering, Stephen Kingsley, Thomas Mekins, William Hilton, Joseph Batchelor, Mr. Steevens, William Ward, Lieut. Howard, William Eastowe, Thomas Brooke, Lieut. Johnson and Joseph Meadcalfe, are chosen a committee to examine the book delivered in by Mr. Bellingham, and compare it with the book of records, and return their objections and thoughts thereof to this house in writing."

[William Ward was a deputy from Sudbury in 1644, but not later.]

May 29, 1644 (Records, ii. 69), it was ordered: —

"That for the better building of shipping within this jurisdiction, and for the avoiding of many inconveniences which now both owners and builders are subject unto, there be a company of that trade, according to the manner of other places, with power to regulate building of ships, and to make such orders and laws among themselves as may conduce to the public good, if any shall appear the next Court and present laws for consideration."

May 29, 1644 (Records, ii. 76-78). The Court established the commission of the Sergeant-major-general, Thomas Dudley. By it provision was made that

"Yourself, together with the Council of War, shall have power to make such wholesome laws, agreeable to the word of God, as you shall conceive to be necessary for the well-ordering of your army, until the General Court shall provide for the same: which being sufficiently published, you, with the said Council, have power to put in execution, be it to the taking away of life or otherwise."

November 13, 1644 (Records, ii. 89), "it is ordered that all the several orders of general concernment agreed on this whole Court, shall be forthwith published to the several towns within this jurisdiction, and that the several towns shall procure a copy of them within three months, under the Secretary his hand."

At the same Court (Records, ii. 91), there were presented the Answers of the Elders to certain Questions submitted to them. One question was, whether the magistrates were, in cases where no express law was provided, to be guided by the word of God. The answer was: —

"We do not find that by the patent they are expressly directed to proceed according to the word of God; but we understand that by *a law or liberty of the country*, they may act in cases wherein as yet there is no express law, so that in such acts they proceed according to the word of God."

Introduction. 73

Here the reference is plainly to Liberty No. 1, and this Liberty is republished, unaltered, in 1660, as the first section of the General Laws.

[22] July 1, 1645 (Records, iii. 26), the Journal of Deputies has the following entry: —

"It is ordered that several persons out of each county shall be chosen to draw up a body of laws and present them to the consideration of the General Court at their next sitting.

"For the county of Suffolk, our honored Governor, [Dudley] Mr. Hibbens, Mr. Cotton, Mr. Mather, Lieut. Duncan and Mr. Prichard are chosen a committee to meet, confer together, and draw up a body of laws and to present them to the next session of this Court.

"For the county of Middlesex, Herbert Pelham, Esq., Mr. Nowell, Mr. Thomas Shepard, Mr. Allen, Capt. Cooke, and Lieut. Johnson," were similarly appointed.

"For Essex, Richard Bellingham, Esq., Mr. Bradstreet, Mr. Nathl. Rogers, Mr. Norton, Mr. Ward, and Mr. Hathorne" were similarly appointed. [This Mr. Ward could not be William, as Sudbury was in Middlesex.]

In each case two magistrates, two ministers, and two deputies seem to have been appointed, except that in Essex, Mr. Nathaniel Ward seems to take the place of one deputy.

[23] October 1, 1645 (Records, ii. 128), it was voted

"Whereas this Court, in a former session, chose and appointed several honored members of this commonwealth as commissioners in their several shires, to meet together in some convenient place within each shire, to consult together, and to return to this Court a result of their thoughts, that this Court may proceed thereupon to satisfy the expectation of the country in establishing a body of laws ; this Court thinks it meet to desire the persons in the order mentioned, at or before the 12th of November next, in their several shires to meet together ; in Boston for Suffolk, in Cambridge for Middlesex, in Ipswich for Essex : and after their first meeting at the time and places above mentioned, by warrant from the Secretary to each committee of each shire, and then as often as they please, to appoint their own meetings for the accomplishment of the end so desired ; and to make their return of what they shall do herein, to the next sitting of the General Court.

"In Captain Cooke's room, at his request, Mr. Joseph Hill of Charlestown ; in Mr. Allen's room, Mr. Knowles ; and Mr. Glover in Mr. Prichard's room. They being out of the way, or shall be suddenly, — Mr. Symonds is

---

[22] The corresponding entry in the Journal of the two houses is in Records, ii. 109, under date of May 14, 1645, and it varies only by saying that these three committees are to report to the next General Court. — W. H. W.

[23] The corresponding entry in the Journal of the Deputies is dated October 7, 1645 (Records, iii. 46–47). — W. H. W.

instead of Mr. Bellingham for Ipswich, because Mr. Bellingham now resides at Boston; and Mr. Bellingham to be for Boston, added to the former.

"And the calling of each assembly to each place is in Mr. Bellingham for Boston, Mr. Pelham for Cambridge, and Mr. Symonds for Ipswich."

The next step seems to have been the appointment of a small sub-committee to digest and arrange the work of the three general committees.

May 22, 1646 (Records, ii. 157), the following vote was passed:[24] —

"This Court thankfully accepts of the labors returned by the several committees of the several shires, and being very unwilling such precious labors should fall to the ground without [that] good success as is generally hoped for, have thought it meet to desire Richard Bellingham, Esq., Mr. [Samuel] Symonds, Lieut. [Nathaniel] Duncan, Lieut. [Edward] Johnson, and Mr. [Nathaniel] Ward, to cause each committee's return about a body of laws to be transcribed, so as each committee may have the sight of the other's labors. And that the persons mentioned in this order be pleased to meet together, at or before the 10th of August, at Salem or Ipswich; and on their perusing and examining the whole labors of all the committees, — with the abbreviation of the laws in force which Mr. Bellingham took great store of pains and to good purpose in and upon the whole, — and make return to the next session of this Court; at which time the Court intends, by the favor and blessing of God, to proceed to the establishing of so many of them as shall be thought most fit for a body of laws amongst us."

It will be remembered that this year was an anxious period for the colonists. Doctor Child and others had raised questions about the powers of the Legislature, and the answer of the General Court had been prepared for transmission to England. Although Winthrop says nothing about this matter of the publication of the laws, his journal shows that the community was excited and uneasy on the point. The above-named committee of six evidently did not work with sufficient promptness, and a change was desired.

Accordingly, [25] November 4, 1646 (Records, ii. 168), the following order was passed: —

---

[24] The Journal of the Deputies of May 20, 1646 (Records, iii. 74, 75), has the corresponding entry. It makes the revising committee to consist of Bellingham and Duncan, Nowell and Johnson, Symonds and Ward, thus adding Secretary Nowell to it. — W. H. W.

[25] The Journal of Deputies of the same date (Records, iii. 84, 85) has this same order, somewhat abbreviated. — W. H. W.

"The Court being deeply sensible to the earnest expectation of the Country in general for this Court's completing of a body of Laws for the better and more orderly wielding all the affairs of this Commonwealth; willing also to their utmost to answer their honest and hearty desires therein, unexpectedly prevented by multitude of other pressing occasions, think fit and necessary that this Court make choice of two or three of our honored Magistrates, with as many of the Deputies, to peruse and examine, compare, transcribe, and compose in good order, all the liberties, laws and orders extant with us; and further to peruse and perfect all such others as are drawn up, and to present such of them as they find necessary for us, as also to suggest what they deem needful to be added, as also to consider and contrive some good method and order, with titles and tables for compiling the whole; so as we may have ready recourse to any of them, upon all occasions, whereby we may manifest our utter disaffection to arbitrary Government and so all relations be safely and sweetly directed and protected in all their just rights and privileges; desiring thereby to make way for printing our Laws for more public and profitable use of us and our successors. Our honored Governor, [Winthrop] Mr. Bellingham, Mr. Hibbens, Mr. Hill and Mr. Duncan as a Committee for the business above mentioned, or any three of them meeting, the others having notice thereof, shall be sufficient to carry on the work."

It will be noticed that only Bellingham and Duncan were retained of the former committee of six. Their powers probably expired with the term of the Legislature. At all events the next General Court revived and continued their powers by the following order, dated May 26, 1647 (Records, ii. 196): —

"The Court understanding that the Committee for perfecting the laws appointed by the last General Court, through streights of time and other things intervening have not attained what they expected, and on all hands so much desired, touching a body of laws, think meet and necessary that our honored Governor, [Winthrop] Mr. Bellingham, Mr. Hibbens, the Auditor General [Duncan], Lieut. Johnson,[26] and Mr. Hills be chosen as a Committee of this Court to do the same, according to the aforesaid order, against the next sessions in the 8th month or the next General Court."

---

[26] In copying this entry Mr. F. C. Gray omitted the name of Johnson, doubtless not recognizing therein the author of "Wonder-Working Providence." In the admirable reprint of that book, issued at Andover in 1867, under the care of William F. Poole, the editor has attempted to show that Edward Johnson was one of the most active and important members of the committee. The main argument is, that Johnson was on the committee appointed May 22, 1646, and on that of May 26, 1647, but was omitted on that of November 4, 1646; that the first and last committees were active and the second inactive: that hence this activity was owing to the presence of Johnson. But I fail to see that the first committee did anything, and Bellingham was undoubtedly the controlling spirit throughout. We shall see later that Joseph Hills of Malden was employed about the printed laws, and did all the clerical part of the revision. — W. H. W.

November 11, 1647 (Records, ii. 209), the following vote was passed: —

"The laws being to be put in print, it is meet that they should be conveniently penned: therefore it is desired that the committee for drawing up the laws will be careful therein; and to that purpose they have liberty to make some change of form, to put in apt words as occasion shall require, provided the sense and meaning in any law or part thereof be not changed."[27]

November 11, 1647 (Records, ii. 212), the following vote was passed: —

"It is agreed by the Court, to the end that we may have better light for making and proceeding about laws, that there shall be these books following procured for the use of the Court from time to time: —

> Two of Sir Edward Cooke upon Littleton;
> two of the Book of Entries;
> two of Sir Edward Cooke upon Magna Charta;
> two of The New Terms of the Law;
> two Dalton's Justice of the Peace;
> two of Sir Edward Cook's Reports."

The next entry, at the same session of November, 1647 (Records, ii. 217-8), is as follows: —

"The laws now being in a manner agreed upon, and the Court drawing to an end, it is time to take order: 1. How all alteration of former laws may be without mistaking compared and fair written: 2d. That all old laws not altered be also written in the same copy: 3dly. That there be a Committee chosen for this business, to be made ready against the first day of the first month next, so as the Court of Assistants, if they see cause may advise for a General Court to prepare them for the press: 4thly. That there be large margins left at both sides of the leaf, and the heads of each law written on the two outsides thereof, and upon the other margent any references and scriptures or the like, and that these be written copywise. The Governor [Winthrop], Mr. Bellingham, Mr. Hill, Mr. Auditor [Duncan] and Mr. Ting are joined in this Committee to act according as in this paper is expressed."

Here, again, the committee seems to be reconstructed, Johnson being dropped and Tyng substituted for Hibbens. The other four,

---

[27] This very important vote must be remembered in comparing the Laws of 1660 with the original records. This Revision of 1649, being approved by the General Court, took the place of former laws, and was undoubtedly taken over without change into the text of the Revision of 1660. It may even be that some law, or part of a law, was enacted for the first time in this Revision, if found to be necessary and acceptable. — W. H. W.

Winthrop, Bellingham, Duncan and Hills seem to have continued the work. The following order of the Court in March, 1647-8 (Records, ii. 227), shows that they had assistance in the clerical portion, and that two standard copies were prepared: —

> "The Court doth conceive it meete that John Wayte of Charlestown Village, shall be allowed, out of the next country rate, for his writing, one book of the laws and for finding paper for both books, £4 ,, 18 shillings."
> Also (Records, ii. 230), "The Court doth desire that Mr. Rawson and Mr. Hill compare the amendments of the books of laws passed, and make them as one; and one of them to remain in the hands of the Committee for the speedy committing of them to the press, and the other to remain in the hands of the Secretary, sealed up, till the next Court."

Two months later, under date of May 10, 1648 (Records, ii. 239):[28] —

> "It is ordered, the copy of the Laws in the two rolls, — which were (by order of the Court) sealed up, with intent that if hereafter any questions should arise about the copy now at the press, it might be examined by this, whereby the faithfulness of the committee might be tried; — and that the other copy (now remaining with Mr. Hill), — should forthwith be sent for, for the use of the Court."[29]

Later, at the same session, May 10, 1648 (Records, ii. 246), it was voted as follows: —

> "Mr. Auditor [Duncan] and Mr. Hill to examine the laws now at press, and to see if any material law be not put in or mentioned in the table as being of force, and to make supply of them."

In the Journal of the Deputies for [30] May 13, 1648 (Records, ii. 263), is the following item: —

> "Ordered, that in the book of Laws, title Appeals, in the last line save one, (*just*) to be entered next before *charges;* and the Auditor General to see it entered in every book."

---

[28] Compare Journal of the Deputies of May 13, 1648 (Records, iii. 125). — W. H. W.

[29] Mr. F. C. Gray notes that something seems to be omitted in this sentence. I think, however, by inserting two dashes as above, the sense is plain and the sentence grammatical. I apprehend that the phrase " and that the other copy " is in accordance with the custom of the times and " that " is a pronoun. Or it may be that the word " that " is merely superfluous. It seems evident that both copies were to be sent for to be used by the Court. — W. H. W.

[30] This same entry is in the Journal of the Deputies (Records, iii. 130). On the same page is a mention of certain propositions to be made to the United Colonies, and the entry is, " Proposition 3, page 24. This consisting of many branches and the Court not having time to consider their own laws and practice in the case have deferred it to a committee to examine and to certify the next Court." See the same entries in Records, ii. 263-4. — W. H. W.

In October, 1648, provision was made for transcribing in an alphabetical or methodical way, all laws, orders and acts of Court, contained in the old books, which were in force but not included in the printed revision.[31]

---

[31] October 18, 1648 (Records, ii. 259, and iii. 141), the following important order was passed: —

" For the better carrying on the occasions of the General Court, and to the end that the records of the same, together with what shall be presented by way of petition &c, or passes by way of vote, either amongst the magistrates or deputies, may hereafter be more exactly recorded and kept for public use: —

It is hereby ordered, that as there is a Secretary amongst the Magistrates (who is the general officer of the Commonwealth, for the keeping of the public records of the same) so there shall be a Clerk amongst the Deputies to be chosen by them from time to time;

That, (by the Court of Elections and then the officers to begin their entries and their recompense accordingly) there be provided by the Auditor, four large paper books in folio, bound up with vellum and pasteboard, two whereof to be delivered to the Secretary and two to the Clerk of the House of Deputies, one to be a journal to each of them, the other for the fair entry of all laws, acts and orders &c, which shall pass the magistrates and deputies; that of the Secretary to be the public record of the country, that of the Clerk's to be a book only of copies.

That the Secretary and Clerk for the Deputies shall briefly enter into their journals, respectively, the title of all bills, orders, laws, petitions &c, which shall be presented and read amongst them, what are referred to committees, and what are voted negatively or affirmatively, and so for any addition or alteration.

That all bills, laws, petitions, &c., which shall be last concluded amongst the Magistrates, shall remain with the Governor till the latter end of that session; and such as are last assented to by the Deputies shall remain with the Speaker till the said time; when the whole Court shall meet together, or a committee of Magistrates and Deputies, to consider what has passed that session, where the Secretary and Clerk shall be present, and by their journals call for such bills &c, as hath passed either house:

and such as shall appear to have passed the magistrates and Deputies shall be delivered to the Secretary to record, who shall record the same within one month after every sessions; which being done, the Clerk of the Deputies shall have liberty, for one month after, to transcribe the same into his book.

And such bills, orders &c., that hath only passed the Magistrates, shall be delivered to the Secretary to keep upon file; and such as have only passed the Deputies shall be delivered to their Clerk to be kept upon file in like manner, or otherwise disposed of as the whole Court shall appoint.

That all laws, orders and acts of Court, contained in the old books, that are of force and not ordered to be printed, be transcribed in some alphabetical or methodical way, by direction of some committee that this Court shall please to appoint, and delivered to the Secretary to record in the first place in the said book of records, and then the acts of the other sessions in order accordingly, and a copy of all to be transcribed by the Clerk of the Deputies as aforesaid.

That the Secretary be allowed for his pains twenty marks per annum, and the Clerk of the Deputies ten pounds per annum, to be paid out of the treasury, till the Court shall appoint their recompense by fees or otherwise."

Under date of Oct. 18, 1650 (Records, iv. part 1, p. 33), there is an entry showing that William Torrey had not then written up the Deputies' book. See also the references (Records, iv. part 1, p. 324) May 19, 1658, to various books of records, when the laws about Constables were collected and codified.

I am sorry to add that none of these various records and compilations of laws are now extant at our State House. The continuous record to 1686 exists and one volume (1644–1657) of the Journal of the Deputies. These are well known, having been printed by the State. Many of the original orders, papers, and minutes are in the files; but the ill-timed zeal of a former Secretary caused the dispersion of these papers into a new classified arrangement, and the continuity of the record is lost. I am informed that, in some cases, books of orders were cut apart and the items scattered into the various new receptacles. Possibly some of these books ordered in 1648 lasted intact for two centuries, to be improved out of existence in our days. — W. H. W.

[32] October 27, 1648 (Records, ii. 262): —

"It is ordered by the full Court, that the books of laws, now at the press, may be sold in quires, at three shillings the book; provided that every member of this Court shall have one without price, and the Auditor-general and Mr. Joseph Hill; for which there shall be fifty in all taken up, to be disposed of by the appointment of this Court."

May 2, 1649 (Records, ii. 273, and iii. 162), the following vote was passed: —

"Mr. Joseph Hill is granted, as a gratuity, ten pounds, to be paid him out of the treasury, for his pains about the printed laws."

Finally we have the distinct evidence of Joseph Hills, as set forth below, that the Book of Laws was prepared by him, and put through the press under his supervision. Hills was a member of the House for Charlestown in 1647, and Speaker in that year. He represented Malden 1650-1656; removed to Newbury soon after, and represented that town in 1667; he died in 1688, aged 86 years. His petition will be found in Mass. Archives, vol. 47, p. 19. It is as follows: —

"In as much as it hath pleased the General Court to engage me in sundry great and weighty services in refference to all the generall laws here established, now in print ffor publique good: In consideration whereof as I conceive, a Gratuity of Ten pounds was Appointed me by the Treasurer, which as it holds forth the good acceptance of the Honored Court, I thankfully acknowledge, as duty binds me.

"Yet apprehending that my Great care, paynes and studies in these difficult Imployments was not truly Informed or understood, I desire briefly to tender you an account thereof as follows.

1. "First it pleased the General Court to employ me in a shire Committee to draw up a Body of Laws in which I took unwearied pains, perusing all the Stat. Laws of England in [Pulton?] at Large, out of which I took all such as I conceived sutable to the condition of this Commonwealth; which with such others as, in my observation, experiences and serious studies I thought needful, all which I drew up in a Book, close written, Consisting of 24 pages of paper, in folio, which upon the Committee's perusal, — viz. Mr. Noel, Mr. Pelham, Mr. Thomas Sheppard and myself, — I was Appointed to draw upp for the use of the Generall Court, which Book was by some means

---

[32] The last clause of this order is printed in the form given in Records, iii. 144, it being rather more explicit. — W. H. W.

lost and could not be found. For further Improvement by another Committee of the Generall Court, viz. Mr. Bellingham, Mr. Nat. Ward, &c., whereupon Mr. Bellingham spake to me to help them to another coppie of the aforesaid Book, which in tender Respect to publique good, to the Honored Court and Committee, I did forthwith again Transcribe out of my First coppie, although it was in harvest time.

2. "After that, it pleased the Generall Court again to Ingage me in the perusing all the laws in the Books of Records, to Consider, Compare, Compose, and Transcribe all laws of publique Concernment, coppie-wise; all which I did draw upp together, and Drew upp in five Books or Rowls, which done were Examined by the Committee and presented to the Gen^{ll}. Court.

3. "Thereuppon I was Ordered by the Court to Transcribe the five Books afforesaid with some other new laws, all which (save onely a few the Auditor did), I, with Great care and vigilancie, performed, and frequented the press, and otherwise took care to Examine them during the Imprinting the same.

4. "Since which it pleased the Gen^{ll} Court to Appoint me with some others to Compose and Transcribe the Second Booke of Laws, coppie-wise, which I allso did; which affter Examination by the Committee was allso presented to the Gen^{ll} Court, which were pleased further to Imploy another Committee, whereof I was one, to fitt them for the press.

"In all which services in reference to publique good, I putt forth my selfe to the uttermost to the Great neglect of my personall and particular occasions, devoting my selfe thereunto for the most part of two years tyme (as neer as I can remember) the benefit whereof doth I hope verie manifestly Redound both to Court and Country, who doubtless uppon a right understanding will not be unwilling to afford such Due encouragement and Recompense as services of such Importance and Advantage to the Countrie doth Require.

"Your Humble Servant,

"JOS. HILLS."

"The Magistrates Referr the consideration of the Petition to theire brethren the Deputies 27 May, 1653.

"EDWARD RAWSON, Secre^t."

"The Deputies think meete to allow Mr. Hills ten pounds out of the next County rate in reference to what is herein exprest, if the honored Magistrates please to Consent thereto.

"WILLIAM TORREY, Cleric."

"Consented to by the Magistrates hereto.

"EDWARD RAWSON, Secre^t."

THE CODE OF 1649.

HAVING already traced the history of the legislation which culminated in the issue of the printed collection of general laws, in 1649, it seems proper to state what has been recovered concerning that volume. Although no copy, or even fragment of one, has been preserved, it is yet possible to form a very good idea of the main features of the book.

First, as to its date. In my Introduction to the reprint of the Laws of 1660, I cited this Code as that of 1649. The only certain dates that we have, show that May 10, 1648 (Rec. ii, 246) the book of laws was "at press"; and October 27, 1648 (Rec. ii, 262) the books were still "at the press." The General Court dissolved at this last date, and met again May 2, 1649. We have thus no official statement as to the month in which the completed volume was issued. In my former Introduction, I assumed the date of 1649, mainly on my understanding of the wording of the title-page of the edition of 1660. This reads as follows: "The Book of the General Laws and Libertyes concerning the inhabitants of the Masachusets, collected out of the Records of the General Court, for the several years wherein they were made and established, and now Revised by the same Court, and disposed into an Alphabetical order, and published by the same Authority in the General Court holden at Boston, in May 1649."

Knowing, as we do, that the Laws of 1660 conformed closely to the pattern of the earlier edition, since that code was also in "alphabetical order" and had a preface, it seemed reasonable to imagine that the title-page of 1660 was substantially the same as that of 1648, and that the phrase "published . . . in May 1649," was copied therefrom.

Dr. George H. Moore, of the Lenox Library, has, however, issued a pamphlet entitled "Memoranda concerning the Massachusetts Laws of 1648," and makes the rather startling suggestion that this date on the title-page of 1660 is a misprint for May, *1659*, and refers to the issue of the Code of 1660.

This seemed plausible; but I find no such "publishment" of that Code by the Court of May, 1659. October 19, 1658, it was ordered that the new code "shall forthwith be printed," and this order is directly referred to on page 1 of the Laws of 1660. The order then proceeds to direct that "the preface to the old law book, with such alterations as shall be judged meet by the Governor [Endecott] and Major-General [Denison], be added thereunto and presented to the General Court to be approved of." It is true, as Mr. Moore states, that in the Massachusetts Archives, Vol. 47, p. 35, there is preserved the manuscript copy of this revised Preface, endorsed "*Preface to the Lawes, p^r Curiam, 1659.*" and at the bottom the usual official endorsement: —

"The magis^{ts} haue past this with refference to the Consent of theire brethren the depu^{ts} hereto

Edward Rawson, Secret'y

14 May, 1659

The depts. Consent hereunto

Tho. Savage, Speaker."

This action is evidently that contemplated by the above order of October, 1658, and is *not* entered on the Journal of the General Court. The question is, whether this action upon the Preface can be construed as a legislative act, by which the laws were "published by the same Authority in the General Court holden at Boston in May, *1659*." Mr. Moore seems very confident of this, but I cannot assent to it, because it would convict Secretary Rawson and all the other revisers of this edition, of gross carelessness upon the very title-page of their most important official publication. I have met with many errors of the press in both editions of the Laws, but I must decline to add this example to the number. Moreover the issue of 1660, page 1, says expressly "The General Lawes of the Massachusets Colony, revised and *published* by order of the General Court in October 1658." Dr. Moore's theory would make the title-page flatly contradict this, and say "*published* by the same authority in the General Court holden at Boston, in May, *1659*."

At present I can only say that neither in May, 1649, nor in May, 1659, is there any entry on the Journal of any "publication" of either edition. But the first Code was undoubtedly ready in print in May, 1649, while the Code of 1660 was not ready in May, 1659, and in fact was not issued till after May 31, 1660; and the Legislature expressly stated, October 16, 1660, that the "said impression of the laws shall be of force after the expiration of thirty days from the date of these presents."

Dr. Moore also cites Johnson's *Wonder-Working Providence*, (London, 1654), and Josselyn's *Observations* (London, 1674), as authorities, who state that the Laws were printed in 1648. Their words, however, do not meet the point at issue, viz., whether or not the Court of May, 1649, made a formal publication of the code. We all agree that the book was in the press early in 1648, and was in process during that year. As to Gov. Hutchinson, also cited by Dr. Moore, his opinion is worthless; since as I have already shown (*ante*, p. 11), Hutchinson thought that Cotton wrote our Body of Liberties.

I must, therefore, persist in thinking that the title-page of 1660 means what it says, that the formal sanction was given in May, 1649; though as I have shown, the printing was begun and probably nearly finished during 1648; and that the title-page was allowed to stand substantially unaltered. A similar instance of blindly following an older copy is shown in the Revision of 1672. That has a new title, but page 1 begins, just like the code of 1660, with the words "The General Laws . . . revised and published by order of the General Court in October 1658," ignoring the orders of 1670, 1671, and 1672 which authorized this edition.

We will next consider the matter of the probable form and size of this Code. It was, of course, printed at Cambridge, that being the only establishment in the Colony.

This press was given by Josse Glover, aided by some gentleman of Amsterdam. From an interesting essay by A. M. Davis, esq., in the Proceedings of the American Antiquarian Society for April, 1888, I learn some new facts about this press. Glover died on his passage hither, and his widow married Dunster. Glover's heirs sued Dunster, and thus we learn something of the books printed. It seems that Glover had a claim against the press for some twenty pounds for expenses, and Dunster also improved it. The actual work was done first by Steven Day, and then by Samuel Green. Dunster sold the press, or rather his claim, to the College when he removed, which was in April, 1655. He was President from 1640 to his dismissal, for doctrinal errors, Oct. 24, 1654.

In the papers connected with the lawsuit are notes about some of the books he printed, and of these the following concern our subject: —

The Freeman's Oath.
The Capital Laws.

The Law Book, 17 sheets, 600 copies, using 21 reams of paper. Sold at 17 pence a book, £42.. 10.. 00. The printing cost £15.. 16.. 03, and the paper £5.. 05.. 00.

This, of course, was printed by Day late in 1648, and was the edition cited as the Laws of 1649. The items correspond very well with the similar entries about the Psalm Book, viz., 33 sheets, 1,700 copies, sold at 20 pence each, amounting to £141.. 13.. 04. Printing, £33.. 00.. 00, paper, 116 reams, £29.. 00.. 00.

It will be seen that the Laws, 17 sheets and 600 copies, would take 10,200 sheets; and the Psalms, 33 sheets and 1,700 copies, would require 56,100 sheets. The ratio is exactly that of the paper specified, viz., 21 reams and 116 reams. I believe a printer's ream was then $21\frac{1}{4}$ quires, and 21 reams would be 10,836 sheets.

The Psalm Book, from remaining examples, we know was printed eight pages to a sheet, size of page $6\frac{1}{4}$ by $3\frac{3}{8}$ inches. There are 37 sheets, including two of preface. The Laws of 1660 are eight pages to a sheet, each 9 by $5\frac{1}{2}$ inches. It seems impossible that the Laws of 1649 could have been printed on as small pages as the Psalms, and, as we have to take either four or eight pages to the sheet, I infer the Laws were four large pages. In this case the 17 sheets would give 68 pages, which would agree very well with our estimate of 56 pages for the text, and allow some pages for title, preface, and table or index. As before argued, it seems impossible that there were twice as many pages in the book, and yet no citations can be found of a page later than page 58 as the extreme.

There is also an entry for Laws, printed after Green took the press, 5 sheets, cost of paper, £1.. 05.. 00; of printing, £5.. 00.. 00. This may have been some of the special laws, or Supplements.

It seems, indeed, surprising, if we have interpreted these entries correctly, that 600 copies should have been printed of the Laws of 1649, and all have disappeared. But if 1,700 copies of the Psalms were printed, the extreme rarity of extant copies is perhaps equally remarkable, especially as more persons would keep the psalm-book than would care for the Code.

We have already (*ante*, p. 79) shown that fifty copies of the Code were taken for the Legislature, and that the rest were ordered sold at three shillings each. The following petition from Massachusetts Archives, Vol. 58, p. 18, shows that a certain portion was turned to waste-paper or burnt. As Mr. Russell, the Treasurer, estimated his loss at £10, this sum would pay for seventy copies or thereabouts. It is fair to presume that he had a discount in buying a large quantity, and I notice in Mr. Davis's notes already cited, that it is stated that the Law Books "sould at 17^d a booke." As the Court fixed the price at three shillings, this other price may represent Russell's purchase, or may be an average of all. It will be safe to say that at least one-quarter of the edition was destroyed before A. D. 1651.

[Mass. Archives, Vol. 58, p. 18.]

"To ye Honored General Court, consisting of Magistrats & deputies

Humbly Showth Whereas By ye Courts Incoradgment I purchased ye Last printed Law Bookes, and by reason of ye Courts Alteration of some things In those bookes made them unvendible Insomuch that your petitioner Lost above Tenn pownds, a great pt. Turned to wast pap'r and many of them Burnt, your Petitioner desires this Court would Tenderly Consider ye same And accordingly releve your petitioner heerin, soe hee shall thankfully remayne

22. 3. 51.   Your servant Richard Russell."

May 13, 1651 (Records, iv, part 1, p. 50), voted as follows: —

"In answer to the petition of Mr. Richard Russell for his allowance in the late law books, which was occasioned by the Court's alteration of some things therein etc., it is ordered, that in consideration of those losses mentioned in the petition and other that he hath lately sustained, he shall have allowed him twenty pounds out of the next rate."

The Preface to the edition of 1660 bears witness to the then scarcity of the earlier book, as it begins "the Book of Lawes, of the first Impression, not being to be had for the supply of the Country, put us upon thoughts of a second."

Mr. Thorowgood was probably not the only English friend who received a copy, and we may still hope that an example remains in some library in England, to appear at some unexpected moment.

We may now proceed to consider the contents of this first printed Code, and the amount of information recoverable is quite remarkable. The Preface to the Code of 1660 says "such Lawes of a general nature as have been made since the first Impression, till this present, and are yet in force, are placed under the former heads, in an Alphabetical order, which method being at first taken up (though perhaps not the most exact) hath this convenience and ease," etc., etc. Again it states "the former Epistle tells you there would be need of alterations and additions."

We therefore know that the first Code was arranged alphabetically under titles, in the same manner as in the later editions; it is certain, however, that these titles were altered in 1660 in some cases, and that some sections or even titles were dropped in 1660. It is also certain that in preparing the Code of 1649 some changes were made in the laws themselves as originally passed and entered on the Journal.

The first and highest authority for the contents of the first edition will be found in the citations made immediately after 1649 in the proceedings of the General Court.

The neighboring colonies of Connecticut and New Haven promptly availed of our Code of 1649 in preparing their respective laws. Connecticut established a Code by vote of May, 1650, and many sections are exactly the same as those in our Body of Liberties and our Revision of 1660. This Code is printed in the Records of Connecticut, Vol. 1, p. 509-563, edited by J. H. Trumbull, Hartford, 1850.

New Haven published her Code at London in 1656, and it is reprinted in the second volume of the Records of New Haven Colony, edited by Charles J. Hoadley, printed at Hartford in 1858. The Code states (p. 571) that in preparing these Laws, Liberties, and Orders "they have made use of the Laws published by the Honourable Colony of the Massachusetts." Herein, again, we find literal transcripts from our Body of Liberties and our Laws.

The following extracts from the printed edition of our Records contain, it is hoped, all the matters useful for our purpose:—

List of References.

1. May 2, 1649 (Records, ii. 281), " Forasmuch as the printed law concerning Dowries . . . . . appears not so convenient as was formerly conceived " . . . . it is ordered " that these words in the 14 line of that order " . . . . be amended.[34]

1.* October 17, 1649 (Records. ii. 287), " the printed law for Elections in page 51, bearing date 1647, is hereby repealed."

2. May 22, 1650 (Records, iv. part 1, p. 4), " whereas the law concerning fencing against great cattle, folio 7. — Harms done by Great Cattle in Fenced Ground shall be viewed and judged. — for explanation whereof this court declareth and ordereth," etc., etc.

2.* May 22, 1650 (Records, iv. part 1, p. 5), " for explanation of that part of the printed law entitled Military Affairs, s. 10," etc.[35]

3. June 19, 1650 (Records, iv. part 1, p. 19), " for explanation and addition of the law, title Profane Swearing," a new law was passed punishing any one for multiplying profane oaths.[36]

4. It appears by a reference, 21 June, 1650 (Records, iv. part 1, p. 20) that the " law, title Gaming, 1646, 1647," is amended by prohibiting bowling or any other play or game in public houses under the same penalties as are " provided for in the aforesaid game of shovel-board." [37]

---

[34] The New Haven Code (p. 587) has the title Dowry just like ours of 1660, omitting the clause (lines 17 and 18), "signified by writing under her hand and acknowledged before some magistrate or others authorized thereunto, which shall bar her from any right or interest in such estate." The New Haven law says that this law shall not apply to any transaction " before this law was published;" and our Code of 1660 says, "before the last of November, 1647." Hence I imagine the New Haven law is substantially ours of 1649. — W. H. W.

[35] This section will be found Records, ii. 222, and reads : " The Surveyor-general hath power to sell any of the common arms where he sees occasion." As it was repealed in 1650, it is not in the Code of 1660. It is the tenth section of the law of November 11, 1647, which was to stand together with two laws of 1645, and all others were repealed. Of course these last-named laws formed the title in our Code of 1649; but Connecticut and New Haven had very different laws. — W. H. W.

[36] The original law was passed November 4, 1646 (Records, ii. 178), and it is copied exactly in the Connecticut code. But in the revision of 1660, the two laws of 1646 and 1650 are printed, and their place is changed to " Swearing and Cursing," or under letter S instead of letter P. No doubt the Connecticut example shows the law of 1649. — W. H. W.

[37] The law against playing shovel-board was passed May 26, 1647 (Records, ii. 195), and is copied almost word for word in the Connecticut code.

But in the revision of 1660 reference is made to laws passed in 1646, 1647, and 1651, and we find that the new title, Gaming, includes " Shovel-board, Bowling, or any other play or game;" also a section against gaming for money, passed November 4, 1646 (Records, ii. 180), and one in regard to dancing in public houses, passed May 7, 1651 (Records, iv. part 1, p. 40).

Now the Connecticut law adds at the end the clause, " The like penalty shall be for playing in any place at any unlawful game," — which clearly was not in the Massachusetts Laws of 1649, as if there, the addition made in 1650, above noted, would have been unnecessary. But I suspect that the law of 1646, against gaming for money, was not in the revision of 1649, as it is most unlikely that the Connecticut law-makers would have stricken it out. Hence I conclude that in 1649 the title Gaming stood just as in the Connecticut code, except the last line. — W. H. W.

5. June 22, 1650 (Records, iv. part 1, p. 22), it was ordered that recording a sale, mortgage, etc., of houses or lands with the records of the shire shall be sufficient " without any further certifying unto the recorder or secretary for the General Court, and that clause in the close of the printed laws, title Conveyances Fraudulent, page 14, requiring the same, is hereby repealed." [38]

6. June 22, 1650 (Records, iv. part 1, p. 23), the Court answered a question " whether by that clause of the law entitled Innkeepers " a certain person was liable to a fine. [39]

7. Records, iv. part 1, p. 26, October 15, 1650, "the former law, title Women, is hereby repealed." [40]

8. May 7, 1651 (Records, iv. part 1, p. 40), " the former law provides, title Cask and Cooper, page the sixth," etc., and is now amended by adding a penalty for defective casks, and a penalty also on any town neglecting to appoint a gauger. [41]

---

[38] The Connecticut code throws no light on this, as under this title it merely prints the two sections about covenous alienation and papers signed under duress.

Section 4 under this title in Laws of 1660 is referred to laws in 1641 and 1642. I fail to find either, but October 7, 1640 (Records, i. 306), the law was passed which is incorporated, partly literally, in this section. At that time there were to be three recorders, and apparently all entries were to be certified every six months to the recorder at Boston. See also Rec. i, 276, where the Recorder has a fee for " receiving the books of men's houses and lands from the towns." —W.H.W.

[39] I feel very sure that the Connecticut code gives our law of 1649, except the section obliging towns to provide one ordinary in each, which was a local law. All the other provisions are to be found in our law of 1660, though in the latter edition are many later sections. But those copied in the Connecticut code are substantially the ones passed here May 14, 1645 (Records, ii. 100) and November 4, 1646 (Records, ii. 172), and they are mostly marked in the margin L. 1, p. 20. — W. H. W.

[40] The new section refers to a man striking his wife, or a woman her husband. The new form is in our Code of 1660, under title " Marriages," p. 51. I do not find the original section in Conn. or N. Haven code, but it was doubtless the same as Liberty No. 80, which E. Hutchinson considers as covered by the title " Marriages." — W. H. W.

[41] The law as it stands in 1660 refers to acts of 1641, 1647, 1651, and 1652. I have already (ante, p. 25) shown that no law of 1641 is found, but Sept. 27, 1642 (Records, ii. 29), a law was passed as follows : " That all vessels of cask used for any liquor, fish or other commodities to be put to sale shall be of London assize and that fit persons shall be appointed from time to time, in places needful, to gage all such vessels or casks; and such as shall be found of due size shall be marked with the gauger's mark and no other; and he shall have for his pains four pence for every tun and so proportionably ; and it is ordered that Mr. Will Aspenwall, Mr. Venner and Thomas Boarman shall be gaugers of cask for this year, and till others be chosen in their room. The gauger's mark shall be ' G.' "

Now the Connecticut code agrees entirely with the first order, word for word, except that it begins " that all cask used for Tar or other commodities to be put to sale shall be assized as follows : viz : every cask commonly called barrels or half hogsheads shall contain twenty-eight gallons wine measure and other vessels proportionable." These words seem to define the term " London assize." It also adds " that every cooper shall have a district brand-mark on his own cask, upon pain of forfeiture of twenty shillings in either case and so proportionably for lesser vessels."

The substance of this last order is in our revision of 1660, but I fail to find it in our Records, either in 1647 or any other year.

I infer, therefore, that 1647 is a misprint for 1649, and that the Connecticut code gives exactly the form in which our law stood in that edition; as it is evident that in 1649 this law was codified and received verbal changes. Compare the New Haven Code, which keeps the term " London assize," and adds also the penalty if the cooper omits to brand. — W. H. W.

9. May 7, 1651 (Records, iv. part 1, pp. 41-42), "for explanation of some words in the printed law, entitled Leather, viz. in that section in the margent entitled Searchers sworn their Duty, by the words (line the fourth) to make search and **view** within the precincts of their limits," etc., etc. Also "concerning those words in the section on the margin entitled Well tanned and dried, penalty, line the fifth," etc., etc. Also "concerning the last words entitled Triers of Leathers seized," etc., etc.[42]

10. May 26, 1652 (Records, iv. part 1, p. 79) an addition is made to the law "as is directed for bread, by order of Court, page 3, title Bakers."[43]

11. May 26, 1652 (Records, iv. part 1, p. 82), "whereas there is a manifest and inconvenient mistake in the penning of the order, title General Court, page the 8th of the last printed book," etc., etc.[44]

12. May 26, 1652 (Records, iv. part 1, p. 84), ordered, "that the printed order about money shall be in force until the first of September next, and no longer."[45]

13. May 26, 1652 (Records, iv. pt. 1, p. 88), "as enjoined by law, title Military, p. 39."

14. Oct. 19, 1652 (Records, iv. pt. 1, p. 106). "Whereas by the law, title Military, page 42, section 6, every captain," etc.[46]

---

[42] Here the Connecticut and New Haven codes are very brief. But the full references above show that our law of 1649 must have been much like that of 1660. — W. H. W.

[43] This means of course the Printed Laws, as in 1660 we find on p. 4 this title, and at the end of it this section as passed in 1652. The New Haven law is almost identical with our law of 1660 (omitting the last section), except that ours has a little clause (p. 5, lines 10 and 11) applying also to butter. I do not find the law authorizing this, and I doubt if it would have been dropped by the New Haven men. Hence I infer it was not in the law of 1649, but was added in 1660. — W. H. W.

[44] This error evidently refers to a law passed October 18, 1650 (Records, iv. part 1, p. 85). This law refers back to law 283, which is the marginal number for a law passed March 3, 1635-6 (Records, i. 169, 170). This primitive law regulated a disagreement between the two houses, where the greater part of each house held its own opinion. In 1650, as above noted, this was declared to mean the greater part of those present and voting. In 1652 this last law was repealed, and it was declared that when there was a difference it should be "determined by the major part of the whole court." Palfrey, iii. 42, says that this means the whole court sitting together, and not action by concurrent votes.

The meaning of the phrase "the last printed book" will be hereafter discussed. — W. H. W.

[45] Here follows a long order establishing the Mint at Boston and making its coin, together with English money, the only legal tender. I presume that the title "Money," in the Code of 1649, was a copy of the law passed Sept. 27, 1642 (Records, ii. 29), which is as follows: —

"Ordered that the Holland ducatour, worth three gilders, shall be current at six shillings in all payments within our jurisdiction; and the rix-dollar, being two and a half gilders, shall be likewise current at five shillings: and the ryall of eight shall be also current at five shillings."

Connecticut had a similar act, but not in its Code. Wampum or Peage was also at times a legal tender, but our law is to be found under those titles. — W. H. W.

[46] These two references to the title Military show that it covered at least pp. 39-42 in the Code of 1649; and I have already shown that there was a section 10 (see *ante*, p. 87,) in this printed law. — W. H. W.

15. Same date (Records, iv. pt. 1, p. 105), " as is provided in the printed law, page first," — in regard to actions triable in any court, etc.⁴⁷

16. Same date (Records, iv. pt. 1, p. 107), " The late order about swine is repealed and the printed law is in force in that respect." ⁴⁸

17. May 18, 1653 (Records, iv. pt. 1, p. 134), the question was decided as to what was meant " by the law, title Weights and Measures."

18. June 2, 1653 (Records, iv. part 1, p. 150), reference is made to " the law, title Masters and Servants," etc., etc.

19. August 30, 1653 (Records, iv. pt. 1, p. 151), a committee was appointed to examine the Treasurer's accounts, etc., " according to the law, page 26, in the second book." ⁴⁹

20. August 30, 1653 (Records, iv. part 1, p. 152), reference is made to " the law, title Impost, page 27."

21. May 3, 1654 (Records, iv. part 1, p. 184), " whereas experience hath manifested some inconvenience in the interpretation of the law, title Appeals, the second printed book, page 1, " wherein it is expressed that all appeals shall be accounted in the nature of a writ of error." ⁵⁰

22. November 24, 1654 (Records, iv. part 1, p. 218), " whereas this Court hath laid an impost on wines imported into any part of this jurisdiction, as in title Impost, in the first printed book,⁵¹ appears," etc., etc.

23. May 14, 1656 (Records, iv. part 1, p. 259), " the Treasurer cannot send forth his warrants to them, as is provided by the law, Charges Public, page the 9th," etc., etc.

---

⁴⁷ This would be under title " Actions," and naturally stand on page 1. — W. H. W.

⁴⁸ The title Swine is found in 1660, and evidently, by the citation, it was in the Code of 1649. — W. H. W.

⁴⁹ The title " Treasurer," in the Code of 1660, cites laws of 1648, 54, 57, 58. I suppose the printed law here above cited was that passed May 10, 1648 (Records, ii. 244). The citation p. 26 of the second book, as it stands printed in Shurtleff's edition, would be exceptional, if that book, as we have already concluded, did not exceed 16 pages. An examination made by Mr. C. B. Tillinghast, State Librarian, shows that the original is doubtless 16, the corresponding figures where they occur as 1653 having the same peculiar " 1 " easily to be confounded with a " 2." — W. H. W.

⁵⁰ This law was passed May 2, 1649 (Records, ii. 279), " to be published forthwith but not to be of force till after the end of the next Quarter Court." It was evidently not in the Code of 1649, but stood on page 1 of the Supplement, or second printed book. I would here note that it is section 2 of title Appeals in the Laws of 1660; and also that section 3 is wrongly cited in the margin as passed in 1643. That section is the law of August 30, *1653* (Records, iv. part 1, p. 152), and at the end of this title in 1660 the citation is 1642, 47, 49, 50, 53, and 54. — W. H. W.

⁵¹ The meaning of the first and second printed books will be hereafter discussed. — W. H. W.

Introduction.

24. May 6, 1657 (Records, iv. part 1, p. 291), " whereas the clause in the law, page thirty-two, mentioning evidence, is obscure, — the jury may bring in a *non licquet*, — which words hath occasioned much trouble and delay in civil proceedings, this Court doth hereby repeal that clause," etc.[52]

25. May 26, 1658 (Records, iv. part 1, pp. 335 and 336), "that the freemen within their several towns have liberty and power according to the last law or order entitled Townships."

"For explanation and emendation of two laws in the printed book, title Townships," etc., etc.

26. October 19, 1658 (Records, iv. part 1, p. 347), in regard to electing magistrates annually, "and that clause of the printed law enjoining the nomination of twenty persons is hereby repealed," etc., etc.

27. May 11, 1659 (Records, iv. part 1, p. 366), in regard to persons aiding the Quakers, etc., " the Court, on perusal of the law, title Arrests, resolve, that the Treasurers of the several counties are and shall hereby be empowered to sell the said persons to any of the English nation at Virginia or Barbadoes."

---

[52] This is a most interesting matter, but I will first explain the text. In the Code of 1660, under title "Jurors," § 2, we find a marginal citation, L. 1. p. 47, and the text establishes Grand Jurors according to the law of March 4, 1634–5 (Records, i. 143). Then follows the clause about jurors not being bound to reveal secrets which do not affect the state, which is Liberty No. 61. Both of these probably were in the Code of 1649, and next to them doubtless stood Liberty No. 31, (the subject of the above amendment in 1657), which allowed the jury in case of doubt to give a *non-liquit*, or a special verdict which left the judgment to the Court.

I do not see why the reference is to Liber 1, p. 47, as the text above is p. 32. But there are so many misprints in our Codes that I suspect this to be one, especially as the page on which it stands in 1660 is numbered 47.

Moreover the marginal references in 1660 are to Lib. 1, p. 32 and p. 31 against the sections preceding and following this very entry of L. 1, p. 47. We have already seen that in the printed laws of 1649 the title "Military" covers pp. 39–42, and the title " Jurors " must have come earlier.

But the whole order in 1657 is worth printing as showing the belief, even then, in the right of juries to judge of the law as well as the facts. It reads : —

" Whereas, in all civil cases depending in suit, the plaintiff affirmeth that the defendant hath done him wrong, and accordingly presents his case for judgment and satisfaction, it behooveth both Court and jury to see that the affirmation be proved by sufficient evidence, else the case must be found for the defendant; and so it is also in a criminal case; for, in the eye of the law, every man is honest and innocent unless it be proved legally to the contrary. All evidence ariseth partly from matter of fact and partly from law or argument. The matter of fact is always feasible to be judged of as well by the jury as by the Court; and concerning the law, or the point of law, in reference to the case in question, it is either more easy and generally known, or more difficult to be discerned. The duty of the jury is, if they do understand the law to the satisfaction of their consciences, not to put it off from themselves, but to find accordingly; but if any of the jury doth rest unsatisfied what is law in the case, then the whole jury have liberty to present a special verdict, viz. : if the law be so or so in such a point, we find for the plaintiff, — but if the law be otherwise, we find for the defendant : — in which case the determination is left to the Court."

Then follows the repeal of the old law and the Court "directeth according to what is above expressed for the future." — W. H. W.

28. May 31, 1660 (Records, iv. part 1, p. 420), the Court declares " that no man whosoever shall be admitted to the freedom of this body politic but such as are members of some church of Christ, and in full communion, which they declare to be the true intent of that ancient law, page the 8th of the 2^{d} month, anno g^r. 1631." [53]

The following table gives the marginal citations in the edition of 1660 which are credited to Liber 1. The variations from a strictly alphabetical arrangement may be explained by a change in the title according to the views of the editor in 1649 and the later issue. It seems probable that we must resort to the idea of misprints to account for pages 57 and 58 under the title "Marshal," as "Watching" and "Wills" were on pp. 52 and 53 : —

CITATIONS IN THE EDITION OF LAWS IN 1660, FROM LIBER 1.

1660.	Title.	Liber 1.	1660.	Title.	Liber 1.
P. 2,	Actions,	do. p. 16.	P. 41,	Indians,	do. p. 28.
	do.	do. p. 49.	42,	do.	do. p. 28.
4,	Attachments, Summons,	do. p. 49.	44,	Innkeepers,	do. p. 30.
11,	Cattle, Trespass,	do. p. 51.	45,	do.	do. p. 30.
12,	Criminal Cases,	do. p. 46.	47,	Jurors,	do. p. 32.
16,	Constable,	do. p. 46.		do.	do. p. 47. [?]
20,	Conveyances,	do p. 16.	48,	do.	do. p. 31.
22,	Courts,	do. p. 16.	52,	Marshal,	do. p. 38.
	do.	do. p. 36.		do.	do. p. 57. [?]
	do.	do. p. 24.	53,	do.	do. p. 58. [?]
23,	do.	do. p. 14.		do.	do. p. 10.
	do.	do. p. 15.		do.	do. p. 45.
	do.	do. p. 36.	66,	Powder,	do. p. 45.
24,	do.	do. p. 15.	67,	Punishment,	do. p. 50.
	do.	do. p. 36.	68,	Records,	do. p. 47.
31,	Fines,	do. p. 38.	73,	Strangers,	do. p. 23.
	do.	do. p. 22.	74,	Sureties (Courts),	do. p. 15.
33,	Freemen,	do p. 23.	79,	Watching,	do. p. 52.
34,	Heresy,	do. p. 2.	81,	Wills,	do. p. 53.
40,	Impress,	do. p. 9.			

[53] In the Code of 1660 this section has a marginal citation of L. 2, p. 8. It precedes a clause declaring that church-members are not exempt from public service as officers, which is cited as L. 1, p. 23. — W. H. W.

Next in importance is a contemporaneous citation of several sections of our Code, first brought to light by Dr. Moore in his recent pamphlet. They are found in a book entitled as follows: "Jewes in America, or Probabilities that the Americans are of that Race. With the removall of some contrary reasonings and earnest desires for effectuall endeavours to make them Christian. Proposed by Tho. Thorowgood, B. D., one of the Assembly of Divines. Cant. 8. 8. Mat. 8. 11. London. Printed by W. H. for Tho. Slater and are *be to* [sic] sold at his shop at the signe of the Angel in Duck lane. 1650." Small sq. 8vo, pp. about 180. A copy is in the Boston Public Library.*

"I shall transcribe some things out of their owne late printed Booke of the Lawes and Liberties concerning the Inhabitants of Massachusets, by which their love to truth, godlinesse, peace, and learning will be evident, together with their liberall and enlarged care to propagate the eternall Gospell of our Lord among the Natives.

"At the title of hæresie (c) this is the preface. Although no humane power be Lord over the faith and consciences of men, and therefore may not constraine them to beleeve or professe against their consciences, yet because such as bring in damnable heresies, tending to the subversion of the Christian Faith, and the destruction of the soules of men, ought duly to be restrained from such notorious impiety, it is therefore ordered and decreed by this Court:

c p. 24.

"That if any christian within this jurisdiction shall goe about to subvert and destroy the Christian Faith and Religion, by broaching or maintaining any damnable heresie, as denying the immortality of the soule, or the resurrection of the body, or any sinne to be repented of in the regenerate, or any evill done by the outward man to be accounted sinne, or denying that Christ gave himselfe a ransome for our sinnes, or shall affirme that wee are not justified by his

---

* The following citation from p. 78, though not directly pertinent to our inquiry, may be worth notice owing to the date:—

"To the Westerne Plantation, indeed, at first men of meane condition generally resorted, but soon after people of better ranke followed; divers of good families and competent estates went into *Virginia* and setled in some Islands thereabouts, but because those of New-England pretended more to Religion than the rest, they are more loaden with uncivill language, but most injuriously; for the transplanting Novangles were many of them severally eminent, some of noble extract, divers Gentlemen descended from good Families; their first Charter mentions three Knights, among other men of worth; and it seemes their example, or somewhat else, was like to prevaile with many others of no meane condition, so that eleven of the then Privy Councell directed their letters in *December*, one thousand six hundred thirty foure, to the Warden of the Cinque ports, taking notice that severall persons went over with their families, and whole estates, forbidding subsidy men, or of the value of subsidy men, to be imbarqued without speciall licence and attestation of their taking the Oaths of Supremacy and Allegiance, submission also to the Orders and discipline of the Church of *England:* And three yeeres after, *viz.* one thousand six hundred thirty seven, a proclamation issued from the King to the same purpose, and in the same words."

death and righteousnesse, but by the perfection of their owne workes, or shall deny the morality of the fourth Commandement, or shall endeavour to seduce others to any the heresies aforementioned, every such person continuing obstinate therein after due meanes of conviction shall be sentenced to banishment.

1646. And before (*d*) having said, that the open contempt of Gods word, and the messengers thereof is the desolating sinne of civill States, &c. It is therefore ordered, and decreed, That if any christian, so called, within this jurisdiction, shall contemptuously behave himselfe towards the word preached, or the messengers thereof—either by interrupting him in his preaching, or by charging him falsely with any error, which he hath not taught, or like a son of *Korah* cast upon his true doctrine, or himselfe, any reproach—every such person or persons (whatsoever censure the Church may passe) shall for the first scandall be convented and reproved openly by the Magistrate at some Lecture, and bound to their good behaviour; and if a second time they breake forth into the like contemptuous carriages, they shall either pay five pounds to the publique treasury, or stand two houres openly upon a blocke or stoole foure foot high on a Lecture day with a paper fixed on his breast, written in capitall letters, AN OPEN AND OBSTINATE CONTEMNER OF GODS HOLY ORDINANCES, that others may feare and be ashamed of breaking out into the like wickednesse. 1646.

<small>d Tit. Ecclesiasticall, p. 19, 20.</small>

"There be some in this *England* that account it piety and Religion to speake evill of Christs Ministers, and cast off his Ordinances; now blessed of God from heaven and earth be our Novangles, Magistrates, Ministers, and people that have so seasonably witnessed against these abominations.

"They are great lovers of peace and government, these therefore be their words in another place; (*e*) For as much as experience hath plentifully & often proved that since the first rising of the Anabaptists about an hundred yeeres past they have bin the Incendiaries of Commonwealths, and the infectors of persons in maine matters of Religion, and the troublers of Churches in most places where they have been, and that they who have held the baptizing of infants unlawfull, have usually held other errors or heresies together therewith (though as heretiques use to doe they have concealed the same untill they espied a fit advantage and opportunity to vent them by way of question or scruple) and whereas divers of this kinde have since our comming into New-England appeared amongst our selves, some whereof, as others before them, have denyed the Ordinance of Magistracy, and the lawfulnesse of making warre, others the lawfulnesse of Magistrates and their inspection into any breach of the first Table, which opinions, if connived at by us, are like to be increased among us, and so necessarily bring guilt upon us, infection and trouble to the Churches, and hazard to the whole Common-wealth: It is therefore ordered by this Court and authority thereof, that if any person or persons shall either openly condemne or oppose the baptizing of infants, or goe about secretly to seduce others from the approbation, or use thereof, or shall purposely depart the Congregation at the administration of that Ordinance, or shall deny the Ordinance of Magistracy, or their lawfull right, or authority to make warre, or to punish the outward breaches of the first Table, and shall ap-

<small>e Tit. Anabaptists, p. 1.</small>

peare to the Court willfully and obstinately to continue therein, after due meanes of conviction, every such person or persons shall be sentenced to banishment. 1644.

"And that wee may discerne how worthy they are that wee should doe all the good wee can for them, for they love the nation where they inhabite, and are very serious in *preparing them for one husband, to present them a pure virgin unto Christ*, 2 Cor. 11. 2. Severall therefore are their decrees in order to their conversion.

ƒ Tit. Indians. p. 28, 29.

(ƒ) "1. Every Towne shall have power to restraine all Indians from prophaning the Lords day. 1633, 1639, 1641.

"2. The English shall not destroy the Indians corne, but shall help them to fence in their grounds.

"3. Considering one end in planting these parts was to propagate the true Religion unto the Indians, and that divers of them are become subjects to the English, and have engaged themselves to be willing and ready to understand the Law of God; it is therefore ordered and decreed, that such necessary and wholesome Lawes which are in force, and may be made from time to time, to reduce them to civility of life, shall be once in the year (if the times be safe) made knowne to them, by such fit persons as the generall Court shall nominate, having the helpe of some able Interpreter.

"4. Considering also that interpretation of tongues is appointed of God for propagating the truth; It is therefore decreed that two Ministers shall be chosen every yeer, and sent with the consent of their Churches (with whomsoever will freely offer themselves to accompany them in that service) to make knowne the heavenly counsell of God among the Indians, and that something be allowd them by the Generall Court to give away freely to those Indians whom they shall perceive most willing and ready to be instructed by them.

"5. They decree further that no Indian shall at any time Powaw, or performe outward worship to their false gods, or to the devill, and if any shall transgresse this law, the Powawer shall pay 5 l. the procurer 5 l. etc. 1646.

"Their love to learning also is meet to be remembered and encouraged, wherein they have (g) observed a chief project of that old deluder Satan to keepe men from the knowledge of the Scriptures, as in former times keeping them in an unknowne tongue, so in these latter times by perswading from the use of tongues, that so at least the true sense and meaning of the originall might be clouded with false glosses of saint-seeming deceivers, and that learning may not be buried in the graves of our forefathers in Church and Common-wealth, the Lord assisting our endeavours, It is therefore ordered by this Court and authority thereof, That every Township encreasing to the number of fifty households, shall appoint one within their Towne to teach all such children as shall resort to him, to write and read, whose wages shall be paid either by the Parents or Masters of such children, or by the Inhabitants in generall by way of supply, as the major part of those that order the Prudentialls of the Towne shall appoint, and where any town shall encrease to an hundred families or householders, they shall set up a Grammar school, the Masters thereof being able to instruct youth so far, as they may be

g Tit. Schools, p. 47.

fitted for the University, and if any town neglect this above a yeere, every such Towne shall pay five pound *per ann.* to the next such Schoole, till they shall performe this order. 1647.

"And an Academy or University is not onely in their aime, but a good while since they had more than begun well, and therefore wee read these words in another (*h*) part of their lawes, Whereas through the good hand of God upon us there is a College founded in Cambridge in the County of Middlesex, called Harvard College, for incouragement whereof this Court hath given the sum of four hundred pounds, and also the revenue of the Ferry betwixt *Charles* Towne and *Boston*, and that the well ordering and mannaging of the said College is of great concernment ; It is therefore ordered by this Court, &c. Then follow directions for the President and Commissioners to establish orders and dispose gifts, etc. 1636, 1640, 1642.

<small>A Tit. College, p. 12.</small>

. . . .

"Our Brethren of New England . . . are not onely furnished themselves with necessaries of all sorts, and have made large steps in an Academicall way, having Acts, Degrees, and Commencements according to the commendable fashion of *England*, as their own words are: The *theses* at their Commencements disputed upon have been printed severall yeeres at *Cambridge* in New England, and thence dispersed here ; but they have also industriously furthered by their godliness, gentleness, and good orders, the conversion of a miserable people that have lien so long in darknesse."

Dr. Moore next cites "Civil Magistrates Power in Matters of Religion Modestly Debated Impartially Stated," &c., &c. By Thomas Cobbet, Teacher of the Church at Lynne in New England. . . . London, 1653. His citation is as follows.

"P. 34, 35—Indeed, our Printed Law Book Alphabetically expressing the Titles or Heads of the Matters about which the Laws are made, reckoneth them thus, for an example, *Dowries, Drovers, Ecclesiastical* (the very thing abused by this Author), *Elections, Escheats*, &c."

It is noteworthy that these sections stand in this order in the Code of 1660, though probably many sections of the Titles *Dowries, Ecclesiastical* and *Elections*, were not printed in the Code of 1649.

Dr. Moore also cites from Snow's History of Boston a paper of instructions to the Selectmen in 1651. Snow however merely copied Shaw's History, p. 125. In this book it stands

"24. 1 mo. 1651. Directions for the Selectmen of Boston commended unto them from the town." . . . First, in generall we require your special care that the good and wholesome orders allready made, which you have the records of, be observed and duly executed, and what other acts and orders shall be established for future benefitt of the towne, that you allsoe cause them to be published and put in execution, and further according to power given *and severall laws of the county*,* to be found in the book of printed lawes, under these titles, Townships, Ecclesiastick, Freemen, Highways, small Causes, Indians, Corn-fields, Masters and Servants, Pipe Staves, Swyne, Weights, Measures, and any other order in force which concerns your place, to regulate yourselves and carry on your worke; and where you finde defect of power to bring your desires to a good issue for well ordering the towne, you may draw some good orders in forme to be aproved by the towne, and so to be presented to the Generall Court, and our Deputyes, for consideration."

. . . .

"Secondly, to enquire of such as present themselves for inhabitants what calling or employment they will undertake, and if they will live under other men's roofs as Inmates, then to deal with them, according to the order of such persons, comprehended under the title of Townshipes."

"These instructions," adds Shaw, "were continued in force by an annual vote of the people for many years."

Although these "Instructions" are not entered on the town book, and Shaw's original is now unknown, there is no reason to doubt his accuracy. At the town meeting, March 10th, 1651, an order was passed "for a Committee to Draw up the power to be given to the Selectmen, which is first to be presented to the Towne and Consented too if they se Cause." (Printed Records, i. p. 103.) — Again, March 14, 1653, a committee of five "ar desired to draw up Instrucktions for the Townsmen (*i.e. Selectmen*) to ackt by, to be an addition to what Instrucktions they already have." (Ibid. p. 114.) — Again, March 4, 1659, (Ibid. p. 150), "It is ordered that the Instructions formerly given to the select men, in writing, bee still in force till the towne present others to them." — March 12, 1660, (Ibid. p. 154), "Itt was voted that the instructions formerly given to the select men should bee in force still."

It is unfortunately true, that no one familiar with the Boston Records will be surprised that Charles Shaw, in 1817, could find and use documents no longer remaining in our archives.

Lastly, William P. Upham, Esq., who has been engaged in sorting and arranging the Court Files of papers for Suffolk

---

* The text here seems to be corrupt. I suggest " *in the severall laws of the country*." — W. H. W.

County, has made the valuable suggestion that in cases tried between 1649 and 1660, citations would doubtless be made from the printed Code. Although it is impossible to cover all the ground at this time, the following examples show the importance and practicability of the idea. I trust it will be followed up by other investigators.

*From the Suffolk Court Files.**

At a General Court held at Boston, 14th of Oct. 1657. In answer to Overseers of Harvard College, Vol II. p 73.   No 275.

"it shall be sufficient unto the validity of college acts, that notice be given unto the overseers in the six Towns mentioned in the Printed Law Anno 1642 &c &c

copy examined

J. Willard, Sec'y"

Goffe & Goffe's Ex. Dec. 1658. Vol II. No 333.
Sam'l Goffe's plea.
Answer, that the deponents to the promise doe professe that had they demanded it then, they doubt not but the said Edward Goffe deceased would have performed it, if he could have done it in a way of concealing it from those whom it might trouble, the desire of woman is evident
Jan 11th '37
Psal. 15 4
If it be contra pleaded it seemeth not valid by our legal acts
that law Anno 52 page 15
"this double portion is so bound or . . . according to scripture acceptation or the law by us inacted, lib. 1, title wils, page 53, which law we think from the scripture law &c &c
"and required by our law in deeds, Law anno 51 May 7"

Harry Bennett vs Wm Fellows:
Pleading, Vol III. p 10. No 351–4 & answer to. Sept. 27. 1659.
"And we shall leave the appellant to your justice to be further p'seded with, according to the Laws, fol 2 title appeals see 2 & fol. 36 title majestrates."

---

* These examples show that the Code of 1649 contained a title *College;* also *Conveyances,* p. 15; *Wills,* p. 53; *Appeals,* p. 2; and *Magistrates,* p. 36. — W. H. W.

Vol II, p. 45, No 257, paper not dated, probably 1655-6
Divorce* Case Jane Halsell vs George Halsell — Petition

(4) "But considering the power of divorce doth properly belong to the Generall Court of Assistance as it is expressed in an order of the generall court = (Maye 16 1656) & a president ther is for it (namely Mr Freeman sometimes of Watertown) & the law submitts it (page 17)
There for I hope &c "

---

* There is no title of *Divorce* in the editions of 1660 and 1672. The references are under *Courts* and *Dowry*, and at the former place the margin quotes *Liber* 1, pp. 14 and 15, and *Liber* 3, p. 5.

As to the powers of the Courts, we find (Rec., i. 276), Sept. 9, 1639, it was ordered "that such of the magistrates as shall reside in or near to Boston, or any 5, 4, or 3 of them, the Governor or Deputy to be one, shall have power to assemble together upon the last fifth day of the eighth, eleventh, second and fifth month, every year, and then and there to hear and determine all civil causes whereof the debt or trespass and damages shall not exceed £20, and all criminal causes *not* extending to life, or member, or banishment, according to the course of the Courts of Assistants, and to summon juries out of the neighboring towns."

October 18, 1648 (Rec., ii. p. 286, and iii. 175), the law was altered so that only two Courts should be held, viz., in the first and seventh months, and the Governor or Deputy was allowed to call a Court to try capital cases, "so that justice be not deferred nor the country charged."

But in the Code of 1660 the law stands " *For the better administration of justice and easing of the Country of unnecessary charges and travaile.* It is ordered by this Court and the Authority thereof, That there be two Courts of Assistants, yearely kept at *Boston*, by the Governour, Deputie Governour and the rest of the Magistrates, on the first Tuesday of the first month, and of the first Tuesday of the seventh month, to heare and determine all and onely actions of appeals from inferior Courts: all Causes of divorce, all Capital and Criminal causes, extending to life, member or banishment. And that justice be not deferred nor the Country needlessly charged, It shall be Lawfull for the Governour, or in his absence the Deputie Governour (as they should judge necessary) to call a Court of Assistants for the tryal of any malefactour in Capital Causes."

It will be noticed that in 1639 the Quarter Courts could *not* try criminal cases extending to life, member or banishment, which powers seem always to have been exercised by the full Court of Assistants. It may be that such was the object of this law, as three magistrates were made a Court by it. The records of the Court of Assistants are printed by Shurtleff, in the first volume of Records, and were entered chronologically with the meetings of the General Court. The latest is dated Sept. 7th, 1641. Happily the Barlow copy of the Records contains further records of these Quarter Courts to March 5th, 1643-4. Then all records are missing prior to the volume dated 1673-1692, in charge of the Clerk of our Supreme Court, as pointed out by Charles Cowley, Esq., in his pamphlet entitled " Our Divorce Courts" (Lowell, 1880).

It will be farther noted that in 1660 the Court of Assistants was to hear and determine "all causes of divorce," a power which does not seem to have been expressly granted before, and which is explained by the case of Halsell quoted above. Mr. Cowley cites the case of James Luxford (3 December, 1639, Rec., i. 283), where the "Court of Assistants or Quarter Court, held at Boston," nine members sitting, decreed that he "being presented for having two wives, his last marriage was declared void, or a nullity thereof, and to be divorced." He was also obliged to give all he had to the wife last married, for her and her children, was fined £100, put in the stocks, and banished. Mr. Cowley could find no other cases.

Such, however, are to be recovered from our records. At the Quarter Court, at Boston, March 5, 1643-4, it is noted that " Anne Clarke being deserted by Denis Clarke her husband, and he refusing to accompany with her, she is granted to be divorced; his refusal was under his hand and seal, which he gave before Mr. John Winthrop, jr, Mr. Emanuel Downing, Mr. Nehemiah Bourne, and Richard Babington. Also he confesseth he liveth in adultery with one by whom he hath had 2, and refuseth to forsake her which he had 2 children by."

Again, at the same Court, John Richardson was ordered to " be sequestered from Elizabeth Fryar, to whom he was married the 12th of the 8th month, and neither to meddle with her person nor estate, till things be cleared by advice from England." The General Court (Rec., ii. 86),

From the Essex Court Files.

Vol. IV f. 17.   March 1657–8
" who ever heard of an accord of Replevin before now.

" The law giveth a replevin : or the thing taken upon an other pledg for ye benefitt of yᵉ former plaintiff : and it is for a trespasse done him. And therefore he Sueth for remedy by vertue thereof, and did give bond to prosecute the same."

" law against near relations to judge " mentioned —

f. 18 — (same case) " that the court will be pleased furderto consider the law in the first booke and page whare tis sayd to this purpose that noe mans goods shall be taken away or any way endamadged vnder cullour of law or countenance of authority vnles it be by the vertue or equity of some expresse law or in defalt thereof by the word of god suficiently warranting the same."

November 13, 1644, on additional testimony. " do declare the last marriage to be void, which was Elizabeth Frier." *(These two cases are in the Barlow manuscript.)*

The next case which I have noted is October 16, 1650 (Rec., IV. part i. p. 32),

" In answer to the petition of William Palmer, desiring a bill of divorce may be granted him from Elinor, his wife, which, since his coming into these parts, hath wholly deserted him and married herself to one William Pope of Salisbury, in the county of Wilts, in England, and hath had children by him, the Court judgeth it meet . . . that the said William Palmer should be divorced, and declared hereby that he is legally divorced."

May 14, 1654 (Rec., IV. part i. p. 190), . . .

" In answer to the petition of Dorcas Hall, desiring a divorce from her husband, John Hall, who is gone from her, &c — the Court finding it fully proved . . . judgeth it meet, that the said Dorcas shall be, and hereby declares that she is, legally divorced from the said John Hall, and is at liberty to marry with any other man."

A similar case of divorce desired is in Rec., IV. pt. i. p. 282, October 11, 1656, as recorded : —

" In answer to the petition of Mary Bachiler, desiring liberty from this Court to dispose of herself, her husband being gone from her, and, as she pretends, since his going, married, &c., the Court judgeth meet to refer the examination to the next County Court at York, and the said Court to make return of what they find to the next Court of Assistants, *who have power to issue and determine the case.*"

In Rec., IV. part i. pp. 259 and 269, it seems that at the session of May, 1656, the General Court referred the petition of William Clements of Watertown, " craving a divorce from his wife, who for several years hath refused marriage fellowship with him, . . . unto the County Court of Charlestown next month."

In Halsall's case, in 1656, the counsel as cited above (*ante*, p. 99) quotes the case of Mr. Freeman of Watertown. Though this does not appear in the General Court's record, it is doubtless a different case from that of William Clements of the same town. Samuel Freeman had a wife Apphia, and it has been thought that his widow married Gov. Thomas Prence of Plymouth. It has now been suggested that she was divorced, and married a second time while Freeman stayed in England, but this surmise needs examination.

Next comes this case of George Halsall and his wife, at the same session (Rec., IV. part i. p. 272), where in answer to the petitions " there having been two committees that have had the hearing of this case, whose apprehensions have been different therein, this Court is not willing to act hereupon, but judge it meet to refer the examination and final determination of this case unto the Court of Assistants, *to whom it doth properly belong.*" Later (Ibid., p. 380), May 28, 1659, the General Court " in answer to the petition of George Halsall, . . . do order, that the determination of it be referred to the next session, and in the mean time forbid either party to marry."

Lastly, November 12, 1659 (Ibid., p. 401), " In answer to the petition of George Halsall,

Essex County Court Papers.

Vol. IV — f. 30 — { case of Gifford & Webb —
June 1658 —

— Henry Webbs Answer —

"2ly The law as I conceave is plaine that the thinge sued for shall be
2 booke 40 page brefely exprest in the warant, that ye plantive might know how to
titel Sumons provide himselfe, wch. is not in this & therefore cannot come prepared to make an answer, vpon wch I conceave there is a mistake.

"3ly the law that gives strangers libertie to trye in any Courte of this
2-b. 15 pag Jurisdiction, restrains it to such as are not residing or inhabiting
titel Strangrs amongst vs. & the general Courte lookt at Mr Giffard as a
stranger. & took bonde of him accordingly. & soe did ye Clark of the writs in this action.

"4ly The law sath y^t al actions of debts acco^t. slander & actions of the
1. b. 1 pag caise &c. shal be tryed w^thin the Jurisdiction of that court wherin
titel Actions the plantive or defendant dweleth. but nether plant. nor defendant
lives in this country as we conceue. ye plant. being determined by General
Courte to be a stranger."

In the case of Cromwell v. Ruck — June 1660 — Vol. V — f. 98 —
"The new law book in pag. 15
"The law sees: wharas the way of passing of houses & landes by salle in England is both peesabell & effectuall namly by deed in writing sealed & deliured wth liueri and Seson or posession given of the same before witness & by deede acknowlidged and recorded or by seesing a ffine : & that divers within this Jurisdiction are apt to rest upon vnsertin bargans or salles for houses or lands of any valew ; this Court taking this thing into Searis consideration doth hereby declare & order for the prevention of all clandestine and vnsartin salles & titells : that henceforth noe sale or Alienation of houses or lands in this Jurisdiction shall be houlden Good in law exsept the same be dune by deed in

---

humbly desiring that Jane, his wife, lately divorced from him by the Court of Assistants, 1656, may be returned to him, &c., the Court, on a hearing of the matter contained in his petition and duly considering of all the evidences by both parties produced in the case, do order, that the judgment of the said Court of Assistants in reference thereto be void, and that the said George Halsall shall have and enjoy the said Joan Halsal, his wife, again."

Here we have full evidence that divorce cases were considered to belong first to the Court of Assistants with an appeal to the General Court. Washburn (Judicial History) points out that this power of appeal existed in all cases.

These nine quoted cases of Luxford, Clarke, Richardson, Palmer, Hall, Bacheler, Clements, Freeman, and Halsall may not comprise all the cases even in the printed Records, as "Divorce" is not an entry in the indexes. The Court of Assistants between 1644 and 1673 may have granted other divorces, of which the record is lost. Halsall's case is most peculiar, as a divorce was set aside after three years.

As the text refers to the fact that divorce cases belonged to the Assistants, and says "the law submits it, page 17," it seems a reasonable surmise that this clause stood in the Code of 1649, under the title *Courts.* — W. H. W.

writen under hand & seal & delivered & posession given upon part in the name of the whole by the vender or his Atorny soe Athorised under hand & seal: vnles the said deed be acknowlidged according to law and recorded." *

From Middlesex Court Files and Records.†

Norcross vs Beers in behalf of the town of Watertown at County Court held at Cambridge, 4ᵈ (2ᵐ) 1654.

"Defendant presents an order in the 50 page of the printed laws which concerns Townships, alleaging our order is repugnant to the Law &c &c"

"Whereas he aledgeth the 13 page of the printed Lawes about recording of Sales, we stand not about title; the thing in controversy is posession in place."

Mr Norcross Declaration:

"was not possession given according to the Lawes of the honored generall court reall but a shadow for the words of the law Page 14 Conveyances fraudulent: noe title is of [validity?] except it be Recorded, the latter book Page 13, that that is Recorded by the Sheer Recorder shall be sufficient security, (without such, not.) Therefore he tould them their order was criminall and repugnant beyond limites provided in that case Page 50.

"whereas the law saith now that [not] above 8ᵗ in 100 that Rate proportionable for all sommes what soever, that is the words of the Law Page 51 Usery."

"they had not showed mee the instructions given them in wrighting to mak that order Tho   I think they can show it Page 51 &c. &c."

———

"Henry Dunster presented for disturbing church services July 30, 1654. County Court Records, Vol 1. p, 60, The Court ordered that Mr Henry Dunster according to the Eclesst: Law page 19. at the next lecture at Cambridge should (by such magistrate as should there be present) be publiquely admonished and give bond for his good behavior."

---

* These Essex Cases prove that in 1649 the Preamble stood first, on page one, being the Liberty for personal protection. Then it contains *Actions*, p. 1, and evidently did not contain title *Strangers*, here referred to the Second Book, p. 13. I suspect the reference above in Webb's answer to title *Summons* means Liber 1, not Liber 2. In Cromwell's case the *new law book*, p. 13, is not the Code of 1660, where the law is on p. 20. The marginal reference there is to Anno 52, p. 13, which, as hereafter shown, was the second Supplement.—W. H. W.

† The Middlesex examples give us references to *Townships*, p. 50; *Conveyances*, p. 13; *Conveyances fraudulent*, p. 14; *Usury*, p. 51; *Ecclesiastical*, p. 19; *Marriage*, p. 38; and probably *Liberties Common*, § 2, p. 35.—W. H. W.

Vol 1. p, 80. "Mr Joseph Hills of Mauldon being p'sented by the Grand Jury for marrying of himselfe, contrary to the Law of this Collony page 38 in ye old Booke. &c &c"
Court April 1, 1656

Symmes vs Broughton, County Court. June 16, 1657, Plaintiffs Reasons.
"The 3rd reason is because the erecting and maintaining of the aforesaid Dams is directly contrary to the righteous established laws of this common wealth wch say expressly pag. 35 of printed laws, That a proprietor shall not by what liberty he hath given him &c &c"

The following Table shows the titles which were certainly in the printed Code of 1649 : —

Preamble	Page 1	Indians	p. 28
Action	" 1	Inn-Keepers	
Appeals	p. 2	Jurors	pp. 31, 32
Anabaptists	" 1	Leather	
Arrests		Liberties, Common	p. 35
Bakers	" 3	Magistrates	
Cask and Cooper	" 6	Marriage	p. 38
Cattle	" 7	Marshal	p. 38
Causes, Small		Masters and Servants	
Charges, Public	" 9	Military Affairs	pp. 39, 42
College	" 12	Money	
Conveyances, fraudulent	" 14	Pipe-staves	
Courts	pp. 14, 15, 24, 36	Powder	p. 40
Cornfields		Punishment	" 45
Divorce	p. 17	Records	" 47
Dowries		Schools	" 47
Drovers		Strangers	
Ecclesiastical	19	Summons	" 49
Elections	p. 51	Swearing	
Escheats		Swine	
Fines	pp. 22, 38	Townships	
Freemen	p. 23	Usury	p. 51
Gaming		Watching	p. 52
Heresy	" 24	Wills	53
Highways		Women	
Impost	p. 27		

After the experimental publication of the Code in 1649, the advantages of a printed authority were evident.

October 17, 1649 (Records, ii. 286, and iii. 173), the following vote was passed: —

"The Court, finding by experience the great benefit that doth redound to the country by putting of the law in print, do conceive it very requisite that those laws that have passed the consent of the General Court since the Book of Laws were in printing or printed, should be forthwith committed to the press; and for that end appoint Richard Bellingham, esq., Mr. Nowell, Mr. Auditor-General [Duncan], Capt. Keayne, and Mr. Hill, or any three of them, a committee to prepare them against the Court of Election; that upon approbation of the return of the committee, they also may be printed; as also therewith to prepare those laws referred to in the end of the printed laws, with a suitable table, to be printed."

October 18, 1650 (Records, iv. part 1, p. 35): —

"It is ordered that Richard Bellingham, esq., the Secretary [Rawson] and Mr. Hills, or any two of them, are appointed a committee to take order for the printing the laws agreed upon to be printed, to determine of all things in reference thereunto, agreeing with the president for the printing of them with all expedition, and to allow the title if there be cause."

These last two entries supply us with a fact which has probably not been noticed for the last century, viz., that not only was there an edition of 1649, but a Supplement thereto in 1650. It will also be possible to form a fair idea of the shape and contents of both of these. As to the existence of the Supplement of 1650, citations given later (under dates of May 26, 1652, Aug. 30, 1653, May 3, 1654, and Nov. 24, 1654) show that the General Court in 1654 referred to and amended laws in the "first printed book" and in the "second printed book." Moreover the Code of 1660 is full of marginal citations from L. 1 and L. 2, the former being quoted up to p. 53 (title "Wills") and the latter to p. 16 (under the same title). And in one case the law cited by the General Court as being on p. 8 of the second book (referring to Freeman) is in 1660 marked as L. 2, p. 8.

Two other facts are significant: First, the annexed Table of the marginal references in the Code of 1660 to Liber 2 shows that the laws copied were all passed prior to 1651. Secondly, that the marginal citations are from Anno 1651 onward, and never backward. That is to say, no year previous to 1651 stands in the margin, though much of the text was enacted in 1648, 1649, and 1650.[33] There are some laws cited as from Liber 2, which were passed earlier than 1648; these are evidently the laws which were omitted in the Code of 1649, but found on examination to be worthy of a place in the General Laws, and therefore put first into the Supplement and then into the Code of 1660.

The title "Ecclesiastical" (p. 28 of 1660) seems to give us a good proof that the Supplement contained amended or omitted laws. Section 14 contains two long sub-sections or paragraphs. Both were passed November 4, 1646 (Records, ii. p. 178, 179); but the first paragraph is on p. 179, and the second on p. 178. Now the Connecticut Code prints the first paragraph complete, but not the second. Hence I infer this first paragraph alone stood in the Code of 1649; but that in the Supplement (the citation being L. 2, p. 5) the previous section, which had been overlooked, was restored.

Note, also, that in the law of 1646 the culprit was to wear a paper inscribed "A Wanton Gospeller"; but in 1660, and by the Connecticut Code, it was changed to "An Open and Obstinate Contemner of God's Holy Ordinances." In my former edition I added that this seems to show that the compilers in 1649 altered the text on that point, and Connecticut copied it. This surmise is made nearly certain by the copy of this act, as quoted by Thorowgood from the Code of 1649 (*ante*, p. 94). I reprint the law as it stands in the Colony Records, ii. p. 177. The clauses in italics are omitted by Thorowgood, one or two words are altered, and the label is to read "AN OPEN AND OBSTINATE CONTEMNER OF GOD'S HOLY ORDINANCES."

Presuming, as we must, that Thorowgood copied *verbatim*, it is quite curious to note that certain phrases, marked in brackets, were omitted in the Code of 1649, more especially as they were

---

[33] I find but two apparent exceptions. In 1660, p. 2, title "Appeals," § 3, the citation is "A. 43, p. 19." This is a typographical error, as the law was passed August 30, 1653 (Records, IV. part 1, p. 152).

The other case is on p. 82 of Code of 1660, title "Wolves," cited as 1648. This law was passed Oct. 18, 1648 (Records, ii. 252), and was to last only four years. It was therefore not in the General Laws of 1649. But it was revived by a law passed August 30, 1653 (Records, IV. part 1, p. 155), and therefore is printed in 1660. The law and the citation are both exceptions.— W. H. W.

restored to the text in the Code of 1660, p. 26, title *Ecclesiastical*, § 14, and as they are also given in full in the Connecticut Code of 1650.

[LAW OF NOVEMBER 4, 1646, COMPARED WITH THOROWGOOD'S CITATION OF 1649.]

"That if any Christian, so called, within this Jurisdiction, shall contemptuously behave himself towards the word preached, or the messengers thereof [*called to dispense the same in any congregation, where he doth faithfully execute his service and office therein, according to the will and word of God*], either by interrupting him in his preaching, or by charging him falsely with any error which he hath not taught [(*in the open face of the church*)], or, like a son of Corah, cast upon his true doctrine or himself any reproach, [*to the dishonor of the Lord Jesus, who hath sent him, and to the disparagement of that his holy ordinance, and making God's ways contemptible and ridiculous, that*] every such person or persons (whatever censure the church may pass) shall for the first scandal be convented and reproved openly by the magistrates at some lecture, and bound to their good behavior; and if a second time they break forth into the like contemptuous carriages either to pay £5 to the public treasury, or to stand two hours openly upon a block 4 foot high, on a lecture day, with a paper fixed on his breast, with this A WANTON GOSPELLER, written in capital letters, that others may fear and be ashamed of breaking out into the like wickedness."

The title "Attachments," in the Laws of 1660, helps to fix the date of the second book. It cites "L. 2, p. 12," for a law passed May 22, 1650 (Records, iv. part 1, p. 5), and farther down it cites "Anno 1651, p. 1," for a law passed May 7, 1651 (Records, IV. part 1, p. 39).

Lastly, as already cited (*ante*, p. 80), Joseph Hills, in May, 1653, states that, after seeing the first volume through the press, he aided others "to compose and transcribe the second Book of Laws, copy-wise," and "to fit them for the press."

We have, moreover, already given a table (*ante*, p. 92), of citations from Liber 1, contained in the Code of 1660. We have now to account for about fifty citations in the volume of 1660, credited to Liber 2. This collation will complete our certainty that Liber 2 was a Supplement, covering the General Laws for 1648 (partly), 1649, and 1650, together with some earlier laws omitted in the Code of 1649, but still in force.

Introduction. 107

It will be seen, from the following table, that this Supplement was arranged under titles in an alphabetical order. The apparent exceptions are doubtless due to the fact that these titles were changed in 1660; and very possibly the order was not strictly observed. But the main fact remains that Liber 2, or the second printed book, contained all the laws passed after the completion of the printed Code of 1649 (or the first printed book), through the sessions of 1650.

Marginal Citations in the Laws of 1660.

1660.	Title.	LIBER 2.	Date of Original Act.
P. 1	Actions	4	Oct. 15, 1650; Rec. iv, *27.
2	Appeals	1	May 2, 1649; " ii, 279.
4	Attachments	12	May 22, 1650; " iv, 5.
6	Bridges	3	March, 1647–8; " ii, 229.
11	Cattle	8	May 22, 1650; " iv, 4.
13	Criminal Causes	4	May 2, 1649; ii, 279.
17	Chirurgeons	3	do " ii, 278.
18	Clerk of the Writs	13	See Footnote a.
21	Counsel	4	do ; " ii, 279.
"	Courts	10	; " ii, 7, 9.
"	do	13	; " ii, 95.
22	do	24	See Footnote a.
23	do (Lib. 3)	5	Oct. 17, 1648; " ii, 286.
24	do	7	Nov. 13, 1644; " ii, 80.
"	do	15	June 31, 1650; " iv, 20.
"	do	4	
26	Dowries	5	} See Footnote a.
27	Ecclesiastical	7	

* References to Records, iv, mean Part 1 of that volume.

Marginal Citations in the Laws of 1660. — Continued.

1660.	Title.	LIBER 2.	Date of Original Act.		
28	Ecclesiastical	5	Nov. 4, 1646;	Rec.	ii, 178.
29	Elections	10	Oct. 17, 1649;	"	ii, 286.
30	Fairs	7	Oct. 18, 1648;	"	ii, 257.
"	Ferries	7	Oct. 27, 1648;	"	ii, 262.
31	Fines	7	May 22, 1646;	"	ii, 153.
33	Freemen	8	May 18, 1631;	"	i, 87.
37	Hides	8	Nov. 4, 1646;	"	ii, 168.
38	Horses	11	May 2, 1649;	"	ii, 280.
39	Imposts	9	Oct. 1, 1645;	"	ii, 131.
41	Indians	15	June 21, 1650;	"	iv, 21.
44	Innkeepers	3	Oct. 17, 1649;	"	ii, 286.
	do	6	Oct. 18, 1648;	"	ii, 257.
46	do	31	See Footnote ª.		
47	Jurors	5	Oct. 17, 1649;	"	ii, 285.
	do	8	May 22, 1650;	"	iv, 3.
51	Married Persons	17	Oct. 15, 1650;	"	iv, 26.
53	Marshall	7	May 26, 1647;	"	ii, 194.
56	Military	12	Mch. 1647–8;	"	ii, 226.
60	do [Ammunition]	1	May 2, 1649;	"	ii, 282.
61	Mines	11	May 10, 1648;	"	ii, 242.
63	Petitions	13	Oct. 27, 1648;	"	ii, 261.
68	Records	15	See Footnote ª.		
	do	7	Nov. 11, 1647	"	ii, 215.
70	Sailors	14	May 22, 1650;	"	iv, 2.

Marginal Citations in the Laws of 1660. — Concluded.

1660.	Title.	LIBER 2.	Date of Original Act.		
71	Sheep	14	Oct. 18, 1648;	Rec.	ii, 252.
73	Strangers	32	See Footnote a.		
74	Swearing	14	June 19, 1650;	"	iv, 19.
75	Townships	10	Mch. 3, 1635–6;	"	i, 172.
78	Wampumpeag	12	Oct. 27, 1648;	"	ii, 261.
			May 2, 1649;	"	ii, 279.
80	Wills	16	Oct. 17, 1649;	"	ii, 287.
81	do	6	May 2, 1649;	"	ii, 281.

a On p. 13, title " Criminal Causes," the reference is L. p. 2. Probably this means Lib. 2.

On p. 18 the reference is in regard to the "Clerk of the Writs." I have already (*ante*, p. 25) noted part of this law as passed in 1641, but I have not found the law establishing their fees. Yet May 31, 1660 (Records, iv. part 1, p. 421), a law was passed which refers to a "former law" on the subject.

On p. 22, title "Courts," the reference is L. 2, p. 24. This is doubtless a printer's error for p. 14, as the preceding reference is to L. 2, p. 13; or to Lib. 1, p. 24, as that is the bottom reference on the same page, § 4. I prefer the latter solution.

On p. 23, § 7, the reference is to L. 3, p. 5, and as this is the *only* reference to Liber 3, I feel sure that it is an error for Liber 2.

On pp. 24 and 26, titles respectively "Courts and Dowries," I cannot find the laws cited. Both matters are fully discussed *ante*, p. 25 and 26.

As to the reference on p. 27 to title "Ecclesiastical," being a law, that "the Treasurer shall defray the expenses of church elders when employed by special order of the General Court, 1642." — This order was passed May 18, 1642. It is on p. 2 of vol. ii, *second edition only*, and is not indexed in either edition.

On p. 46, title "Innkeepers," § 12, the reference is to L. 2, p. 31; evidently an error for Liber 1, as on the previous page § 8 is referred to L. 1, p. 30.

On p. 68, title "Records," the reference is L. p. 15. Undoubtedly Liber 1 is meant, and I imagine that it therein stood under title "Courts."

On p. 73, title "Strangers," the citation is L. 2, p. 32. This must be an error for L. 1, p. 23, as just above it the citation is L. 1, p. 23. The text is dated 1641, and both paragraphs are in the Body of Liberties.

On p. 81, title "Wills," § 3, the reference is to L. 2, p. 6. I suspect an error for L. 2, p. 16, as that is the citation for § 1 on the previous page.

It is, of course, undesirable to explain difficulties by presuming typographical errors. But the fact remains that the edition of 1650 contains many such about which there can be no dispute. The first three instances noted above are all the references to any page in Liber 2 above 16; and it seems impossible that there could have been 24 or 32 pages in the book, and yet that none of those intervening pages were used in preparing the Code of 1660. — W. H. W.

Nor does our information stop here, but it is demonstrable that two more Supplements were issued, the second containing Laws of 1651, 1652, and 1653, and the third embracing those of 1654, 1655, 1656, and 1657. This information was given in the Introduction to my former edition, pp. 112–113, but is now put in its proper relation to the preceding pages.

In a report dated Sept. 1, 1673 (Archives, Vol. 48, No. 125), I notice the following words.

See Laws in 48
49 fol 8 of 2^d print
52 fol 11 3^d print
&c.

"It is the sense already given by the General Court, see the Result of s^d question in 44 the old printed b. fol. 13, where the Governor hath onely a casting voice in case there bee an equall number on different sides."

Following out the clue thus given I turned again to the marginal citations in the Code of 1660. We have already discovered that Liber 1 meant the Code of 1649 and Liber 2 the Supplement of 1648–1651. But there were also many later references, all made to A 51, A 52, &c., including A 58, and evidently meaning *Anno* 1651 to *Anno* 1658. These years were accompanied almost invariably by the words p. 1, p. 2, p. 20, up to p. 26. The following table gives the list:—

Marginal Citations, Code of 1660.

1660.			1660.		
Page 1,	. .	. A 52, p. 7. (A).*	Page 16,	. .	. A 56, p. 11. (F).*
2,	. .	. A. 51, p. 1.	"	. .	. A 54, p. 6
"	. .	. A 43, p. 19	17,	. .	. A 51, p. 4
"	. .	. A 54, p. 2	19,	. .	. A 54, p. 2
3,	. .	. A 51, p. 5	"	. .	. A 57, p. 26
4,	. .	. A 51, p. 1	20,	. .	. A 52, p. 15
5,	. .	. A 52, p. 8	"	. .	. A 51, p. 2
6,	. .	. A 51, p. 4	22,	. .	. A 52, p. 11
6,	. .	. A 55	24,	. .	. A 54, p. 2
7,	. .	. A 58	25,	. .	. A 53.
7,	. .	. A 52, p. 10.	"	. .	. A 54, p. 3
9,	. .	. A 51, p. 2	27,	. .	. A 58.
"	. .	. A 52, p. 17	28,	. .	. A 54, p. 6
11,	. .	. A 53, p. 20	29,	. .	. A 52, p. 15
13,	. .	. A 51, p. 6	"	. .	. A 58.
"	. .	. A 54, p. 2	32,	. .	. A 52, p. 11
14,	. .	. A 51, p. 1.	"	. .	. A 52, p. 9, 10.
"	. .	. A 57, p. 23	33,	. .	. A 51, p. 3

Marginal Citations, Code of 1660. — Continued.

1660.		1660.	
Page 34,	A 57, p. 7, 8. (G).*	Page 59,	A 55.
35,	A 54, p. 7	60,	A. 56, p 12
"	A. 56, p. 13	"	A 56, p 12
"	A 57, p. 26	"	A 54, p 1
"	A 58	"	A 56, p. 12
36,	A 53, p. 19	61,	A 53
"	A 58	"	A 52, p 12
39,	A. 53, p. 19	62,	A 54, p. 5
40,	A 52, p. 16	"	A 52, p. 9
41,	A 57, p. 22	63,	A 54, p. 5
"	A 57, p. 23	"	A 54, p 1
42,	A. 56, p. 18	65,	A 58, p 22 (H).*
43,	A. 58	"	A 56, p 10 (E).*
"	A 52, p. 10	"	A 57, p 24
"	A 58	66,	A 52, p. 3 (B).*
44,	A 51, p. 4	"	A 55, p. 10
"	A 53, p. 19	67,	A. 57, p 25
45,	A 54, p. 2	68,	A 52, p 13
"	A. 58	"	A 57, p. 21
46,	A 57, p. 21	"	A. 54, p. 24 (D).*
47,	A 54.	69,	A 52, p 9
"	A 51, p. 5	"	A 53, p. 18
"	A 53, p. 19	70,	A 52
"	A 57, p. 25	71,	A 54, p 1
"	A 56, p. 14	"	A 56, p 12
49,	A 51, p. 3	"	A 53, p 18
53,	A. 53, p. 20	72,	A 55 p 11
55,	A 52, p. 12	73,	A 51, p 7
"	A 55	74,	A 1658.
56,	A 56, p. 12	75,	A 51, p 4
"	A 53, p. 13 (C).*	76,	A. 58
57,	A 52, p. 13	"	A 53, p 18
"	A 56, p. 12	"	A 54, p 2
58,	A 53	77,	A 58
"	A 52, p. 14	78,	A. 52, p 12
"	A 53	"	A. 57, p 25
59,	A 53	80,	A 55
"	A 56, p. 12	81,	A 52, p 15
"	A 54, p. 3	82,	A. 48.

* These references are explained in the following pages, — they being the apparent exceptions to a perfect system of pagination.

The preceding table gives all of the marginal citations which are by year-dates, according to the pages of the Code of 1660. They are all repeated in the margins of the edition of 1672, without correction even of obvious errors, and with a few additional blunders.

Thus, in 1672, there were *omitted* the following citations of 1660, viz., p. 10, A. 51, p. 4; p. 12, A. 55; p. 16, A. 52, p. 17, and the following errors were added: —

In 1660, p. 19, A. 57, p. 26; In 1672, p. 3, A. 55, p. 26.
" " p. 41, A. 57, p. 23; " " p. 75, A. 52, p. 23.
" " p. 47, A. 53, p. 19; " " p. 86, A. 55, p. 19.
" " p. 63, A. 54, p. 5; " " p. 120, 54, p. 4.
" " p. 65, A. 58, p. 22; " " p. 123, A. 58, p. 28.

These citations, however, could not be arranged on any system as pages in a single book. Even allowing that titles were altered, the contradictions were too many. But by re-arranging these eighty-four citations we find that they fall into two consecutive series.

The acts of 1651 are cited as pp. 1, 2, 3, 4, 5, 6.
" " 1652 " " 7, 8, 9, 10, 11, 12, 13, 14, 15, 16, and 17.
" " 1653 " " 18, 19, 20, and five times unpaged.
" " 1654 " " 1, 2, 3, 4, 5, 6, and 7.
" " 1655 " " 10 and 11, and four times unpaged.
" " 1656 " " 10, 11, 12, 13, 14, and 18.
" " 1657 " " 21, 22, 23, 24, 25, and 26.
" " 1658 " eleven times, always without a page.

There are a few discrepancies which I will note, and which seem to be mainly owing to printers' errors. They are as follows: —

In the first series (1651, 1652, and 1653) we find on (A.) p. 1, Anno 52, p. 7, and on p. 73, Anno 51, p. 7, and on p. 34, Anno 57, p. 7 and 8. This last citation is clearly wrong, as the law was the well-known law against Heresy, passed in 1652. By a double error, the date at the end of the section is 1651 instead of 1652. The law cited on p. 2 was also passed in 1652. Hence, as three out of four citations of this p. 7 refer to 1652, I conclude that the fourth citation, of 1651 as p. 7, is a clerical error for some other page, from 1 to 6.

(B.) On p. 66 we find Anno 52, p. 3, but the act was passed in 1651, and is cited at the end as 1651. Clearly this is a printers' error, and should be Anno 51, p. 3, agreeing with the series.

(C.) On p. 56 we find Anno 53, p. 13, but the law was passed in 1652, and is so cited on p. 57. This is also a printers' error, and should be 1652, p. 13.

In other words the serial arrangement is harmonious for about forty times, and the three apparent exceptions are explained above as obvious errors of the press.

As to the second series, we find that the year 1654 covers pages 1, 2, 3, 4, 5, 6, 7. But we find also (D.) on p. 68, Anno 54, p. 24. But the law was passed in 1657, and here again the printers' error, if corrected, makes the series right, as p. 24 comes under the year 1657.

In 1655 the citations are four times by the year alone; on p. 66 as Anno 55, p. 10; on p. 72 as Anno 55, p. 11.

In 1656 the citations are pp. 10, 11, 12, 13, 14, and 18. Here pp. 10 and 11 are assigned to both years, 1655 and 1656. (E.) But the citation p. 65 of Anno 56, p. 10, is an error, for the law was passed in 1655, and is so noted at the end of the section.

(F.) The reference on p. 16 to Anno 56, p. 11, is wrong, as the act was passed in 1655. It should be Anno 55, p. 11. But very curiously the reference on p. 72 to Anno 55, p. 11, is also wrong, as the law about spinning was passed in 1656. The reference must be to *Anno* 1656, some page between 12 and 18.

But with the balance of errors, I presume that pages 10 and 11 both belong to the year 1655.

In 1657 the citations are, 21, 22, 23, 24, 25, and 26, but we note one exception.

(G.) On p. 34 we find Anno 57, pp. 7 and 8. This has already been explained (see item A.) as an error for 1652.

Lastly, we find

(H.) on p. 65, Anno 58, p. 22, but the law was passed in 1657, and is so cited at the end of the section. Evidently a printers' error, especially as this is the only case where *Anno* 1658 is followed by a page-number.

We may, therefore, say that the second series is also regular and continuous.

Having already identified the "second printed book" with a Supplement covering the omissions and laws through 1650, I now consider the "third printed book" to have been a second Supplement, of some 19 pages, covering the laws of 1651, 1652, and 1653, printed in accordance with the order of May 3, 1654, cited (*post*, p. 116). Then I doubt not in 1657 a third Supplement, or "fourth printed book" of some 26 pages, was issued, covering the laws of 1654, 1655, 1656, and 1657, according to the orders cited, (*post*, p. 117). After this the issuing of Supplements was probably stopped while the Revision of 1660 was in hand.

In other words, it is almost absolutely certain that the Code of 1649 was followed by Supplements until the next revision, as we have proof that the Code of 1660 and every subsequent revision down to the present time has been so supplemented.

In our Records, (Vol. iv. part 1, pp. 324–327), will be found a summary of the laws relative to constables, made in 1658. These twenty-six sections are each referred to some previous law, and the citations are from *Lib.* 1, pp. 13, 14, 16, 19, 26, 27, 31, 32, 37, 38, 39, 46, 48, 51 and 55; *Lib.* 2, p. 10; *Lib.* 3, pp. 2, 3 and 9; *Lib.* 4, pp. 16, 18, 20 and 26. This may be a mere coincidence, or it may confirm our theory that before 1660 there were these four books of printed laws: especially as *Liber* 1 runs to p. 55. I have not been able to thoroughly investigate the references, some of which are very puzzling.

The preceding pages complete the citations from the Records respecting the Code of 1649 and the Supplement of 1650; there remains only to copy the entries in regard to the Laws between 1650 and 1660, when the Code was printed, and the latter votes preceding and following the Revision of 1672.

May 23, 1650, the following order[54] was passed (Records, iii. 193): —

"Whereas this Commonwealth is much defective for want of laws for maritime affairs, and forasmuch as there are already many good laws made and published by our own land, and the French nation, and other Kingdoms and commonwealths; this Court doth therefore order that the said laws, printed and published in a book called *Lex Mercatoria*, shall be perused and duly considered, and such of them as are approved by this Court shall be declared and published to be in force within this jurisdiction after such time as this Court shall appoint.

---

[54] This is from the House Journal, and is more in detail than the regular joint record in Records, iv. part 1, p. 10. — W. H. W.

"And it is further ordered that Mr. Bellingham, Mr. Nowell, Mr. Willoughby, Capt. Hathorne, the Auditor-general [Duncan], and Mr. John Allen, shall be a committee to ripen the work, and to make return of that which they shall conclude upon, unto the General Court; and the time of their meeting to be the first third day of the sixth month next."

June 22, 1650 (Records, iv. pt. 1, p. 23, and iii. 204), the following vote was passed:[55] —

" It is ordered by this Court and the authority thereof, that henceforth the Secretary for the General Court, shall, within two months after the end of every session, send unto the clerk of every shire court, as also unto the present or late deputies of each town, or to the constable where no deputy is, a copy of all general orders made in each Court, for which he shall receive of the Treasurer for every such copy after the rate of eight pence per page, which the Treasurer shall charge upon each town together with their country rate from time to time, viz, for the copies sent unto the particular towns.

" And it is farther ordered by the authority aforesaid, that the deputies, or constable of each town where no deputy is, shall cause the same to be audibly read, in a public town meeting, warned by the constable of each town, within ten days after their receipt thereof, on penalty of five pounds upon any deputy or constable for neglect of their respective duties.

" And it is farther ordered by the authority aforesaid, that such reading thereof in any shire or market town in each shire, shall be a sufficient publication thereof from time to time; provided also that the Treasurer shall have a copy without payment from time to time."

October 23, 1651 (Records, iv. part 1, p. 69, and iii. 252) : —

" Whereas, in the year 1650, there was a committee chosen to peruse a book called *Lex Mercatoria*, to extract such laws from thence as might be suitable for our use in this commonwealth, which said committee have not yet met according as was then concluded : that the said order may be further prosecuted, it is ordered by this Court, that the accomplishing of that work shall be referred to Mr. Nowell and the Auditor-general [Duncan], who are hereby chosen a committee and desired to peruse the said book, and to collect from thence such laws as they shall judge meet for our use, according as that order doth direct, and to make return to the next General Court."

---

[55] Records, iv. part 1, p. 63, mention that the Secretary for this service of transcribing orders and for other services, is to receive forty pounds annually.

August 30, 1653 (Records, iii. 317, and iv. part 1, p. 152), it was ordered " that the several gross sums of all the incomes, viz. : upon the annual rate upon imposts, vintners, entering of actions, fines, forfeitures &c. as also of all expenses, viz. of all Courts, commissioners, gratuities, allowances, payments, debts, &c. be exactly by the Auditor certified to the General Court annually, and expressed in all the copies of the laws sent unto the several towns, made in the first session of the Court of Election, whereby the true state of things in that respect may be obvious to all that are concerned therein." — W H. W.

October 26, 1652 (Records, iv. part 1, p. 119) : —

"It is ordered that Richard Bellingham, Esq., and William Hibbens, Mr. John Glover and the Secretary [Rawson,] or any three of them, shall be a committee to peruse the laws that have passed this Court, and to determine which of them shall go to the towns."

June 2, 1653 (Records, iv. part 1, p. 149), voted as follows : —

"Mr. Bellingham, Mr. Glover and Mr. Hill are appointed with the Secretary [Rawson] to peruse the laws that is passed this Court, comparing them with the original copies."

Sept. 10, 1653 (Records, iv. part 1, p. 180) : —

"It is ordered that the Deputy Governor [Bellingham], Mr. Hibbens, Mr. Glover, and the Secretary [Rawson], Mr. Hills, or any two of them with the Secretary, shall be a committee to examine the laws that passed this Court.

"It is ordered that the Secretary shall take care that the old book of records shall be fairly written out, for which he shall have satisfaction by the page, as the Court allows."

May 3, 1654 (Records, iv. part 1, p. 182) : —

"It is ordered by this Court, that henceforth the Secretary, shall, within ten days after this present sessions and so from time to time, deliver a copy of all laws that are published unto the president,[56] or printer, who shall forthwith make an impression thereof, to the number of five, six, or seven hundred, as the Court shall order : all which copies the Treasurer shall take of and pay for in wheat or otherwise, to content, for the number of five hundred after the rate of one penny a sheet, or eight shillings a hundred for five hundred sheets of a sort, for so many sheets as the books shall contain.

"And the Treasurer shall distribute the books to every magistrate one, to every Court one, to the Secretary one, to each town where no magistrate dwells one, and the rest among the towns that bear public charge within the jurisdiction, according to the number of freemen in each town.

"And the order that engageth the Secretary to transcribe copies for the towns and others, is in that respect repeated, the Court allowing him ten pounds this year only, in respect of what benefit hereby is withdrawn from him."

"And it is further ordered, that Mr. Samuel Symonds, Major Dennison, and Mr. Joseph Hills shall examine, compare, reconcile, and place together, in good order, all former laws both printed and written, and make fit titles and tables for ready recourse to any particular contained in them, and to present the same unto the next Court of Election, to be considered of, that so order may

---

[56] This reference, like the earlier one on p. 80, is to Henry Dunster, President of Harvard College, who had an interest in the only press in the colony.

be taken for the printing of them together in one book, whereby they be more useful than now they are or can be."

May 14, 1654 (Records, iv. part 1, p. 195) : —

"It is ordered, that the honored Governor [Endicott], the Secretary [Rawson], Capt. [Thomas] Clarke, and Mr. [Joseph] Hill, or any three of them, shall be a committee to peruse and view the laws passed this session, according to former order."

June 9, 1654 (Records, iv. part 1, p. 196) : —

"Upon conference with Mr. Dunster and the printer, in reference to the imprinting of the Acts of the General Court, whereby we understand some inconveniences may accrue to the printer, by printing that law which recites the agreement for printing, it is therefore ordered that the said law be not put forth in print, but kept amongst the written records of this Court." [57]

October 14, 1656 (Records, iv. part 1, p. 281) : —

"It is ordered that the Deputy Governor [Bellingham], Capt. Clarke, Mr. Secretary [Rawson], and Capt. Savage, shall examine the laws of the General Court for two years past, and cause such laws as are of public concernment to be written out, whereby they may forthwith be committed to the press and sent to the several Courts."

May 6, 1657 (Records, iv. part 1, p. 292), the following vote was passed: —

"Whereas it is found by experience that the passing and enacting of divers grants, orders and laws upon the first proposal, hath occasioned many inconveniencies which might have been prevented by mature deliberation, and that it is the laudable custom of the Parliament of England to pass no bills which have not been there read and debated, it is therefore ordered and enacted by this Court, that no grant of land, law or order (except transient acts) shall henceforth be of force but such as, after reading and mature consideration on three several days, shall be approved and consented to by the major part of Magistrates and Deputies."

May 6, 1657 (Records, iv. part 1, p. 299) : —

"It is ordered by this Court, that all laws of public concernment, not yet printed, be forthwith transcribed by the Secretary, and sent to the press to be printed at the public charge ; the printer to be paid by the Treasurer."

---

[57] October 18, 1659 (Records, iv. part 1, p. 301) : "It is ordered by this Court, that the Treasurer shall, and hereby is empowered to, disburse out of the Treasury what shall be necessary tending towards the printing of the laws unto Samuel Greene, referring to his pains therein or otherwise." Perhaps the terms of payment to the printer, in view of these "inconveniences" were in this later case kept as a secret of state. — W. H. W.

May 26, 1658 (Records, iv. part 1, p. 337) : —

"It is ordered, that Major General Daniel Denison diligently peruse, examine and weigh every law and compare them with others of like nature, and such as are clear, plain and good, free from any just exception, to stand without any animadversion, as approved ; such as are repealed or fit to be repealed, to be so marked and the reasons given ; such as are obscure, contradictory, or seeming so, to be rectified and the emendations prepared ; where there is two or more laws about one and the same thing, to prepare a draught of one law that may comprehend the same ; to make a plain and easy table ; and to prepare what else may present in the perusing of them to be necessary and useful : and make return to the next sessions of this Court."

October 19, 1658 (Records, iv. part 1, p. 350) : —

"It is ordered by this Court and the authority thereof that the Book of Laws, as they have been revised and corrected and put in form by order of this Court, together with the alterations and additions here under expressed, shall forthwith be printed, and be of force in one month after the same ; and that there shall be a perfect table made there unto what remains yet to be done, to be prepared for the press by our honored major-general ; and that in the meantime the laws stand in force as now they be."

Then follow seven amendments to the laws, two being in the negative, and the following vote : —

"It is ordered, that when the present copy of the Laws is finished by the Major-General [Denison], that they be sent to the Treasurer, who shall take care that they be printed as speedily as may be : also, that the preface to the old law book, with such alterations as shall be judged meet by the Governor [Endecott] and Major General, be added thereunto, and presented to the General Court to be approved of: and Mr. Danforth is appointed to oversee the impression."

May 28, 1659 (Records, iv. part 1, p. 381) : —

"It is ordered, that the Treasurer dispose of Mr. Norton's books now at the press, delivering every member of this Court one, and to the several towns in proportion to their rates, and twenty or thirty to Mr Norton, presenting this Court's acknowledgment to him for his pains at present ; and giving every minister one : the like order about the laws."

October 18, 1659 (Records, iv. part 1, p. 391) : —

"It is ordered by this Court, that the Treasurer shall and hereby is impowered to disburse out of the treasury what shall be necessary tending towards the printing of the laws, unto Samuel Greene, referring to his pains therein or otherwise."

Although not in strict chronological order, I here insert two orders showing the compensation made to the persons employed on the Code of 1660.

October 16, 1660 (Records, iv. part 1, p. 441): —

"Whereas, at the request of this Court, Mr. Thomas Danforth hath attended the service of this Court, in surveying the laws at the press, and making an index thereto, this Court judgeth meet, as a gratuity for his pains, to grant him two hundred and fifty acres of land, to be laid out in any place not legally disposed of by this Court."

Also (Ibid. p. 441): —

"Whereas Mr. Edward Rawson was employed by this Court for the drawing up of the book of laws before it was performed by Major-General Denison, this Court, being willing to acknowledge the labors of such as are employed for the public behoof, doth judge meet, as a gratuity for his pains, to grant him two hundred and fifty acres of land in any place not yet disposed of by this Court."

May 31, 1660 (Records, iv. part 1, p. 422): —

"For the more equal distribution of the law books, when they shall be printed, it is ordered by this Court and the authority thereof, that the printer shall deliver the said books to the country Treasurer as soon as they are past the press, who, immediately upon receiving of them, shall deliver or cause to be delivered to every magistrate one; to every deputy of this General Court one; to the Secretary and Clerk of the Deputies one apiece for themselves; to the Recorder or Clerk of every County Court three apiece to be kept for the use of the several Courts:

"And the remainder of the said books, the Treasurer shall send to every county treasurer such a proportion as is due to each county according to what charge they bear in the country rates.

"And the county Treasurers are hereby enjoined to send unto every town in the respective countries their town's proportion, according to the rule above mentioned, and deliver the same to some meet person employed by each town to receive them, engaging to satisfy the Treasurer for them according to his disbursements, that so no charge be put upon the country for the same, as Capt. Gooking, the Treasurer of the country, and Treasurer of each county shall determine, both for price and quality of pay.

"And that provision be made for the eastern parts, it is ordered, that before the division there be fifty books laid apart for their supply, they making like payment to the country Treasurer for the same; and that Portsmouth and Dover have twenty books laid aside for them on the same terms.

"And it is further ordered, that Mr. Thomas Danforth, who was to have the oversight of the impression, make an index to the said book with all convenient speed, that so the work may be no longer delayed."

October 16, 1660 (Records, iv. part 1, p. 432): —

"It being a matter of some concernment to the country rightly to understand when this last impression of the laws are to be in force and begin to take place, this Court doth therefore order and declare, willing and requiring all persons concerned to take notice, that the said impression of laws shall be of force after the expiration of thirty days from the date of these presents, and that in the meantime the old books to stand good and to be attended to as before."

We have thus completed the record up to the issue of the edition of 1660, which has been issued by the City in a fac-simile reprint. The evidence thus collected seems to show that Nathaniel Ward was the principal compiler of the Body of Liberties; that Bellingham was probably the chief inciter of the edition of 1649; that Joseph Hills prepared the Supplement of 1650; and that Secretary Rawson, Capt. Thomas Clark of Boston, and especially Major General Daniel Denison[58] were chiefly concerned in collecting, condensing, and arranging the code of 1660.

In the nature of things, no finality is ever to be reached in law-making. The code of 1660 was immediately subjected to amendments and additions, and various yearly supplements were considered necessary. The copy preserved in the library of the American Antiquarian Society at Worcester, being the one formerly owned by Secretary Rawson, contains most of these supplementary sheets, but nine pages were supplied from the copy in the Law Library of Harvard College. In the meantime the following extracts from the Records will show what steps were taken by the Legislature: —

May 22, 1661 (Records, iv. part 2, p. 4):—

"It is ordered and by this Court declared, that the order made in the third month, 1654, appointing the printing of the general orders of Court of

---

[58] Daniel Denison was born in England, in 1612, and came here with his father, William D., in 1631. He settled in Ipswich in 1635, and was a deputy from that town for several years, being Speaker in 1649, 1651, and 1652. He was an Assistant from 1653, till his death in 1682, and Commissioner of the United Colonies for seven years. He was very prominent in military affairs and major-general much of the time from 1653 to 1680. He was town-clerk of Ipswich, and in 1653 was chosen Secretary in the absence of Edward Rawson. He married a daughter of Gov. Thomas Dudley, and was essentially one of the ruling caste in the colony. He must have received a good education in England as his letters and state papers show. He left a treatise in manuscript entitled, "Irenicon, or Salve for New England's Sore," which was published after his death by his pastor, Rev. Wm. Hubbard. A good memoir of him is in the N.E. Historical and Genealogical Register for July, 1869. — W. H. W.

each session within ten days, be again revived, and be in force so far as it refers to the annual printing of laws, any law to the contrary notwithstanding."

October 19, 1664 (Records, iv. part 2, p. 136) : —

"Mr. Thomas Danforth, Capt. Thomas Clark, Mr. Wm. Parkes are appointed a committee to join with the Secretary [Rawson], if he be well, to peruse the laws of public concernment, made this year or formerly, not published, and to take care that they be speedily printed and sent to the several towns of this jurisdiction ; and, in case of the secretary's sickness, to proceed without him, and that Mr. Danforth supply his place in all other cases."

At the May session in 1665 the General Court was greatly disturbed by the demands of the Royal Commissioners, Nicolls, Carr, Cartwright, and Maverick, who presented twenty-six changes which they desired to have made in the Book of the General Laws and Liberties of 1660. Their principal objects were to substitute for all expressions of the supremacy of the Commonwealth, an acknowledgment of the Royal authority; to procure a recognition of the Church of England, and to destroy the long-standing limitation of citizenship to church-members.

An examination of the edition of 1672 shows that only one or two points were conceded by the Court, either then or prior to that issue, and that the recognition of his majesty's supremacy was allowed in one clause whilst the power of the local authority was asserted in a score. The right of strangers to become citizens was nominally conceded, but on conditions which afforded the minimum of relief to all but church-members. See Code of 1672, p. 56.

October 11, 1665 (Records, iv. part 2, p. 282) : —

"This Court doth appoint Mr. Thomas Danforth, the Secretary [Rawson], and Mr. [Anthony] Stoddard, to survey the laws that have been made this year, of public concernment, and cause them forthwith, with such other not yet printed, to be printed."

October 19, 1666 (Records, iv. part 2, p. 330) : —

"Mr. Thomas Danforth, the Secretary [Rawson], and Capt. [Francis] Norton, are appointed a committee to peruse the laws of this year, and determine which of them shall be printed."

May 31, 1670 (Records, iv. part 2, p. 453) : —

"Whereas there is a great want of law books for the use of several Courts and inhabitants of this jurisdiction at present, and very few of them that are extant are complete, containing all laws now in force amongst us, it is therefore ordered by this Court, that Major Eliazer Lusher, Capt. Thomas Clarke, Capt. Edward Johnson, Capt. Hopestill Foster, Capt. George Corwin, and Capt. Joshua Hubbard, or any four of them whereof Maj. Lusher to be one, shall, and hereby are appointed to be a committee to, peruse all our laws now in force, to collect and draw up any literal errors, or misplacing of words or sentences therein, or any liberties infringed, and to make a convenient table for the ready finding of all things therein, that so they may be fitted for the press; and the same to present to the next session of this Court, to be further considered of and approved by the Court."

This committee seems to have attended to its duty, for at the next session, October 12, 1670, "the Court having perused and considered of the return of committee to whom the review of the laws was referred, etc., by the General Court in May last," proceeded to make a number of verbal changes, all of which will be found in the Records, iv. part 2, pp. 467-9. The following vote may be noted: —

"To some queries, whether, if at any time there appear contradictions betwixt laws or parts of laws, some being made formerly, some latter, shall the late law be accounted of force in all parts, and all laws or parts of laws formerly made be accounted null wherein they are contradicted by any latter law, though they be not repealed or not, — as instance in troopers fined by a former law 5 shillings, by a latter 10 shillings —. It is ordered by the Court that the latter stand."

A few days later, the following order, now preserved in Mass. Archives, vol. 58, p. 66, was passed by the House. It shows a wonderful ignorance of the undoubted fact that the Body of Liberties of 1641 had been thoroughly incorporated into the text of the printed laws, both in 1649 and 1660, while it also shows that there was a popular belief that such a Bill of Rights had existed. Probably the Magistrates refused their assent because they were better informed. It seems clear by the letter from Joseph Hills, dated May 24, 1682, hereinafter printed by me, that the Book of Liberties existed in a separate manuscript about 1648: —

"There being a new Impression of the Lawes shortly to be made, & that there was longe since a booke of libertyes agreed upon & confirmed as the undoubted right of the freemen of this Jurisdiction, the Deputies conceive It Necessary & have therefore Voted, that the s^d booke of liberties be printed together with the new Impression of Lawes but distinct & apart & to be set in the front of the s^d booke & that no law which shall hereafter be made shall interfere with or any way infringe or Contradict any of the s^d liberties upon any pretence whatsoever. The Deputies have past this desiringe the consent of o^r Hono^rd mgis^ts hereto. 27 (8) 1670.

WILLIAM TORREY, Cleric.

The Magis^ts consent not hereto.

EDWARD RAWSON, "Secret."

May 31, 1671 (Records, iv. part 2, p. 488) : —

"Mr. Richard Russell, Mr. Thomas Danforth, and Mr. William Stoughton, or any two of them, are appointed with Capt. Thomas Clarke and Capt. [William] Davis, to be a committee, and are empowered to cause the book of laws to be printed, and an exact table to be made thereto with a marginal note of the word 'Repealed' unto all laws that stand repealed; and the Treasurer is required to pay for the impression and dispose of the books, as to him shall seem expedient for the public good and advantage."

May 15, 1672 (Records, iv. part 2, p. 514) : —

"It is ordered that the former committee, with the Secretary, formerly appointed to send out the laws to the press, be hereby ordered to peruse the laws now this Court made, and to make a preface and table and what else is requisite, and send all out to be printed presently."

May 15, 1672, the following order was passed which has a certain connection with the preservation of the laws. (Records, iv. part 2, p. 515) : —

"The Court, in order to the further prosecution thereof, doe order, that Major William Hathorne and Major Eliazer Lusher make diligent enquiry in the several parts of this jurisdiction concerning any thing of moment that have past, and in particular of what hath been collected by Mr. John Winthrop, Senr, Mr. Thomas Dudley, Mr. John Wilson, Senr, Capt. Edward Johnson, or any other; that so, matter being **prepared**, some meet person may be appointed by this Court to put the same into form, that so, after perusal of the same, it may be put to press."

At the same date, an important order about printing was passed. (Records, iv. part 2, p. 527) : —

"In answer to the petition of John Usher, the Court judgeth it meet to order, and be it by this Court ordered and enacted, that no printer shall print any more copies than are agreed and paid for by the owner of the said copy or copies; nor shall he or any other, reprint or make sale of any of the same, without the said owner's consent, upon the forfeiture and penalty of treble the whole charges of printing and paper &c. of the whole quantity paid for by the owner of the copy, to the said owner or his assigns."

These extracts bring the matter up to the issue of the edition of 1672, already reprinted in *fac-simile* by the city of Boston. To complete the record I transcribe all the later references to be found in the Records, up to the overthrow of the First Charter in 1686, and the beginning of the Inter-Charter period under Andros.

May 7, 1673 (Records, iv. part 2, p. 559) : —

" Mr. John Usher having been at the sole charge of the impression of the book of laws, and presented the Governor, magistrates, secretary, as also every deputy, [*and*] the clerk of the deputies one, and Capt. Davis one, the Court judgeth it meet to order, that for at least this seven years, unless he shall have sold them all before that time, there shall be no other or further impression made by any person thereof, in this jurisdiction, under the penalty this Court shall see cause to lay on any that shall adventure in that kind, beside making full satisfaction to the said Mr. John Usher or his assigns, for his charge and damage therein. Voted by the whole Court met together."

October 15, 1673 (Records, iv. part 2, p. 562) : —

" It is ordered by this Court and the authority thereof, that all laws and orders of this Court which are thought fit to be published at the end of every sessions, shall be forthwith sent to the press and also read in the market-place at Boston upon the fifth day, being a lecture day, within ten days after the end of such sessions, which being performed, is and shall be accounted sufficient publication; and further, that printed copies shall be disposed at the discretion of the Treasurer, and care taken for the same by the secretary and marshal-general, as the law directs, folio 231."

October 24, 1674 (Records, v. p. 27) : —

" It is ordered, that Major Thomas Clarke and Mr. Humphrey Davy, with the secretary [Rawson], be a committee to peruse the acts of this Court, and determine what they judge meet to be printed."

May 28, 1679 (Records, v. p. 223) : —

" It having pleased the only wise God to remove by death our late honored Governor [Leverett], who, as we are informed, was at considerable charge for procuring a new seal, which is used with a screw, much more convenient than the hand seal, it is therefore ordered by this Court, that the

Treasurer of the country do treat with and purchase of the executrix of said late Governor, the said seal and screw, and deliver the same to our present honored Governor, [Bradstreet] and also receive of the said executrix the old seal, together with a duplicate of our patent lying now in her hand, which seal, duplicate and screw henceforward shall remain in the Governor's hand for the time being, for the use of the country."

It has been already shown, by the Reprint of the Revision of 1672, that the Secretary continued to issue consecutive pages annually of a supplement. After the lapse of some six years, however, the ever-attractive subject of a new codification was again mooted. October 15, 1679 (Records, v. 244), the following vote was passed: —

"Upon perusal of the result of the late Synod, wherein they seem to intimate, at least, as if there were some doubt concerning some of our laws, whether they were sufficiently warranted by the word of God, and other laws not so well worded as may be effectual to the end intended, or honorable to this Court; as also some may be wanting to the ends therein contained; it is therefore ordered, that the honored Thomas Danforth, esq., Deputy Governor, Joseph Dudley, esq., Capt. John Richards, Mr. Anthony Stoddard, and Capt. Daniel Fisher, be a committee to consider our laws already made, that may need emendation or may not so clearly be warranted from the word of God, and to draw up such laws and orders as, being presented by them at the next Court of Election, may then be considered, and upon mature deliberation be confirmed: which this present Court cannot have time to do."

May 19, 1680 (Records, v. 268), it was voted as follows: —

"On a motion made to this Court, for the reprinting of the laws, etc., the Court approves of the motion, and do order that William Stoughton, esq., Joseph Dudley, esq., Peter Bulkeley, esq., or any two of them, with Capt. Daniel Fisher, Mr. Anthony Stoddard, Capt. John Waite, Lieut. William Johnson and Capt. Elisha Hutchinson, or any three of them, be a committee to consider our laws already made, and that need emendation, and what else is necessary referring thereunto, together with his Majesty's letter, now under consideration, as it relates to this matter."

October 13, 1689 (Records, v. p. 294): —

"This Court having in May last appointed a committee for the revisal of our laws, and nothing of that nature being yet done, it is ordered by this Court, that the Committee formerly appointed for that work do effectually apply themselves to the same, and make return of what they do therein to the next Court of Election, and that the charges of this work be defrayed by the country Treasurer."

Under the same date (Records, v. p. 301): —

"Humphrey Davy, esq., John Richards, esq., Capt. Elisha Hutchinson appointed, with Edward Rawson, Secretary, a committee to peruse the acts of this Court and the Laws, and determine what to send out to the press."

January 4, 1680–81 (Records, v. 303): —

"Whereas, notwithstanding what hath already passed this Court, concerning the revisal and amendment of our laws, respecting such things as are objected against them from England, &c. yet nothing is effected, the effectual proceedings therein being no small part of the work of this Court respecting our agents to be sent to England, it is therefore ordered, that the remaining part of that committee, viz. Joseph Dudley and Peter Bulkley, esquires, Mr. Stoddard and Capt. Hutchinson, together with John Richards, esq. Mr. Joseph Cooke and Mr. Joseph Lynde, the senior magistrate appointing time and place, as a committee apply themselves to that work, and make return to the next adjournment of this session, any former order notwithstanding."

October 18, 1681 (Records, v. p. 331): —

"The Court agree to proceed to the consideration of what is necessary to be done touching such laws as are objected against, and others of like nature, and to do therein what shall be incumbent on them and most conducible to their peace and safety."

At this time a serious attempt was made to conciliate the king, by making alterations in the more objectionable laws of the colony. In May, 1681 (Records, v. 321–2), the Legislature amended some laws. At a session held February 16, 1681–2, the court passed a long and humble address to the king, and ordered that the Acts of Trade and Navigation should be published and observed. They established naval officers for Boston and Salem, and passed the following votes, March 17, 1681–2 (Records, v. 339): —

"It is ordered by this Court and the authority thereof, that the 12th section of the capital laws, title *Conspiracy, Rebellion,* and the 18th section of said laws, title *Rebellious Son,* be and are hereby repealed: also the law referring to *Christmas,* page 57, 58, and the word *Commonwealth,* where it imports jurisdiction, is hereby repealed, and the word *Jurisdiction* is hereby inserted."

"If any man conspire and attempt any invasion, insurrection or public rebellion against the King's majesty his government here established, or shall endeavor to surprise any town or towns, fort or forts therein, or shall treacherously and perfidiously attempt the alteration and subversion of our frame of polity or government fundamentally, he shall be put to death."

The following petition from Joseph Hills (Mass. Archives, Vol. 100, p. 282), contains some information not given in his earlier one (printed *ante*, p. 79). It was first published by Dr. George H. Moore, in the Historical Magazine for February, 1868, p. 81 : —

"To the Hon'ed Generall Court holden at Boston 24 May, 1682.

"The petition of Joseph Hills, humbly shewing, How it hath pleased the righteous God to lay upon y^r petitioner, a smart hand of visitation in the later part of his pilgrimage, totally bereaving him of the sight of his eyes, for more than 4 yeares now past, (besides sundry yeares dimnesse before) by meanes whereof he hath been utterly uncapable of getting or saving anything towards his necessary subsistence, being now also more than 80 yeares of age besides other infirmities of body, which long have and are like to accompany him to his grave.

"Your petitioner hath not been backward to his ability to be serviceable with his person & estate to the comon wealth : for besides other ordinary services, it pleased ye court to make him one of the county comitty to draw up some orders necessary for ye country in which service I went over all ye Statutes in Fulton at large, collected such as I deemed just & necessary, drew them up in a small book in folio, and transmitted them according to order to the grand comitty at boston, (viz) Mr. Winthrop, Mr. Ward & others, after this it pleased the court to appoint a comitty to draw up a body of lawes for the Colony, (viz) Mr. Winthrop & sundry others whereof your petitioner was one, to examine all ye Court records, from ye first to that time, which for avoyding of far greater charge, it being the worke but of one, fell to my lott to be active in, in which I went over ye 2 old bookes of recordes, ye book of libertyes, & ye greate booke then & since in ye handes of Mr. Rawson, which lawes I brought together under theyr proper heades coppy-wise, with exact markes of ye severall emendations one way or other made therein, which (after examination & approbation of ye Court) I was ordered to prepare for the presse, which I did, putting them together under theyr proper heads with ye dates of ye sundry lawes in the foot thereof, in the year 1648, in an alphabetical order, with an apt table for ye more ready recourse to each law :

"for which last service it pleased the court to make me some allowance, which was to my satisfaction, though short of the elaborate care, paines and time spent therein. these thinges I should not have touched upon, but that there are few of ye Court as now constituted, that had ye opportunity to have ye cognizance thereof.

"The premises considered, my petition is that I may be freed from all publick assessments, to ye country, county (and secular things for ye towne if it may be), for my infirme person and little estate now left, during the remaining part of my pilgrimage in this vale of teares.

"So with my dayly prayers to god, only wise Just & mercifull, to guide you in all your momentous concernments, I crave leave to subscribe my selfe

Your very humble servant

JOSEPH HILLS."

"In answer to this petition, the Mag'. judge meet that the petitioner bee freed from Country and County rates during his life, their B". the Deputyes hereto consenting.

P. BULKELEY, p. order.

June 1, 82

"Consented to by the Deputys

WILLIAM TORREY, Cleric."

The order as it stands under date of October 11, 1682, is as follows (Records, v. p. 377) : —

"In answer to the petition of Mr. Joseph Hills, bereaved of his sight for several years &c, the Court judgeth it meet to order that the petitioner be freed from country and county rates during his life."

October 11, 1682 (Records, v. p. 378) : —

"Whereas it hath been thought necessary and a duty incumbent on us, to take due notice of all occurrences and passages of God's providence towards the people of this jurisdiction since there first arrival in these parts, which may remain to posterity, at that the Reverend Mr. William Hubbard hath taken pains to compile a history of this nature, which the Court doth with thankfulness acknowledge; and as a manifestation thereof, do hereby order the Treasurer to pay unto him the sum of fifty pounds in money, he transcribing it fairly into a book, that it may be the more easily perused, in order to the satisfaction of this Court."

October 24, 1684 (Records, v. p. 464) : —

"It is ordered that Elisha Cook, Esq., Mr. Saffyn, and Mr. Fairweather with the Secretary, be a committee to peruse and fit the laws for the press, and to peruse the Address and the Court's letter to Mr. Humphreys."

(Mass. Archives, Vol. 47, No. 66.) "This Court considering that there is great need for to reprint the Laws in which there is a necessity for the Emendation of severall things: Do therefore think it meet that a Committee be chosen out of both Houses to consider of some expedient for the easing of what may be or hath been gravaminous for many yeares, and to make a report thereof to this Court upon Tuesday next att Eight o clock in the morning; and the Court to be adjourned in the meane while.

Voted by the Deputys the Honored Magistrates Consenting.

JOHN SAFFIN per Order.

Not consented to

EDWARD RAWSON Secret."

8 May, 85.

May 6, 1685 (Records, v. 473): —

"It is ordered, that John Richards, Samuel Nowell and Elisha Cooke, Esquires, with Mr. Oliver Purchase, Mr. John Saffin, Capt. John Smith, Capt. Richard Sprague, and Mr. Henry Bartholomew, shall and hereby are appointed a committee to revise the laws, and especially such as have been made since the last committee had the perusal and revisal of the body of them, and to make a return to the next Court of Election."[59]

May 27, 1685 (Records, v. p. 476): —

"It is ordered that the committee appointed at the last sessions of General Court, so called upon to make their report to the Court of their revising the laws, especially those more lately made, in order to their consideration at this Court, and that the work of revising the whole book of laws, passing, [perusing?] and preparing them for the press, be forthwith attended and set about."

"In obedience to the order of the honored General Court, dated 6th instant, empowering us a committee to revise the laws, especially those lately made, etc., — we accordingly have met and perused the said laws, and transferred them to their proper heads in the former transcript, where they will be found, sometimes wholly in their own words, sometimes in such necessary parts as were intended for alteration or explanation; which are either printed in said transcript in sheets, printed or written as there was occasion; to which we refer, reserving only the liberty of inserting the prefaces where reason may require.

JOHN RICHARDS, SAMUEL NOWELL, ELISHA COOKE, JOHN SAFFYN, RICHARD SPRAGUE."

Same date (Records, v. p. 479): —

"The Court went on, day by day, to revise and peruse the transcript of the laws."

"For greater expedition in the present revisal of the laws, this Court doth order that they shall be sent to the press sheet by sheet; and that the Treasurer make payment to the printer for the same, paper and work, June 10th, 1685: and that Elisha Cook and Samuel Sewall, Esquires, be desired to oversee the press about that work."[60]

---

[59] Sewall notes in his Diary (i. 71) that the committee was chosen "at the earnest suit of the deputies, which would have had them make a report of next Tuesday, but agreed to be next Election Court." As the Court met on Wednesday, May 6th, and dissolved on May 8th, the order to report even on Election Day, May 27th, did not afford much time. The report, however, according to the record, was called for as soon as the deputies had organized. — W. H. W.

[60] This entry is duplicated exactly under date of June 4, 1685 (Records, v. p. 484). — W. H. W.

It is somewhat surprising to find the foregoing references to a new revision of the Laws as being contemplated by the Legislature in 1681 and again in 1685, since there can be no doubt that the scheme utterly failed. The relations of the Colony to the English Government may, however, explain the mystery. The enemies of the Colony, especially Randolph, were exceedingly busy in their attacks upon the Charter. December 17, 1681, Randolph arrived with a letter from King Charles II., dated October 21, 1681, concluding as follows: "In default whereof, we are fully resolved in Trinity Term next ensuing, to direct our Attorney-General to bring a *quo warranto* in our Court of King's Bench, whereby our Charter granted unto you, with all the powers thereof, may be legally evicted and made void." (Palfrey, iii. 351.)

The General Court promptly assembled, altered some laws, prepared an address to the king, and notified him that the Colony had already sent Joseph Dudley and John Richards as agents to him. These agents arrived in London, August 20, 1682, but, hampered as they were by secret instructions, they were unable to accomplish anything. Randolph hastened home during the winter, and June 27, 1683, the writ of *quo warranto* was issued. He arrived in Boston with a copy of the writ, October 23, 1683, having been preceded by the agents by three days. The Legislature was convened on November 7, 1683, and the documents were presented to them. (Records, v. 421.) Their only action was to empower Mr. Robert Humphreys, of London, a barrister, to appear for them before the court.

Early in 1684, however, the Crown lawyers changed their plans and abandoned the *quo warranto*. Instead of this a *scire facias* against the Governor and Company of Massachusetts Bay was issued from the Court of Chancery, April 16, directed to the Sheriff of Middlesex, who made his return that he could not find the defendants, or anything belonging to them, within his bailiwick. May 12, a second writ was issued and the same return made. June 21, the Lord Keeper (North, Lord Guilford) made a decree vacating the Charter, suspending it, however, till the autumn term, to give time to the defendants to plead to issue.

Of course the Legislature of Massachusetts could not do this within the time, even had it been so inclined; and on October 23, 1684, the final judgment was entered, despite the motion for a stay of proceedings made by Mr. Humphreys. Palfrey (iii. 392-3) gives these facts and discusses the probable reasons why the Crown took this particular mode of cancelling the Charter.

Soon after this judgment, Charles II. died, and James II. succeeded to the throne, February 6, 1685. From the time that the news of both events reached Boston, the colonial government was of necessity known to be only provisional. Bradstreet and Danforth were chosen as Governor and Deputy-Governor, but the General Court transacted little important business. May 14, 1686, Randolph arrived with an exemplification of the judgment and commissions for a new government. There were to be a President, Deputy-President, and sixteen Councillors, and their authority extended over Massachusetts, New Hampshire, Maine, and the King's Province. Joseph Dudley was made President and William Stoughton, Deputy. On May 20, 1686, the General Court dissolved.

Finally, on December 20, 1686, Sir Edmund Andros arrived at Boston with a commission to govern all New England, and the Colonial period of Massachusetts was at an end.

In view of the political troubles in 1685, as hereinbefore recited, it seems impossible that any progress can have been made in printing a revisal of the whole code of laws. Samuel Sewall was one of the committee appointed in May, 1685, to oversee the printing; but his Diary says nothing about any work done. He makes certain entries, however, which may throw light on the abandonment of the scheme. Thus he writes, June 20, 1685, (Diary i., 83) that the Court adjourned till July 7, on a dispute between the branches as to the proviso to the title " Courts", section 2, of the Laws of 1672. Later on, he records very decided disputes between the branches as to what course should be pursued, now that the Charter was cancelled, in case Col. Kirke or any one else should arrive with a commission to be Governor.

Although the formal record of the Legislature as printed gives no light upon the matter of a new edition of the Laws in 1685, the Archives fortunately contain certain votes which failed between the branches and which fully explain it. They are preserved in Volume 47, title Laws.

As we have seen, the out-going Legislature on May 16 appointed a committee to revise the laws, and the new Legislature meeting May 17 promptly called for and received a report.

The following vote does not appear on the record, although it is of much interest as showing what was contemplated: —

(Mass. Archives. Vol. 47, No. 73.) "The Magistrates have voted that there be eight hundred copies of the Lawes printed for the Country's use (and that no more be printed under the penalty of 5ˢ for each book) the said eight hundred to be delivered to the Treasurer. The Magistrates have past this, their brethren the deputys hereto consenting.

13 June 1685   EDWARD RAWSON Secret.
Consented unto by the Deputys

JNO. SAFFIN per Order."

The temper of the branches was evidently very irritable. The next two votes failed to meet their joint approval, though the matter of the Preface was only the pretext, as will appear later.

(Mass. Archives, Vol. 47, No. 75.) "The Deputyes Consent that a suitable preface be drawn up and agreed upon to be Printed together with the lawes when the whole body of them are fully Revised and Considered of, and such as this Court doe not see meet to Repeale be transcribed and fitted for the press, as is understood to be the Intent and Agreement of this Court.

Voted by the Deputys the honored Magistrates Consenting

June 18, 1685   JNO. SAFFIN per Order
not consented to by the Magistrates

EDWARD RAWSON, Secret."

(Mass. Archives, Vol. 47, No. 76.) "The Magistrates consent not hereto, and do therefore desire that a suteable preface may be drawn up for the printing of those wherein wee have agreed, and that all further agitation concerning those wherein wee can't agree be forborn at present.

The Magistrates have past this, their brethren the deputys thereto consenting.

18th of June, 1685   EDWARD RAWSON Secret.
The Deputys Consent not
18 June 1685   JNO. SAFFIN, per Order"

(Mass. Archives, Vol. 47, No. 77.) "The Deputys Consent not to the repealing of the proviso in the Latter end of the second section of the Law title Courts, nor any part of that section unless our honnoured Magistrates please to Consent with them in passing of this bill annexed, and then the said Proviso to bee repealed.

The Deputys have past this, our honnoured Magistrats heerto consenting.

June the 19th, 1685   Richard Sprague per Order
8 July 1685   not consented to by the Magistrates

EDWᴅ. RAWSON, Secret."

Sewall, who was deeply interested and in a position to know, records as follows, in his Diary, i. 83: —

"Satterday, June 20th, 1685.[61] The Court not agreeing about the Proviso in the end of the 2¹ Section of the Law, title 'Courts,' adjourns till Tuesday, July 7th, except Occasions be, and then the Governour is to call them sooner. The final difference between the Magistrates and Deputies is: The Governour and several with him would Repeal the Proviso, letting the rest of

---

[61] This matter of the Proviso to the Law about Courts had long been in dispute between the branches. I have already (ante, p. 89, foot-note 44) mentioned it, but a fuller account may be needed. The papers preserved in Vol. 48 of Mass. Archives show what was done in 1672. Without going into small details of errors and corrections in old laws, it seems that in 1652 (Rec. iv. part 1, p. 82) it was decided that when the branches differed in any case of judicature, whether civil or criminal, such case should be determined by the major part of the whole court. This was reënacted as a proviso in the code of 1660, the verbal change being, "shall be determined by the major vote of the whole Court met together."

This citation, together with the matters therein referred to, shows that in the *first* printed Book of Laws (*i. e.* Code of 1649), the law of 1644 was placed. The marginal note to this paper (cited *ante*, p. 110) shows that the law was on p. 13 of that edition; that the laws of 1648 and 1649 were in the *second* printed book, folio 8: and the law of 1652 was in the third printed book, fol. 11.

The vote in 1652 (Records, iv. part 1, p. 82) reads thus: "Whereas there is a manifest and inconvenient mistake in the penning of the order, title General Court, page the 8th of the last printed book, that leaves all or most of the cases formerly issued in the General Court doubtful and uncertain, and takes away the negative vote, both of Magistrates and Deputies, in making laws, as well as in cases of judicature, which was not intended, much less consented to, it is therefore ordered, that for time to come, if there fall out any difference betwixt the Magistrates and the Deputies, in any case of judicature, either civil or criminal, it shall be determined by the major part of the whole Court, and the forementioned law is hereby repealed."

It seems clear that in the second printed book, which was the first Supplement to the Code of 1649, some error had happened in transcribing the laws of 1648, 1649, on this topic. I find nothing relative thereto in the laws of 1648, unless it be the order about the records, already printed, (*ante*, p. 78): but in 1649, the following law was passed; October 17, 1649, (Records, ii. p. 285). "It is ordered, that in cases wherein there hath been difference, the next General Court should hear the case together and determine the case by the major vote."

We must also note the following curious entry under date of October 18, 1650 (Records, iv. part 1, p. 55).

"It is ordered, that the interpretation of the law 283, concerning the greater part of the Magistrates and the greater part of the Deputies, are to be understood of the greatest number of those that are present and vote."

The reference to law 283 takes us back to the order so numbered in the margin, which is dated March 3, 1635-6 (Records, i. p. 169-170), which reads . . . . "And whereas it may fall out that in some of the General Courts, to be holden by the magistrates and deputies, there may arise some difference of judgment in doubtful cases, it is therefore ordered, that no law, order or sentence shall pass as an act of the Court, without the consent of the greater part of the magistrates on the one part and the greater number of the deputies on the other part; and for want of such accord, the cause or order shall be suspended, and if either party think it so material, there shall be forthwith a committee chosen, the one half by the magistrates, and the other half by the deputies, and the committee so chosen to elect an umpire, who together shall have power to hear and determine the cause in question."

This citation by the Magistrates of the law of 1644, which was in the *first* printed Book of the Laws (*i. e.* Code of 1649) seems to refer to the vote of March 7, 1643-4 (Records, ii. 58) which is as follows: —

"Forasmuch, as, after long experience, we find divers inconveniences in the manner of proceeding in Courts by magistrates and deputies sitting together, and accounting it wisdom to

the Law stand as it does; the Deputies have voted the Repeal of the Proviso, and withall that the Remainder of the Law have this alteration, viz.: instead of 'greater part of the Magistrates'—'greater number of the Magistrates present'—: so to make the law new, as it might be construed contrary to the Charter. The Governour, Mr. Stoughton, Dudley, and several others would not consent."

The Legislature met on July 7 and adjourned on the 10th. It met again July 21 and adjourned on the 24th; having received

---

follow the laudable practice of other states who have laid groundworks for government and order in the issuing of business of greatest and highest consequence.—
"It is therefore ordered, first, that the magistrates may sit and act business by themselves, by drawing up bills and orders, which they shall see good in their wisdom, which having agreed upon, they may present them to the deputies to be considered of, how good and wholesome such orders are for the country, and accordingly to give their assent or dissent; the deputies in like manner sitting apart by themselves and consulting about such orders and laws as they in their experience shall find meet for common good, which agreed upon by them, they may present to the magistrates, who, according to their wisdom, having seriously considered of them, may consent unto them or disallow them; and when any orders have passed the approbation of both magistrates and deputies, then such orders to be engrossed, and in the last day of the Court to be read deliberately, and full assent to be given: provided also, that all matters of judicature which this Court shall take cognizance of, shall be issued in like manner."

It seems inexplicable that in 1650 the Legislature should be amending a law of 1635, when a totally different law had been passed in 1644, put into the Code of 1649, and clearly established. All that later portion of the law of 1635, which provides in case of a disagreement, for committees and an umpire, must have been superseded, if indeed it ever was in force. PALFREY, (I. 617–622) treats at large of this vote of 1644, which provided for the first time that the two houses should sit separately. The contest beginning in 1636 with Mrs. Sherman's pig, had at last involved the whole frame of government, and especially what was called the negative vote of the magistrates. The outcome as Palfrey says was that "the negative vote was not taken away but duplicated;" each branch had a negative upon the acts of the other.

Yet he does not seem to explain this vote of 1650, though he cites the vote of 1652. A careful perusal of § 2, title *Courts*, Code of 1660, seems to make it clear that the Code fairly expresses the intent of the laws of 1644, 1649 and 1652.

The marginal citation in 1660 are *Liber* 1, pp. 16 and 36, and *Anno* 52, p. 11. We may surmise therefore that Liber 1, (the code of 1649) contained the law of 1644. The Supplement undertook to quote the law of 1649; and if it repeated faithfully the words of that act that "in *cases* where there hath been difference, the next General Court should hear the case *together*,"—it would indeed as said in 1652 "take away the negative vote both of magistrates and deputies, *in making laws* as well as in *cases* of judicature"—since the words "cases where there hath been difference" would apply to all joint legislative acts as well as to appeals. Hence in 1652, the act of 1649 is amended by the provision that differences in regard to cases of judicature *only*, were to be settled in joint convention.

The law of 1660 represents the practice therefore from 1652, and in 1672 the same section and proviso were re-enacted.

But this method of forcing an agreement was very disagreeable to the magistrates who fought against it in 1672 and 1673, reluctantly yielding the point at last, though their powers were thereby greatly curtailed. From the numerous messages between the branches at that time I make the following citation from one drawn by the Magistrates, as it seems to state their views most thoroughly. It is in Vol. 48, No. 114:—

"The present question — which is not concerning the power and authority of the General Court, consisting of Magistrates and Deputies, or whether that Court hath not the ultimate determination of all cases and causes proper to their cognizance. But whether the freemen or their delegates (which we acknowledge) may by their greater number over-rule the conclusion the advice of the elders of the several towns, as requested by vote (Records, v. p. 492). Sewall says that thirty-one ministers met at Boston and their opinion was that "the Government ought not to give way to another till the Generall Court had seen and judged of the Commission: so should be called if not sitting at the Arrival of a Commissioned Governor." The Court re-assembled August 12 and adjourned the same day to September 16, when it was ordered that the session be ended and a second session be called for October 14. After a short session it adjourned October 22 (Sewall, i. 101) to November 17, sat one day then, and adjourned to February 16, 1685–6. Sewall adds that in case orders came from England the Secretary or the Treasurer was "to send forthwith to the Members of the Court, and to such others as Freemen may chuse, to convene two days after the Date of such Signification, to which time the Court is adjourned in such case."

and finally determine any and every case without the consent and against the judgment of any of the magistrates, or whether the consent of some of the magistrates with the deputies be not absolutely necessary to make any valid act in the General Court. The magistrates affirme this latter to be the plaine literal sense and true meaning of the patent, the foundation of our Government, consonant to right reason and the best security of the people's, especially the freemen's, liberties.'

" 'That branch of the law made in [16]52, if it may be called a regulation or irregulation or direction of the manner and way of issuing causes of judicature in cases, which did (doubtless through inadvertency) repeale the order of [16]44 which concludes another manner of determining all causes in the General Court, and is in the first printed book of lawes. But the General Court nor their manner of proceeding is constituted by the order of [16]52 upon which the deputies insist, there being General Courts in act for 20 yeares before." &c &c

Little of this controversy in 1672 is to be found on the records of the General Court of course, as the various votes failed to receive joint assent. I find however an order dated May 15, 1672 (Records, iv. part 2, p. 516) as follows: " It is declared by the Court that they will attend the hearing of any case that is orderly depending and under the cognizance of this Court, provided that the directions given by the patent for the determination and issue thereof be attended."

May 7, 1673. (Rec. iv. part 2, p. 559), a committee, consisting of Samuel Symonds, Simon Bradstreet, William Stoughton, John Oxenbridge, Uriah Oakes, Joshua Hobart, John Richards, Henry Bartholomew, John Hull, and Samuel Torrey was appointed to consider whether by the Charter there was a negative in any part of the General Court. This seems to be three magistrates, two clergymen, and five deputies, including their clerk. The report dated Sept. 1, 1673, is in the Archives, Vol. 48, No. 125. It seems that eight members were present, and three did not vote. The report against there being such a negative power in either branch is signed by Symonds, Oxenbridge, Bartholomew, Hobart, and Richards. It does not appear to have been accepted, but the papers are voluminous, and quite worthy of being put in print. The question involved is, of course, the same as we are considering, viz., whether the Charter allowed a convention of the whole court, wherein all of the eighteen magistrates might be of one opinion and yet be overpowered by the numerical superiority of the forty or more deputies.

As we have seen, in 1672, the Magistrates raised the ingenious idea whether one at least of their number must not be on the side of the majority, and that suggestion deservedly failed. Now, in 1685, following out the same idea which had animated the magistrates from the start, they desired to do away the joint convention plan and obtain an absolute veto. In 1672, they claimed that their idea was " the plain literal sense and true meaning of the patent." In 1685 (post, p. 136) they demanded that the law be repealed and that " all things of that or the like nature shall be issued and determined as the patent directs," which would have given them the victory.

We have seen that the matter was unsettled at the adjournment in June, 1685, and the fight was at once renewed in July. On the 8th of that month the magistrates rejected the order then pending. The next two papers show the result of the four days' session, July 7, 10: —

(Mass. Archives, Vol. 47, No. 79.) "As a fynall Conclusion and determination of the question that hath bene soe long in debate, It is hereby ordered and inacted that the second section of the law tytle Courts be and is hereby repealed soe farr as it relates to the way and manner of yssueing and determining all things in the generall Court as the makeing of lawes and decrees &c, and that hereafter all things of that or the like nature shalbe yssued and determined as the Pattent directs.

The Magistrates have past this their brethren the Deputys hereto consenting

    8 July 1685   EDWARD RAWSON Secret.

And if our Brethren the Deputyes do not see cause hereto to consent wee desire a speedy end may be putt to this Court."

(Mass. Archives, Vol. 47, No. 80.) " Boston July 9, 1685. The Magistrates doe order that there be a present stopp to the printing of the Lawes till farther order ; our brethren the Deputies hereunto consenting.

                                                   JA. RUSSELL pr Order."

" The Deputys Consent not hereto ; but since so much time and payns hath been already Expended in Reviseing of the lawes and proceeding so farr in the press with them, Desire that all such lawes as are not agreed upon by the vote of this Court to be Repealed, with those which have been amended or altered by Consent of both houses, be carried on to a full impression

    July 9, 1685   JOHN SAFFIN per order

Not consented to by the Magistrates

                                                   EDWARD RAWSON, Secret."

We have thus arrived to one certain fact. The magistrates had ordered the printing of the laws to be stopped, and the printer doubtless obeyed. When the Court reassembled, Sept. 16, 1685, the following ineffectual order was introduced: —

(Mass. Archives, Vol. 47, No. 81.) " The Deputies beinge informed that there is a present stop in the presse about the Lawes, having bin ordered thither by this Court, and of the expectation of this house and generallytie of the Freemen being that they would ere this time have bin finished, Doe judge meete to order, that, that worke be forthwith proceeded in, to the perfecting of that Impression. And those Gentlemen appoynted and desired to oversee the press be ordered to take all due care thereof, desiring the consent of our honored magistrates herein

    17 Sept. 1685   WILLIAM TORREY, Cleric.

Not consented to by the Magistrates

                                                   EDWARD RAWSON, Secret."

Introduction. 137

On October 14, 1685, the Legislature met again, and the deputies renewed their attack, as follows: —

(Mass. Archives, Vol. 47, No. 84.) "The Deputys having once and again pressed the prosecution of the printing of the Lawes, and understanding there is a stopp in the progresse of that work, they haveing bin sent to the press by order of the whole Court, there being great expectation of the Freemen and others throughout the Jurisdiction of a new Impression thereof to come forth, — doe again manifest their desires that they may be proceeded in to a full Issue, according to our former Votes, sent up the 9th of July last; desiring our honored Magistrates' consent hereto.

16th. 8th. 1685   WILLIAM TORREY, Cleric.
Not consented to by the Magistrates
                                               EDWARD RAWSON, Secret."

Finally, Sewall writes under date of Saturday, October 17: "Court adjourned till Tuesday morning next, partly because of the designed Training. Before adjournment, the Deputies sent down a smart Bill alleging that they were no blamable cause of the Laws not being printed."

This "smart bill" was not entered on the full record, of course, and therefore is not to be found in the printed volume. Fortunately the document is preserved in the State Archives, Vol. 47, No. 82, subject, "Laws." It is as follows: —

"The Deputys, understanding that it is imputed to them that there is a stop in the going forwards with the impression of the Lawes through theire default in denying to Consent to the determining of maters according to our Charter, hold themselves bound for theire owne vindication to Signifie they ar wholy ignorant that ever they have soe declared themselves by any vote or otherwise; but as they alwais have, soe still doe, Manifest theire redyness to Attend the same, soe far forth as they have understood, and as was judged and practised by theire Judicious predecessors, many of them the first patentees, and still desire the procedure to the full impression of the Lawes according to former vote of ye whole Court.

17th October 1685   the deputies have past this with reference to the consent of our honored Magestrats for a proscedur.

                                       SAMUELL TOMPSON per order

Not consented to by ye Magists.
                                               EDW. RAWSON Scert."

As I no longer hold the opinion expressed in my former Introduction, that the matter in dispute was trivial and obscure, it may be added that the principle for which the Magistrates contended has since triumphed. Under the Second Charter each body in practice was independent of the other. In the Constitution of the Commonwealth, the Senate and House have a negative each on the other; the same rule prevails in Congress: and such seems now to be the accepted plan for all legislative bodies composed of two branches.

However, our interest at present is confined to the effect which this dispute had upon the projected issue of a new code of laws.

It may be safely concluded that very little progress had been made towards printing the new revision up to the adjournment in October, 1685, that the two branches were at a stand, with considerable personal feeling evinced; and that, with the well-known disinclination of the magistrates to take any responsibility in the unsettled state of the government, the disagreement between the branches afforded a sufficient pretext for abandoning the project.

We may, therefore, probably conclude that the various Supplements to the Code of 1672, as already reprinted from the Hutchinson copy, contain all the official publications of the Colonial Laws of a general nature, except Tax and Excise Acts, prior to the dissolution of the First Charter government.

In conclusion, I have to ask the reader of this Introduction to pardon its length, urging the apparent necessity of bringing into one collection all available facts in regard to the method adopted by our ancestors in preparing and publishing those general laws which are still, in part, in force in this Commonwealth.

As to the whole book, I hope I may apply the words of Judge Sewall, when sending to a friend a copy of the Statutes at Large for 1684, "You will find much pleasant and profitable Reading in it."

WILLIAM H. WHITMORE.

CITY HALL, BOSTON, October, 1890.

INDEX

TO THE

INTRODUCTION TO THE COLONIAL LAWS.

A

ALLEN, JOHN
  appointed from Middlesex county, 1645, on commission to draft body of laws . . . 73
  on committee, 1650, to revise maritime laws . 115
ANCIENT CHARTERS AND LAWS
  published by the State in 1812 . . v
  instance of omission in (*note*) . . vi
ANDROS, SIR EDMUND
  arrives, 1686, with commission to govern all New England . . 131
ANTIQUARIAN SOCIETY
  American, at Worcester, Rawson's copy of laws of 1660 preserved in . 120
  essay in Proceedings of, on Cambridge press 83
ARMY
  laws for the well-ordering of, sergeant-major-general and council war of authorized to make and execute . 72
ASPINWALL, COL. THOMAS
  owner of Lechford's copy of Records of General Court . . . vii
  bought in England . . xiii, xiv
ASPINWALL, WILLIAM
  Cotton's pamphlet reprinted by, in London, 1655 12
  adoption of, disclaimed by . 12

ASSISTANTS
  chosen under provisions of charter of 1629 2
  court of, extent of powers exercised by 3, 99
  empowered to make laws and choose officers . . 3
  Records of, published by State vi
    1641–1644, contained in Lechford's copy . x, xiii
  powers of, in divorce cases . . 99–101
ATHENÆUM, BOSTON (see BOSTON ATHENÆUM).
AUDITOR GENERAL (see DUNCAN, NATHANIEL).
  appointed on committee, 1647, to perfect draft of laws . . 75
  1647, to prepare laws for press 76
  1648, to examine laws in press . . . 77
  to insert amendment, to receive one copy of the book of laws, without price, 79
  1649, to prepare supplement of 1650 . . . 104
  1650, to revise maritime laws 115

B

BACHELER, MARY
  divorce 100
BARLOW, SAMUEL L. M.
  owner of Lechford's copy of Records of General Court . . . vii
BARTHOLOMEW, HENRY
  appointed, 1685, to revise body of laws 129
BATCHELOR, JOSEPH
  appointed, 1644, to examine Bellingham's revision of laws . . 72
BELLINGHAM, RICHARD
  share of, in preparation of Body of Liberties 18
  deputed, 1635, to make draft of laws . . . 4, 5
  1637, to make codification, to examine laws . 8
  1642, to revise orders of court for publication . 71
  1644, examination of book of laws presented by . 72

BELLINGHAM, RICHARD, continued.
  deputed, 1645, from Essex county, on commission to draft body of laws . . . 73
  1646, on sub-committee, examine draft of body of laws . . 74, 75, 80
  1647, to prepare laws for the press . . . 76
  1649, to prepare supplement of 1650 . 104
  to arrange for printing, 104
  1650, to revise maritime laws, 115
  1652, to serve in court of election . . viii
  to select laws to go to the towns . 116
  1653, to examine laws . 116
  1656, to revise laws for publication . . 117
  probably the chief incitor of the revision of 1649 . . . 120

BODY OF LIBERTIES (see LIBER-
    TIES, BODY OF).
BOOKS
  of laws (see LAWS, PUBLICATION).
  list of, ordered for use of court,
    1647, in making laws 76
BOSTON
  sends deputies to general court, 1634, 3
  deputies of 1639 to prepare code of
    laws 7
  1642 to revise orders of
    court for publication . 71
  commissioners for Suffolk, to pre-
    pare draft of laws, to meet at . 73
  Shaw's History of, citation from . 96, 97
  titles of code of 1649 cited in records
    of selectmen 97
BOSTON ATHENÆUM
  manuscript copy of Body of Liberties
    preserved in 10
  William S. Shaw, librarian of . . 10

BOSTON PUBLIC LIBRARY
  now owns Lechford's copy of Records
    of General Court . . . vii, xvii
  Thorowgood's "Jewes in America"
    to be found in 93
BRADSTREET, THOMAS
  appointed, 1645, from Essex county,
    on commission to draft body of laws, 73
  governor, chosen, 1685 . . . 131
    seal of colony and dupli-
    cate of patent placed in
    hands of 124
BRIDGES, CAPT. ROBERT
  MS. records, 1644, in handwriting of, xi
BROOKE, THOMAS
  appointed, 1644, to examine Belling-
    ham's revision of laws . . . 72
BULKELEY, PETER
  deputed, 1637, to revise drafts of laws
    presented from the towns, 6
    1680, to revise laws . 125, 126

C

CAMBRIDGE
  commissioners for Middlesex, to
    prepare draft of laws, to meet at . 73
  code of 1649 printed at . . . 83
CAPITAL LAWS (see LAWS, CAPITAL).
CHARLESTOWN
  sends deputies to general court, 1634, 4
  deputies of 1639, to prepare code of
    laws 7
  Joseph Hill, member of house for . 79
CHARTER
  ancient (see ANCIENT CHARTERS).
  of March 4, 1629, provisions of . 2
  attacks upon, by Randolph . . 130
  cancellation of 130
CHICKERING, FRANCIS
  appointed, 1644, to examine Belling-
    ham's revision of laws . . . 72
CHRISTMAS
  law in relation to, repealed, 1681 . 126
CLARKE, DENNIS AND ANNE
  divorce 99
CLARKE, CAPTAIN THOMAS
  appointed, 1654, 1656, to revise laws
    of current session . 117
  1664, 1670, to prepare
    laws for publication 121, 122
  1671, to cause book of
    laws to be printed . 123
  1674, to determine what
    acts of general court
    shall be printed . . 124
  chiefly concerned in arranging the
    revision of 1660 120
CLEMENTS, WILLIAM
  divorce 100
CLERK
  of deputies, office established and
    duties prescribed, 1648 . . . 78
COBBET, THOMAS
  citation from his "Civil Magistrates
    Power," etc. 96
COMMISSIONERS, ROYAL
  changes in code of 1660 demanded by 121
COMMON LAW
  of England, compared with the Body
    of Liberties 17
COMMONWEALTH
  word "jurisdiction" substituted for,
    1681 126

COMPANY OF THE MASSACHU-
    SETTS BAY
  records of, previous to removal to
    New England vii
CONNECTICUT
  code of laws of, modelled on Body
    of Liberties and revisions of
    1649 and 1660 . . . 86
  correspondences with Mass.
    code of 1649 (note) . 87, 88, 89
CONSPIRACY
  law in relation to, repealed, 1681 . 126
COOKE, CAPT. GEORGE
  appointed from Middlesex county,
    1645, on commission to draft body
    of laws 73
COOKE, ELISHA
  appointed, 1684, to prepare laws for
    press 128
  reports, 1685, a revised draft . . 129
  requested, 1685, to oversee printing
    of revised body of laws . . 129
COOKE, JOSEPH
  appointed, 1680, to revise laws . 126
CORWIN, CAPT. GEORGE
  appointed, 1670, to prepare laws for
    publication 122
COTTON, REV. JOHN
  author of pamphlet erroneously cited
    as Body of Lib-
    erties . . . 1
    published anony-
    mously in Lon-
    don, 1641 . 12
    reprinted by Wil-
    liam Aspin-
    wall, 1655 . 12
    by Gov. Hutch-
    inson . 11
  requested, 1636, to make draft of
    "fundamentals" 5
  unfounded claim to be author of
    Body of Liberties discussed . 12–20
  compilation by, presented to general
    court 6, 7
  no action taken 6
  appointed from Suffolk county, 1645,
    on commission to draft body of
    laws 73
COUNCIL OF WAR (see WAR).

COURT OF ASSISTANTS (see As-
    SISTANTS, COURT OF).
COURTS
    as to powers of (*note*) . . . 99
    Essex county, citations of code of
        1649 in files of 100
    Middlesex county, citations from
        code of 1649 in files of . . 102
    Suffolk county, citation of code of
        1649 in files of 98
COURT, GREAT AND GENERAL
    Records of, published by State . vi
        Lechford's copy now in
            Boston Public Library . vii
    under charter of 1629, composition,
        times of meeting, authority of . 2
    confers upon governor and assistants
        the power of making laws, etc. . 3
    sole authority in itself to make laws,
        etc., voted 4
    system of election, sessions, etc.,
        established, 1634 4
    only two sessions annually, May and
        October 5

D

DANE, NATHAN
    appointed, 1812, on committee to
        prepare for publication "Ancient
        Charters and General Laws" . v
DANFORTH, THOMAS
    appointed, 1658, to oversee printing
        of laws 118
        compensation 119
    ordered to make an index to revision
        of 1660 119
    appointed, 1664-5-6, to prepare laws
        for publication . 121, 123
        1671, to cause the book of
            laws to be printed . . 123
        1679, to revise laws . . 125
    chosen deputy governor . . 131
DAVIS, A. M.
    essay on subject of printing press at
        Cambridge 83, 85
DAVIS, CAPT. WILLIAM
    appointed to see revision of 1672
        through the press . . . 123
DAVY, HUMPHREY
    appointed, 1674, to determine what
        acts of general court
        shall be printed . . . 124
        1680, to revise laws . . 126
DAY, STEVEN
    work done by, on printing press at
        Cambridge 84
DEAN, JOHN WARD
    memoir of Rev. Nathaniel Ward, by . 18
DENISON, MAJ.-GEN. DANIEL
    1654, to edit laws for publication . 116
    1658, to revise and report to general
        court 118
    to make alterations in preface
        to laws 82
    chiefly concerned in production of
        revision of 1660 . . . 120
    notice of (*note*) 120
DIVORCE
    early decrees of . . . 99-101
DORCHESTER
    sends deputies to general court, 1634, 4
DOVER
    twenty copies of revision of 1660
        allotted to 119

COURT, GREAT AND GENERAL,
    continued.
    commission appointed by, to frame
        a body of grounds of laws,
        1635 . . . . . 4, 5
    to revise drafts of laws presented
        from the towns, 1637 . . 6
    to draw up a code, 1639 . . 7
    Ward's code adopted by . . 9
    legislation by, 1641 to 1672 . . 71
    authorizes publication of code of
        1649 82
    each member to receive one copy of
        revision of 1649 without price . 79
    distribution of copies of revision of
        1660 among 119
    order of, 1682, exempting Joseph
        Hills from taxation . . 128
    prepares address to the king, 1682 . 130
    disagreement between the branches
        as to what shall constitute a ma-
        jority vote . . . 131, 133
COWLEY, CHARLES
    pamphlet, "Our Divorce Courts" . 99

DOWNING, MR.
    authorized to get copies of laws and
        liberties, etc. 9
DUDLEY, JOSEPH
    appointed, 1679, 1680, to revise laws,
        125, 126
    sent to the king, 1682, as agent of
        colony 130
    made president, 1686, under commis-
        sion of James II. . . . 131
DUDLEY, THOMAS
    deputed, 1635, to make a draft of
        laws 4, 5
        1639, to prepare a code . . 7
    share of, in preparation of Body of
        Liberties 18
    appointed to revise Body of Liberties,
        1643 71
    sergeant-major-general, 1644, em-
        powered to make laws for the well-
        ordering of the army . . 72
    appointed from Suffolk county, 1645,
        to draft body of laws . . 73
DUNCAN, LIEUT. NATHANIEL
    (Auditor-General, 1645-1657).
    appointed from Suffolk county, 1645,
        on commission to draft
        body of laws 73
        1646, on sub-committee to
            examine draft of body of
            laws 74, 75
        1647, on committee to pre-
            pare laws for the press . 76
        1648, to examine laws in
            press 77
        1649, to prepare supple-
            ment of 1650 104
        1650, to revise maritime
            laws 115
DUNSTER, HENRY
    president of Harvard college, 1640-
        1654 84
    marriage to widow of Josse Glover . 83
    ownership of printing-press . . 84
    presented, 1654, for disturbing
        church service 102
    directed to print the laws . . 116
    other publications by . . . 84

E

EASTOWE, WILLIAM
  appointed, 1644, to examine Bellingham's revision of laws . . . 72
ELDERS
  answer of, to questions submitted, 1644, by general court . . 72
ENDICOTT, JOHN
  owner of Lechford's copy of records . ix, x
  deputy, authorized to get copies of laws and liberties, etc. . . . 9

ENDICOTT, JOHN, continued.
  governor, appointed, 1654, to revise laws of current session . . . 116
  authorized, 1658, to make alterations in preface to laws . . . 82, 118
  new seal and press provided by . 124
ESSEX COUNTY
  commissioners appointed from, 1645, to draft body of laws . . 73
  citations from code of 1649, in court files of 100

F

FAIRWEATHER, MR.
  appointed, 1684, to prepare laws for press . . . 128
FINES
  imposed by court of assistants . . 3
FIRST BOOK OF THE LAWS (see LAWS).
FISHER, CAPT. DANIEL
  appointed, 1679, 1680, to revise laws 125
FORCE'S TRACTS
  Cotton's pamphlet reprinted in, 1844 1
FOSTER, CAPT. HOPESTILL
  appointed, 1670, to prepare laws for publication 122
FREEMAN, SAMUEL
  divorce 99, 100
FREEMAN'S OATH, THE
  issued from press at Cambridge . 84

FREEMEN
  sole power to choose and admit, vested in general court . . 4
  admission by inferior courts . . 25
  powers of, to be exercised by deputies chosen to general court . . 4
FRYAR, ELIZABETH
  divorce case 99
FUNDAMENTALS
  draft of, commission appointed to prepare 5
  presented to general court, 1636 6
  freemen to collect and present to governor, 1637 . . 6
  commission appointed to codify, 1639 . . . 7
  compared with Magna Charta . . 16
    with common laws of England . . . 17
  fac-simile pages 66

G

GENERAL COURT (see COURT, GREAT AND GENERAL).
GLOVER, JOHN
  appointed, 1645, substitute in place of Mr. Prichard on commission to draft body of laws . . 73
  1652, to serve in court of election . . . viii
  1652, to select laws to go to the towns . . . 116
  1653, to examine laws . . 116
GLOVER, JOSSE
  printing-press given by . . 83
GOODELL, ABNER C.
  editor of General Laws of the Province 6
GOOKING, CAPT.
  Treasurer, to determine price of volumes of laws of 1660 . . 119
GOVERNOR
  provided for in charter of 1629 . 2
  with deputy and assistants, empowered to make laws, etc. . . 3
  to summon general court four times a year 4
  deputed, 1635, to make a draft of laws 4, 5

GOVERNOR, continued.
  deputed, 1637-39, to revise and codify models of laws presented by the freemen 6, 7
  1643, to revise orders of court, 1642, and Body of Liberties . . . 71
  1645, from Suffolk county on commission to draft body of laws . . . 73
  1646, on committee to perfect draft of body of laws 75
  1647, on committee to prepare laws for the press . 76
  1654, to revise laws of current session . . 117
  seal, duplicate of patent, etc., to remain in hands of . . . 125
GRAY, FRANCIS CALLEY
  discovers and prints, 1843, Body of Liberties xvi
GREEN, SAMUEL
  work done by on printing-press at Cambridge 84
  order for Treasurer, 1659, to pay for printing laws (note) . . 117, 118

H

HALL, JOHN AND DORCAS
   divorce 100
HALSALL, GEORGE AND JANE
   divorce 99, 100, 101
HARVARD COLLEGE
   president of (see DUNSTER, HENRY).
   Law library of, pages of supplements to code of 1660 supplied from 120
HAWTHORNE, WILLIAM
   deputed, 1637, to revise drafts of laws presented from the towns . 6
   requested to procure copy of Liberties 9
   appointed from Essex county, 1645, on commission to draft body of laws . . . 73
   1650, to revise maritime laws . . . 115
   1672, to collect matter for supplement to laws . 123
HAYNES, JOHN
   governor, 1635, deputed to make a draft of laws 4, 5
HIBBENS, WILLIAM
   appointed, 1643, to revise Body of Liberties . . . 71
   1645, from Suffolk county, on commission to draft body of laws . . . 73
   1646, on committee to perfect draft of body of laws . . . 75
   1652, to select laws to go to the towns . 116
   1653, to examine laws 116
HILL, JOSEPH
   substitute for Capt. Cooke on commission to draft body of laws . 73
   appointed, 1646, on committee to perfect draft of body of laws . . 75, 79, 80
   1647, on committee to prepare laws for the press . . 76, 80
   to make final examination of the book of laws upon publication . . 7
   1648, to examine laws in press . . 77, 80
   to receive one copy of book of laws, without price . 79
   1649, allowed £10 for services . . 79
   on committee to prepare supplement of 1650 . . 104

HILL, JOSEPH, continued.
   appointed, 1649, to arrange for printing . . . 104
   supplement prepared and put through the press under supervision of . 99, 120
   1652, to examine and revise records . viii, 116
   1653, statement of services and petition for recompense . . 79
   allowed £10 . . 80
   1653, 1654, to examine laws passed by general court . 117
   1656, presented for "marrying of himself" 103
   1682, petition to general court for exemption from taxes on account of poverty, blindness, etc., 127
   public services of . 79
HILTON, WILLIAM
   appointed, 1644, to examine Bellingham's revision of laws . . 72
HOADLEY, CHARLES J.
   editor of records of New Haven colony . , . . 86
HOWARD, LIEUT.
   appointed, 1644, to examine Bellingham's revision of laws . . 72
HUBBARD, CAPT. JOSHUA
   appointed, 1670, to prepare laws for publication . . 122
HUBBARD, REV. WILLIAM
   grant of £50 to, in acknowledgment of services in compiling history of colony . . . 128
HUMPHREYS, ROBERT
   appears at London for colony . . 130
HUTCHINSON, CAPT. EDWARD
   owner of Lechford's copy of Records x, xii
HUTCHINSON, ELISHA
   collection of papers, Cotton's pamphlet reprinted in, 1769 . . 1
   possessor of MS. copy of Body of Liberties . . . 10
   fac-simile reprint of . . 32
   possessor of Lechford's copy of records . . . x, xii
   appointed, 1680, to revise laws 125, 126
HUTCHINSON, GOV. THOMAS
   owner of Lechford's copy of records of general court . . . vii, xiii
   Rev. John Cotton's book reprinted by 11
   cited by Dr. Moore in pamphlet on date of code of 1649 . . . 85

I

IMPRISONMENT
   inflicted by court of assistants . . 3
INDEX
   to revision of 1660, Thomas Danforth ordered to make 119
   to Body of Liberties . . . 63
IPSWICH
   magistrates residing at, appointed to revise Body of Liberties, 1643 . 71
   commissioners for Essex, to prepare draft of laws, to meet at . . 73

J

JOHNSON, LIEUT. EDWARD
  appointed, 1644, to examine Bellingham's revision of laws . . . 72
  1645, from Middlesex county, on commission to draft body of laws . 73, 75
  1646, 1647, on sub-committee to examine draft of body of laws . . . 74
  1652 to examine and revise records . . . viii

JOHNSON, LIEUT. EDWARD, continued.
  appointed, 1670, to prepare laws for publication . . . 122
  author of "Wonder-Working Providence" (*note*) . . . 75

JOHNSON, LIEUT. WILLIAM
  appointed, 1680, to revise laws . 125

JURISDICTION
  substituted, 1681-2, for word "Commonwealth" in laws . . . 126

K

KEAYNE, CAPT.
  appointed on committee to prepare supplement of 1650 . . . 104

KINGSLEY, STEPHEN
  appointed, 1644, to examine Bellingham's revision of laws . . . 72

KNOWLES, MR.
  substitute in place of Mr. Allen on commission to draft body of laws 73

L

LANDS
  granted by court of assistants . . 3
  sole power to dispose of, vested in general court, 1634 . . . 4

LAWS
  of Province, 1692 to the revolution, published by state . . . vi
  public and general, of Colony and Province, published by state in 1812 . . v
  incompleteness of, . . vi
  edition of 1649, lost, but may be reconstructed 1
  spurious code of 1
  the work of Rev. John Cotton . . . 1
  proposed but never accepted . . 2
  authority of general court to make, under charter of 1629 . . . 2
  governor, deputy and assistants impowered to make . . . 3
  sole power to make, vested in general court . . . 4
  to be made at October session . . 5
  passage of, concurrence of majority of magistrates and deputies required 5
  body of grounds of, commission appointed to frame, 1635 . . . 5
  fundamentals, commission appointed, 1636, to make draft of 5
  reported to general court, no action taken . . . 6
  freemen to collect and present to governor, 1637 . . . 6
  commission appointed to codify for general court . 6, 7
  code prepared by Nathaniel Ward adopted in 1641 8

LAWS, *continued*.
  manuscript copies of . . . 9, 10
  of 1641 and 1660, Body of Liberties traced in . . . 21, 27
  of 1660, sections of Liberties not incorporated in . . . 27, 28
  common, of England, Body of Liberties compared with . . . 17
  capital, ordered to be printed, 1642 . 71
  in Body of Liberties . . 54
  issued from press at Cambridge . . . 84
  amendments to, 1681 . . 126
  printing of, by Dunster, Day and Green, on press at Cambridge . 84
  code of 1649:
  commission appointed, 1642, to examine and perfect orders of last court, 71
  1643, to consider the Body of Liberties . 71
  1644, to examine Bellingham's report . 72
  ship-owners and builders, 1644, to make and present laws for consideration of general court . 72
  general laws of 1644, ordered published to the town . . 72
  commissioners appointed, 1645, to present draft . . 73, 80
  sub-committees appointed, 1646, to examine draft . 74, 75
  authorized, 1647, to make change of form as occasion may require . 76
  books procured, 1647, for use of court in making laws . . 76
  orders, 1647, to committee preparing laws for press . . 77
  examined and put to press, 1648 . 77
  amendment, 1648, while in press . 77
  allowance to John Wayte for copying book of . . . 77
  labors of Joseph Hills upon . . 79

LAWS, *continued.*
code of 1649:
 transcription of old laws not included
  in printed revision, 1648 . . 78
 distribution of printed copies, . . 79
 referred to as the "first printed
  book" 104
 forms, size, and contents of . . 83, 86
 probable size of edition . . . 84
 date of publication, examination of
  Dr. Moore's pamphlet on . . 81
 order to sell in quires at 3s. the
  book 79
 price quoted at 17d. a book . . 85
 destruction of copies . . . 85
 arranged alphabetically under titles, 86
 correspondences in New Haven and
  Connecticut codes (*note*) . 87, 88, 89
   in titles of revision
    of 1660 (*note*) . . 90
 citations from, in proceedings of
  general court . 86–92
  in Thorowgood's
   "Jewes in America" . . 93
  of titles in records of selectmen of Boston . . 97
  in code of 1660 . . 92
  in Essex court files . . 100
  in files of Middlesex court, 102
  in Suffolk court files. . 98
 table of titles known to be in printed
  code 103
 Bellingham probably chief inciter of
  edition 120
supplement of 1650:
 committee appointed to prepare,
  with table 104
    to print . 104
 referred to, as the "second printed
  book" 104
 correspondences in Connecticut code
  of 1650 105
 citation from title "Ecclesiastical,"
  by Thorowgood . . . 106
 date as fixed by citation in later
  books of the laws . . . 106
 marginal citations of, in code of
  1660 107
 supposed contents of . . 106, 107
 prepared and put through the press
  by Joseph Hills . . . 120
supplements of 1654 and 1657:
 reference to, in records, 1673, of
  general court . . . 110
  in marginal citations,
   code of 1660 . 110–113
 known as "third printed book" and
  "fourth printed book" . . 114
 committee appointed, 1650, to revise
  Lex Mercatoria . . . 114
 copy of general orders of each court
  to be sent to each town . . 115
 publication of, by reading in town
  meeting 115
 committee to examine, 1652 . viii, 116
 orders of each session to be printed
  and distributed, 1654 . . 116
  committee appointed to edit . 117
 legislative procedure, readings on
  three several days required before
  enactment 117
 all general laws to date, 1657, ordered transcribed and printed . 117

LAWS, *continued.*
revision of 1660:
 Major-General Daniel Denison, 1658,
  ordered to revise the laws, . 118
  to prepare for the press and
  make alterations in preface, . 118
 to be of force thirty days from Oct.
  16, 1660 120
 orders, 1659, 1660, for printing and
  distribution 119
 Thomas Danforth ordered to make
  an index 119
 amendments and additions published
  in yearly supplements . . 120
 changes in, demanded by the Royal
  Commissioners . . . 121
 marginal citations in, from liber 1 . 92
 Secretary Rawson's copy preserved
  in Library of Am. Antiq. Soc. at
  Worcester 120
 pages of supplement supplied by copy
  in Harvard Coll. Law Library . 120
edition of 1672:
 orders preparatory for . . . 121
 committees appointed to prepare . 122
 printing and disposition of . . 123
 order to prepare preface and table . 123
 copyright voted to John Usher for
  seven years 123, 124
 supplements issued annually in consecutive pages . . . 125
 new codifications proposed and committees appointed, 1679, 1680 125, 126
 amendments, 1681–2, to conciliate the
  king 126
 committee appointed, 1684, to prepare for press 128
 proceedings in revision of . . 129
 reported and ordered to press . . 129
 explanation of the failure to print the
  new revision of the body of laws . 130
 cancellation of the charter, 1684 . 130
 arrival of Andros, 1686, and end of
  colonial period . . . 131
 votes which failed between the two
  branches of the general court 131, 132
 grounds of the dispute between the
  magistrates and deputies . 133–136
 history of the dispute (*note*) . . 133
 printing of the laws stopped . . 136
 final disagreement . . . 137
LECHFORD, THOMAS
 copy of Records described . vii, ix, x
 ownership by Gov. Endicott and
  others . . . . . ix, x
 manuscript copies of Body of Liberties made by 8
 changes in Ward's draft suggested by, 19
LEGISLATION (see LAWS).
 from 1641 to 1672 . . . 71
LEX MERCATORIA
 committee appointed, 1650, to revise, 114
LIBERTIES, BODY OF
 a spurious code cited as . . . 1
  the work of Rev.
   John Cotton . . 1
  published in London,
   1641 . . . 1
  reprinted, 1655, 1798,
   1844 . . . 1
 proposed, but never
  accepted . . . 2
 disclaimed by William Aspinwall . 12

BODY OF LIBERTIES, *continued.*
  prepared by Rev. Nathaniel Ward
    and adopted in 1641 . . . 8, 120
  manuscript copies of . . . 8, 9, 10
    sent to the several towns, 9
    established for three years . . 9
    evidence showing actual contents of, 15
    comparison with Magna Charta and
      common laws 16
    existed in a separate MS. about 1648, 122
    traced in the edition of laws of 1641
      and 1660 21–27
    sections not incorporated in statutes
      of 1660 . . . . . 27, 28
  fac-simile reprint of Hutchinson
    manuscript of . . 32
    table of contents . . 30
    index . . . 63
  fac-simile references to, in fac-simile, 66

BODY OF LIBERTIES, *continued.*
  reference to, by elders, in answer to
    question of general court . . 72
  revisions of 71
  not entered on the records of general court v
  rediscovered by F. C. Gray and
    printed by him in 1843 . . xvi
LIBRARY, PUBLIC, OF BOSTON
  (see BOSTON PUBLIC LIBRARY).
LUSHER, MAJ. ELIAZER
  appointed, 1670, to prepare laws for
    publication 122
    1672, to collect matter for
    supplement to laws . 123
LUXFORD, JAMES
  divorce case 99
LYNDE, JOSEPH
  appointed, 1680, to revise laws 126

M

MAGNA CHARTA
  comparison of Body of Liberties
    with 16
MAJOR GENERAL (see DENISON,
  DANIEL).
  authorized, 1658, to make alterations
    in preface to laws . . . 82
  preparation of code of 1660 for
    press by 116, 118
  chiefly concerned in arranging code
    of 1660 120
MAJORITY
  in vote of magistrates, disagreement
    as to what shall constitute . 131, 133
MALDEN
  Joseph Hill, member of House for . 79
MANUSCRIPT
  Body of Liberties, copies made in . 8, 9, 10
  miscellaneous, list of, prefixed to
    the Hutchinson volume . . 10
  comparison of the Elisha Hutchinson MS. with laws and liberties, 16
  by Thomas Lechford, of records
    piror to 1640 . . . vii, ix, x
MARITIME LAWS
  acts of trade and navigation ordered,
    1681, to be published and observed, 126
  committee appointed, 1650, to revise 114, 115
MASSACHUSETTS BAY, COMPANY
  OF THE (see COMPANY OF THE
  MASSACHUSETTS BAY).

MASSACHUSETTS HISTORICAL
  SOCIETY
  Cotton's pamphlet reprinted in Collections of I
MATHER, REV. RICHARD
  appointed from Suffolk county, 1645,
    on commission to draft body of laws, 73
MEADCALFE, JOSEPH
  appointed, 1644, to examine Bellingham's revision of laws . . 72
MEKINS, THOMAS
  appointed, 1644, to examine Bellingham's revision of laws . . 72
MIDDLESEX COUNTY
  commissioners appointed from, 1645,
    to draft body of laws . . 73
  citations from code of 1649 in court
    files of 102
  sheriff of, 1684, return made by, on
    writ of *scire facias* against Governor and Company of Massachusetts
    Bay 130
MOORE, DR. GEORGE H.
  of the Lenox Library, examination
    of pamphlet concerning date of
    code of 1649 81
  extracts from Thorowgood's "Jewes
    in America" 93
  citation from Thomas Cobbet . . 96
  citation from Snow's "History of
    Boston" 96
  petition of Joseph Hills, 1682, published by 127

N

NEWBURY
  Joseph Hill, member of House for . 79
NEW HAVEN
  colony, code of laws of, modelled on
    Body of Liberties and revisions of
    1649 and 1660 86
  correspondences with Mass. code of
    1649 (*note*) 87
NEWTOWN (Cambridge)
  sends deputies to general court, 1634, 4
NORTH, LORD GUILFORD
  issues decree vacating charter, 1684, 130
NORTON, CAPT. FRANCIS
  appointed from Essex county, 1645,
    on commission to draft body of
    laws 73, 79

NORTON, CAPT. FRANCIS, *continued.*
  appointed 1649, disposition of books
    of 118
  1666, to prepare laws for
    publication . . . 121
NOWELL, INCREASE
  clerical aid by, in keeping Records . vii
  appointed 1645, from Middlesex
    county, on commission
    to draft body of laws . 73
  1649, to prepare supplement of 1650 . . 104
  1650, to revise maritime
    laws 115
NOWELL, SAMUEL
  reports, 1685, revised draft of laws . 129

O

OFFICERS
  executive, court of assistants empowered to choose 3
  sole power to appoint or remove, vested in general court . . 4

ORDINANCES
  authority of general court to make, under charter of 1629 . . . 2

P

PALMER, WILLIAM AND ELINOR
  divorce 100
PARKES, WILLIAM
  appointed, 1664, to prepare laws for publication 121
PELHAM, HERBERT
  appointed from Middlesex county, 1645, on commission to draft body of laws 73, 79
PETERS, REV. HUGH
  deputed, 1636, to make draft of "fundamentals" . . 5
  1637, to codify drafts presented from the towns . 6
PHILLIPS, REV. GEORGE
  deputed, 1637, to revise drafts of laws presented from the towns . 6
POPE, WILLIAM
  divorce case 100
PORTSMOUTH
  twenty copies of revision of 1660 allotted to 119
PRENCE, GOV. THOMAS
  second marriage . . . 100
PRESCOTT, WILLIAM
  appointed, 1812, on committee to prepare for publication " Ancient Charters and General Laws " . v
PRESIDENT (see DUNSTER, HENRY)
  of Harvard College, laws to be printed by 116
PRICHARD, HUGH
  appointed from Suffolk county, 1645, on commission to draft body of laws 73

PRINCE SOCIETY
  reissue of Hutchinson's collection of papers by 1, 12
PRINTING PRESS
  at Cambridge, given by Josse Glover and others 83
  issues from, by Dunster, Day and Green 84
PROVINCE
  laws of, published by State . . vi
PROVISO
  in title " courts," as to majority vote, disagreement between magistrates and deputies 131, 133
PRUDENTIAL AFFAIRS
  origin and significance of term (*note*), 12
  prudential equivalent to prudent (*note*) 14
PSALM BOOK
  issued from press at Cambridge . 84
PUBLICATION
  of capital laws 71
  of revision of laws, 1649, 1660 . 71
  of general laws of 1644, ordered to be made to towns . . . 72
  of code of 1649, ordered . . . 77
  of supplement of 1650 . . . 104
  of general laws by reading in public town meeting 115
  of laws, psalms, etc., by H. Dunster, Day and Green 84
  of revision of 1660 120
PURCHASE, OLIVER
  appointed, 1685, to revise body of laws 129

R

RANDOLPH, EDWARD
  bearer of letter, 1681, from Charles II. 130
  arrives with commissions for a new government 131
RAWSON, EDWARD
  clerical aid by, in keeping records . vii
  appointed, 1647, to make final examination of the book of laws before publication, 77
  1649, to arrange for printing supplement of 1650, 104
  1652, 1653, 1654, to select laws to go to the towns, 116, 117
  grant of land for services, 119
  1664, 1665, 1666, to prepare laws for publication . . . 121
  to make preface and table to revision of 1672 . . . 123

RAWSON, EDWARD, continued.
  appointed 1674, 1680, to determine what acts of general court shall be printed . 124, 126
  1680, to revise laws . 126
  1684, to prepare laws for press 128
  chiefly concerned in arranging the revision of 1660 . . 120
REBELLION
  law in relation to, repealed, 1681 . 126
RECORDS
  of colony, 1629–1686, published by State v
  of general court, published by the State vi
  edited by Dr. Shurtleff . . vi
  amended in second issue . xiv, xv

RECORDS, *continued.*
  of general court, Lechford's copy
    now in Boston
    Public Library . . . vii, xvii
  entry in Lechford's
    note book concerning . . . ix
  ownership by Gov.
    Endicott and
    others . . ix, x
  comparison of
    Shurtleff's Vol.
    III. with Lechford's copy . x, xi, xii
  old volumes cited
    in 1652 . . viii
  provision for transcribing . . viii, 78
  transcribed by Joseph Hills . . 80
  list of references
    in, to laws subsequent to code
    of 1649 . . 87
  entries in regard
    to laws enacted
    between 1650
    and 1660 . . 114
  subsequent to publication of revision of 1660 . 120

RECORDS, *continued.*
  of court of assistants, 1641-1644, contained in Lechford's copy . . x, xiii
  of county courts, references in, to
    code of 1649, Suffolk . 98
    Essex . . 100
  of county code of 1649, Middlesex . 102
  of selectmen of Boston, citations of
    code of 1649 in . . . 97
  of Connecticut colony . . . 86
  of New Haven colony . . . 86
RICHARDS, JOHN
  appointed, 1679, 1680, 1685, to revise
    laws . . : . 125, 126, 129
  reports, 1685, revised draft . . 129
  sent to the king, 1682, as agent of
    colony 130
RICHARDSON, JOHN
  divorce case 99
ROGERS, NATHANIEL
  appointed from Essex county, 1645,
    on commission to draft body of
    laws 73
ROXBURY
  sends deputies to general court, 1634, 4
  deputies of, 1639, to prepare code of
    laws 7
RUSSELL, RICHARD (*Treasurer*)
  allowance, 1651, for loss incurred
    upon edition of laws of 1649 . . 85
  appointed to see revision of 1672
    through the press . . . 123

S

SAFFIN, JOHN
  appointed, 1684, to prepare laws for
    press 128
  reports, 1685, a revised draft . . 129
SALEM
  sends deputies to general court,
    1634 4
SAUGUS
  sends deputies to general court,
    1634 4
SAVAGE, CAPT. THOMAS
  appointed, 1656, to revise laws for
    publication 117
SEAL
  of colony, purchase and custody of . 124
SECOND BOOK OF THE LAWS
  (see LAWS).
SECRETARY
  (Increase Nowell, 1636-1650. Edward Rawson, 1650-1685.)
  to transcribe old records, 1652 . . viii
  to print laws 71
  to compare amendments . . . 77
  to prepare journal 78
  to print supplement, 1649 . . 104
  of committee on *Lex Mercatoria* . 115
  to examine laws, 1656 . . . 116
  to send laws to press, 1657 . . 117
  grant of land for services . . 119
  to examine laws, 1665-66 . . 121
  to make preface, etc., 1672 . . 123
  to revise laws, 1684 . . . 128
  1674, 1680, to determine what acts of
    general court shall be printed 124, 126
SERGEANT-MAJOR-GENERAL
  (*Thomas Dudley*)
  authorized, 1644, to make laws for
    the well-ordering of the army . 72

SEWALL, SAMUEL
  requested, 1685, to oversee printing
    of revised body of laws . . . 129
  extracts from diary of, as to dispute
    between magistrates and deputies, 131, 133
SHAW, CHARLES
  citation from his History of Boston . 96, 97
SHAW, WILLIAM S.
  librarian of Boston Athenæum, 1813
    to 1822 10
SHEPHERD, REV. THOMAS
  deputed, 1636, to make draft of
    "Fundamentals" . . . 5
  1637, to codify drafts presented from the towns . 6
  appointed from Middlesex county,
    1645, on commission to draft body
    of laws 73, 79
SHIPPING
  owners and builders to make and
    present laws, 1644, to general
    court 72
  acts of trade and navigation ordered,
    1681, to be published and observed, 126
  revision of maritime laws . . 114
SHURTLEFF, DR. NATHANIEL B.
  editor of records of general court
    and assistants vi
  printed edition of records amended
    in second issue . . . xiv, xv
SMITH, CAPT. JOHN
  appointed, 1685, to revise body of
    laws 129
SNOW, DR. CALEB H.
  citation from his "History of Boston" 96
SON, REBELLIOUS
  law in relation to, repealed, 1681 . 126

SPENCER, WILLIAM
    deputed, 1637, to revise drafts of laws
        presented from the towns . . 6
SPRAGUE, CAPT. RICHARD
    appointed, 1644, to examine Belling-
        ham's revision of laws . . . 72
    reports, 1685, revised draft of laws . 129
STEVENS, WILLIAM
    appointed 1644, to examine Belling-
        ham's revision of laws . . . 72
STODDARD, ANTHONY
    appointed, 1665, to prepare laws for
        publication . . . 121
        1679, 1680, to revise
        laws . . . 125, 126
STORY, JOSEPH
    appointed, 1812, on committee to pre-
        pare for publication "Ancient
        Charters and General Laws" . v

STOUGHTON, WILLIAM
    deputed, 1639, to prepare code of laws 7
        1671, to see revision of
        1672 through the press . 123
        1680, to revise laws . . 125
    made deputy governor, 1686, under
        commission of James II. . 131
SUFFOLK COUNTY
    commissioners appointed from, 1645,
        to draft body of laws . . 73
    citations from code of 1649 in court
        files . . . 98
SYMONDS, SAMUEL
    appointed, 1641, on sub-committee
        to examine draft of
        body of laws . . 74
    1654, to edit laws for
        publication . . 116

T

TAXES
    levied by court of assistants . . 3
    sole power to levy, vested in general
        court, 1634 . . . 4
THOROWGOOD, THOMAS
    copy of code of 1649 received by . 86
    citations from code of 1649 in his
        "Jewes in America" . . 95
    title "Ecclesiastical," in code of
        1649, quoted by . . . 106
TREASURER (RICHARD RUSSELL)
    allowance, 1651, of £20 for loss
        incurred upon edition of laws of
        1649 . . . 85
    to have copy of laws without pay-
        ment . . . 115

TREASURER (RICHARD RUSSELL),
    continued.
    distribution of books of laws (1650)
        by . . . 119
    to pay for printing of, and to dispose
        of revision of 1672 . . 123
    to purchase seal and screw of execu-
        trix of Gov. Leverett . . 124
    to pay Rev. William Hubbard £50
        for services in compiling history
        of colony . . . 128
TRUMBULL, J. HAMMOND
    code of Connecticut laws printed by, 86
TYNG, WILLIAM
    appointed, 1647, on committee to
        prepare laws for the press . 76

U

UPHAM, WILLIAM P.
    examination of Lechford's copy of
        records by . . . ix, xiii
    suggestion as to citations from code
        of 1649 in Suffolk court files . 97

USHER, JOHN
    publication of revision of 1672 by,
        copyright voted for seven years, 123, 124

V

VANE, HENRY
    governor, 1636, deputed to make draft of "Fundamentals" . . . 5

W

WAR
    council of, authorized to make and
        execute laws for the well-ordering
        of the army . . . 72
WARD, REV. NATHANIEL
    deputed, 1637, to revise drafts of
        laws presented from the
        towns . . . 6, 7
    1645, from Essex county,
        on commission to draft
        body of laws . . . 73
    1646, on sub-committee, to
        examine draft of body of
        laws . . . 74, 80

WARD, REV. NATHANIEL, continued.
    model of form of government framed
        by . . . 7, 120
        adopted in 1641 . . . 8
        known as "Body of Liberties". 8
    memoir of . . . 18
    strange words used by (note) . . 19
WARD, WILLIAM
    appointed, 1644, to examine Belling-
        ham's revision of laws . . 72, 73
WAITE, CAPT. JOHN
    of Charlestown, allowance to, for
        copying book of laws, 1647 . . 77
    appointed, 1680, to revise laws . 125

WATERTOWN
  sends deputies to general court, 1634, 4
WHIPPING
  inflicted by order of court of assistants 3
WILLOUGHBY, FRANCIS
  appointed on committee, 1650, to revise maritime laws . . 115
WINTHROP, JOHN
  deputed, 1635, to make a draft of laws, 4
  1636, deputy governor . 5
  1637, 1639, governor . . 6, 7
  share of, in preparation of Body of Liberties 18
  appointed, 1646, on committee to perfect draft of body of laws 75

WINTHROP, JOHN, continued.
  appointed, 1647, on committee to prepare laws for the press 76
  1642-43, to revise orders of court and Body of Liberties . . . 71
WORD OF GOD
  causes to be determined by, in absence of statute law . . . 5
  committee appointed to revise laws in accordance with . . . 125
  magistrates to proceed according to, in absence of express law . . 72
  ordinances of war to be established agreeable to 72

www.ingramcontent.com/pod-product-compliance
Lightning Source LLC
Chambersburg PA
CBHW030818190426
43197CB00036B/592